Art After Metaphysics

by

John David Ebert

Copyright © 2013 John David Ebert
All rights reserved.

ISBN: 1492765481
ISBN 13: 9781492765486

Acknowledgements

Special thanks are due to the following individuals for reading various portions of the manuscript and providing encouragement and support: Chris Boyd, Michael Aaron Kamins, Jacques de Beaufort, Breffni O'Byrne, Sara Monika Leanda and Henry Warwick.

Table of Contents

A Few Words About the Cover vii

Part One: Chronological Divisions 1

On the Four World Ages of European Art 3

Part Two: Geographical Regions 29

New York 31

    Jackson Pollock 35

    Mark Rothko 55

    Jean-Michel Basquiat 67

The Greater German Grouping 79

    Joseph Beuys 83

    Gerhard Richter 99

    Anselm Kiefer 113

Zdzislaw Beksinski 119

Odd Nerdrum 131

London *145*

Francis Bacon 149

Damien Hirst 163

Anish Kapoor 177

Rome & Paris *191*

Jannis Kounellis 195

Christian Boltanski 207

A Final Word 217

A Few Words About the Cover

For this book's cover illustration I have chosen a work by contemporary British artist Chris Boyd, entitled *The Book of Darecebu*. It is a strange and enigmatic book which Boyd says was inspired by his witnessing of the volcanic eruption of Mount Pinatubo in the Phillipines where he spent a good deal of his childhood growing up. ("Cebu" is located there). The book has a central gaping hole that appears to be crackling with lavic energies that might erupt at any moment. It is a perfect metaphor for Zygmunt Bauman's "liquid modernity," the age in which we now find ourselves living, in which all the cultural forms (or what Cornelius Castoriadis called "imaginary significations") are melting down into a kind of slag heap of broken models, discarded signifiers and retro-fitted artifacts that might characterize the denizen of a *Mad Max* landscape who constructs his own world out of the debris of the previous civilization like a *bricoleur*.

But what struck me about the image is its evocation of the great Medieval book-as-work-of-art from the time of Charlemagne's court library at Aix-la-Chapelle, when huge manuscripts were transformed into twelve pound books with ivory plaques on their covers that were surrounded by expensive gold and various kinds of gems. These books were made by the monks at Charlemagne's court, some of whom were survivors of the various Viking raids of the Irish monasteries – Alcuin was one such individual, for instance – who carried with them to Charlemagne's court the knowledge of the making of illuminated manuscripts.

Aix-la-Chapelle (which Spengler once compared, brilliantly, to a sort of Mycenaean fortress stronghold like Pylos which borrowed its culture forms from the southern and more cosmopolitan civilization of Minoan Crete, just as Charlemagne's palace borrowed culture forms, such as the candy-striping on the architecture, from the more cosmopolitan civilization of the Spanish-Islamic Moors of Cordoba) was then a sort of cultural refuge that gathered together the knowledge of the time and began the painful and intricate process of reconstructing Western civilization. (Whereas, today the opposite is taking place, in which the Western tradition reconstructed by Charlemagne's monks is now being taken apart piece by piece by French deconstructionists).

The covers of these books as artworks unto themselves were often ivory-carved images replete with Christian iconotypes such as the Crucifixion or the Assumption of Mary to Heaven, or to one or another of the four Evangelists, which served as a common iconography of the time. The Gospel Book of Charlemagne, or the Epernay Gospel or the Book of Pericopes date from about this time, and the iconotypes lovingly carved into their covers served as the basic structural forms of the entire age. They were transcendental signifieds that anchored all meaning in a concrete system of references that prevented truth from sliding around into semiotic chaos.

But today, all the transcendental signifieds are gone. For the signifiers of contemporary art all refer back to a series of semiotic vacancies like scars on the walls of Being that once used to organize the Western mind, but which do so no longer. Boyd's *Book of Darecebu*, with its central rupture where, once upon a time there used to be such grand signifieds as the Apocalypse or the Crucifixion, now features only a semiotic vacancy at the ontological center of Western Being.

Being has been gutted. Its transcendental signifieds have all melted down, and now exist in a magmatic flow of laval forms that are failing to crystallize into any perceivable shape. Boyd's *Book of Darecebu* thus points out what the current task amounts to for today's contemporary artist: namely, to construct new signifieds from out of the melted slag heap of the West's discarded pile of signifiers.

It is an intimidating task, but we currently have men, and women, on the job, working to fashion new signifiers for the dawning Age of Uncertainty and Anxiety that is now looming over the horizon upon us.

The volcanic reference on Boyd's book cover, furthermore, suggests the possibility of imminent catastrophe that our age now finds itself currently under (just as the Vikings of Charlemagne's time constituted a looming threat): a sort of permanent state of emergency in which floods, famines, fires, tsunamis and explosions have surrounded us on all sides.

What catastrophe will take place next and where will it happen?
My backyard?
Or yours?

PART ONE:

CHRONOLOGICAL DIVISIONS

On the Four Ages of European Art

Art, then, *after* metaphysics...

The metaphysical age was an invention of Heidegger's that spans a chasm of European intellectual history from Plato to Nietzsche in which all the West's grand metaphysical narratives were constructed but which, from about the time of Nietzsche's annunciation of the death of God, began to collapse and disintegrate like Valhalla at the end of Wagner's opera *Gotterdammerung*. Heidegger saw himself as a sort of epilogue or appendix to this grand age of metaphysical certainties, for with the replacement of Being by technological enframing, all that he saw remaining as the "task of thinking" for contemporary philosophers was varying degrees of *aletheia*-type "truth-making," in which entities brought into the clearing are, from henceforth, like the blurred photographs on the canvases of Gerhard Richter; that is to say, lacking the pristine clarity of *absolute* Truth, such entities could only hope to attain to one or another *degree* of truth.[1]

But then, *before* the metaphysical age that Heidegger saw beginning with Plato's divorce of Being from Becoming, there was a long, long stretch of myths, religions and ideas which the contemporary philosopher Peter Sloterdijk has demarcated as the *pre*-metaphysical age, an age in which being-in-the-world meant to *be* in the body of the Great Mother.[2] Hence the conception of the earth in the times of the Mesopotamians and the Egyptians as a sort of embryo surrounded by the amniotic fluid of a vast world ocean and enclosed – at least in Egypt – by a sky goddess whose belly was full of stars (Nut, for instance; or later, Hathor, the cow goddess of the daytime sky). The pre-metaphysical age had an immanental, rather than a transcendental, understanding of Being, and correspondingly all religious journeys through the cosmos had a decidedly *downward* tendency, from Inanna's prototypical journey to the underworld of Irkalla to the fate of the soul in the various afterlife scenarios of the Egyptian underworlds presided over by the mummified god-king Osiris.

But then, according to Sloterdijk, being-in-the-world during the metaphysical age was a being-in-the-Father, and so it is precisely during this epoch that the concept of the paternal womb comes into being as an attempt to appropriate the birth-giving powers of the Great Mother by a whole horde of Father demiurges and progenitors: Zeus, for example, giving birth to Athena, or God the Father giving birth to the Logos from out of the uterine depths of his own mind (Mary is only the chosen biological vessel of this dual-substance being, for her task is now limited to creating the *physical* body of the already pre-existent Logos-being). It is during this period of the great metaphysical age that all religious journeys, from the myth of Plato's cave to the ascenionist literature of the church fathers, have an *upward* valency, for the old midden heap of underworlds left over from the previous pre-metaphysical age have lost all their appeal and become associated with the realm of carnality and physicality. Osiris, for instance, was the god of the constructed physical body, whereas Christ becomes the lord of the spiritual body, and all must now follow in the wake of the paths broken by him through the heavens.

In the post-metaphysical age that begins with Heidegger, however, being-in-the-world now means a being-*thrown* into the world, in which, as Sloterdijk points out, a real outside now appears for the first time[3]: the individual finds himself thrown into the world in a sort of horizontal direction, full of angst and care, and unprotected by any overarching metaphysical immune system (hence, perhaps, the significance of Edvard Munch's 1895 painting *The Scream*). There are neither journeys upward, nor any downward to make, for the individual must now crawl about the surface of the earth in quest of drastic solutions to the crisis of shell-lessness. (Artificial substitutes for *Transcendenz* now begin to appear: drugs or sex, for instance, which are designed to replicate the ecstasies of the ancient transcendent journeys which, once upon a time, were part of the very fabric of the metaphysical age).

And so art, then, in a post-metaphysical age, is an art that has lost touch with Being, for Being now has degenerated into technological enframing, and consequently, no great meaning systems exist any longer for the art to realize and manifest. As Jacques Derrida pointed out in his early essay on "Structure, Sign and Play in the Discourse of the Human Sciences," there is now an absent ontological center at the heart of the West's understanding of Being which once *used* to be occupied by what he termed "transcendental signifieds"[4] (basically the Kantian Ideas of the Reason: God, Soul, Freedom and Immortality). But with the death of God as pronounced by Nietzsche, the transcendental signifieds which once functioned to anchor and orient all the West's signifiers (as made evident, for instance, in art) have crumbled and collapsed. They have been delegitimized and deconstructed, and so now there is only a semiotic vacancy where the grand signifieds once used to anchor and guarantee all systems of meaning and all philosophical narratives whatsoever. Philosophy, consequently, can no longer function with any kind of absolute metaphysical certainty, and art – contemporary art, in particular – now suffers from a crisis of meaning.

But in order to understand how the situation of contemporary art came about – whose signifiers all refer, not to Being, but to a series of semiotic vacancies – we have to pause for a moment to examine the history of the West's transcendental signifieds, which have changed and evolved through time. Once, long ago, those transcendental signifieds that anchored all meaning systems were composed of what I term "iconotypes," which refer to the main structuring motifs of Medieval art, motifs such as the Incarnation, the Assumption of Mary to heaven, the Last Supper, the Crucifixion, etc. Those iconotypes formed the very ontological fabric of the cosmos itself, but they underwent a series of transformations in which, during the various epochs of Western art, they took on different meanings. It is important to be able to recognize the transformed iconotypes as they reappeared in each epoch to perform different functions, but yet remained as the structural features holding together the very interior of each epoch.

The Age of Medieval Art

The history of Northern European civilization from about the time of the Carolingian period onward has been marked by a series of *four* distinctly different world pictures. There have, accordingly, been precisely *three* crisis points whereby one world picture dissolved and disintegrated as it transformed into the succeeding one. The first of those crisis points, and also the longest, took place between the years from 1400 – 1600 AD; the second began to set in around 1860 or so; and the third can be demarcated with the conclusion of World War II in 1945. Each one of these points functions as a kind of interregnum analogous to the various intermediate periods of ancient Egypt whereby, for instance, the Old Kingdom was demarcated from the Middle Kingdom by the First Intermediate Period; the Middle Kingdom from the New Kingdom by the Second Intermediate Period, and so on. During each of these crisis points, furthermore, the structures of the previous world age underwent a collapse and transformation, while the ontology of the world picture changed and then crystallized once more into a stable world image. The art of these four ages reflects the ontological transformations that took place in them, and not, as art scholars too often assume, the other way about. The art does not *cause* the changes, in other words; it reflects them, and makes their nature visible.

The four world ages, then (and yes, I realize this is a grand metanarrative, but sometimes they are still useful) begin with the Medieval macrosphere which extends from about 600 AD to 1400 AD; then comes Heidegger's Age of the World Picture[5] which occupies the period from 1400 until about 1860; after that comes Jean Gebser's Modernist integral hypersphere,[6] which extends from 1860 to 1945; and after that, the epoch of contemporary hypermodernity (termed "post-history" by Vilem Flusser,[7]) which we still find ourselves occupying up to the present day.

In the first of these world ages, then – that of the Medieval macrosphere – the cosmos is actually composed out of a series of images or iconotypes which anchor meaning and enclose and protect human society within a cosmic dome (made, according to Aristotle, out of "ether," a shining, self-luminous substance which has the property of turning the cosmic spheres with perfect circular motion). These iconotypes were inherited by the West largely, though not, of course, exclusively, from the Byzantine tradition of icon painting, for it is in the Byzantine iconic tradition that all the most famous iconotypes are first worked out: Christ Pantocractor, who gazes down at us with his all-seeing eyes from atop the dome of the world-ceiling, as in the church of Daphne near Athens, dating from about the year 1100[8]; the image of Mary with the Christ child on her lap (which comes from Egypt, and is a transformation of the goddess Isis with the child Horus who sits on her lap[9]; and since Isis, in appropriating the imagery from the cow goddess Hathor was associated with the sky, so the blue cloak that becomes associated with Mary is a signifier that points to the blue dome of the daytime sky, such that we are always protected within the womb of Mother Mary); the Last Supper, the Baptism of Christ by John, the Annunciation to Mary, and so forth. All these iconotypes come from the Byzantine tradition, including the cult of the saints which, as Hans Belting points out in his book *Likeness and Presence*, was itself a transformation of the Roman funerary portraits composed in Lower Egypt (specifically in the Faiyum) in the second and third centuries AD.[10]

During the so-called Iconoclastic controversy that took place in Byzantium during the years 727-843 AD, the aesthetic theory for this entire first world age was worked out: for whereas the iconoclasts argued that it was blasphemy to represent images of Christ and the Incarnation, since such an artistic act presumed to separate the inseparable dual nature of the Logos (both human *and* divine) into a merely physical nature in the image, the iconophiles argued – successfully, as it turned out – that the whole point of the Incarnation was that the Eternal Word was made visible in an earthly *image*, thus establishing the prototype for making the divine physically visible and therefore annulling the Old Testament ban on images.[11] And besides, they argued, the iconic images were not substanstially *identical* with their divine models, but only earthly mirrors of them, like reflections seen in water. They were not identical to their models, but similar to them, and could thus be represented, especially for the illiterate, as a means of making contact with the spiritual world as a daily reality for the masses. Thus, the aesthetic theory for the iconotypes – although rejected by the West during Carolingian times – nonetheless holds for them right down to the shift into the Age of the World Picture: they are emanations and avatars from the realm of spiritual being and so participate in a supernatural reality.

Thus, during the age of the Medieval macrosphere, the artist is a cosmocrator who, in painting the iconotypes, is imitating the divine act of bringing forth entities. Its mode for communicating its Vision is therefore Pentecostal, in the sense that it is a continuous echo of a single primordial event that is constantly incarnated into the present moment in the construction of each of these images.

The medieval artist, furthermore, in painting these iconotypes as frescoes onto the walls of churches is, as it were, painting them onto the walls of the world dome, the actual cosmosphere constructed by God that was thought to have surrounded and captured the earth within a bounded uterine structure. Thus, Giotto, in painting the life of the Virgin on the north wall of the Arena Chapel, is actually painting the iconotypes onto the walls of this cosmic dome, just as the Paleolithic artist, in painting his various animal forms onto the walls of his cave, was actually painting them onto the world ceiling (the animals, according to Michael Rappenglueck, may actually have been constellations[12]). In the West, though, the iconotypes (the Medieval version of Derrida's "transcendental signifieds") are not so much physical constellations of the night sky as they are *temporal* constellations that compose the very fabric of history itself, for the iconotypes are almost all Events that occurred in time as singularities: the *Last* Supper, the *Annunciation* to Mary, the Incarnation, the Crucifixion.

They function, furthermore, during this age to prevent the play of signification from sliding around into semiotic chaos, as has happened today. They act, in this sense, as immune structures protecting and immunizing the Western psyche against the impacts of the Real that lay out beyond the Symbolic order (in those days, bounded by the world dome). This is perfectly illustrated by Jean Fouquet's 1460 painting of *The Descent of the Holy Ghost on the Faithful,* in which the hand of god is shown puncturing the dome of the blue sky, whereupon it sends out ripples through the fabric of the heavens that chase away hordes of chattering devils and demons that are shown fleeing from it in all directions. The world dome that encloses and protects the human being during this age, that is to say, is an immunological structure that keeps the mind anchored in the realm of meaning, in which all signifiers refer to the iconotypes as their primary transcendental signifieds which prevent the Derridean "play of signification" – or *differance* – from ever taking place.

But the iconotypes, as it turns out, are not quite as stable as they appeared to be to the inhabitants of this first World Age of Northern European civilization, for they are, in fact, constantly undergoing transformation. In some of the earliest Byzantine icon paintings, for instance, the so-called "donor" or "patron" of the painting is usually depicted as a tiny little figure in one of the corners kissing, perhaps, the foot of the Virgin, who towers above him.[13] But gradually, over time, the donor – who is an actual "real" person – grows larger and larger, slowly pushing his way into the pictures, as in the case of Jan Van Eyck's Ghent altarpiece of about 1432, in which the two saints represented in the bottom panels of the reverse side are just about the same size and in the same dimension as the two donors of the painting (wealthy burghers named Jodocus Vidjt and Lysbette Vorluut) who are depicted praying to either side of them. The donors, real individuals from the three dimensional world, in other words, are slowly pushing their way into the canvases, where they will eventually usurp and replace the two-dimensional icons. (All icons are two-dimensional by their very nature, for they are flat and abbreviated hieroglyphs of complex processes from the real world). Finally, in Hans Memling's Nieuwenhove diptych of 1487, the composition is constructed of two portraits of the same size: on the left is Mary with the Christ child; on the right is the wealthy burgher who has commissioned the portrait, shown in devotional attitude toward Mary, but notably painted exactly the same size. By the end of the Quattrocento, in other words, the donor and patron is beginning to replace the portraits of the saints with the new "iconotype" of the Western portrait study, of which Jan Van Eyck was indeed the first great master.

In Joos van Cleve's 1511 painting of the *Virgin and Christ Child*, moreover, we notice yet another new "iconotype" creeping in at the corner of the canvas, for in this painting the Virgin is shown entertaining the Christ Child, while in the lower right hand corner, there is a plate of fruit depicted together with some silverware and a half-empty glass. The still life (a kind of secular iconotype), in other words, which the Dutch masters of the seventeenth century will apotheosize, is now making its way into the canvases.

But by 1511, the transformation of one world age into the next is nearly complete. At this time, Michelangelo is in the middle of painting the Sistine ceiling (like the Paleolithic artist, he is painting the iconotypes onto the very dome of the heavens). The art of the Sistine ceiling is part of the grand climax of the Medieval iconotypes whose age, by 1500, had already had its day. (Hieronymous Bosch, at just about this time, is one of the last painters to envision the world dome on the closed outer panels of his *Garden of Earthly Delights*: it is precisely on the walls of Bosch's translucent sphere that Michelangelo paints his iconotypes).

The art of the High Renaissance consists, in essence, of the apotheosis of the iconotypes: Leonardo's *Annunciation* of 1475 is the greatest of all Annunciations ever painted. It cannot be improved upon, although this will not stop other artists from trying. His *Last Supper* of 1495 is the apotheosis of all Last Suppers: *no one* ever improved upon it, and Tiepolo's and Baroccio's mannerist Last Suppers are but pale shadows by comparison. Indeed, if Leonardo had finished his *Adoration of the Magi*, it too would have achieved the apotheosis of that particular iconotype, for even the mere sketch, unfinished as it was, had an enormous influence upon subsequent artists. The same might be said for his unfinished *St. Jerome in the Wilderness*.

Michelangelo, meanwhile, had already apotheosized the iconotype of David in 1504, and his frescoes on the Sistine ceiling are composed of a series of final statements on very ancient iconotypes: God animating Adam, for instance; or the Expulsion from the Garden; Noah and the Flood; or Yahweh himself, whom Michelangelo fixes in our mind's eye for all time as *the* great representation of that bearded old cosmocrator.

Once the iconotypes have achieved their final statements in the works of Leonardo, Raphael, Michelangelo and Titian, they begin, throughout the course of the Mannerist art of the 16th century, to fade out of existence. Tintoretto, that great Renaissance deconstructionist, spends the vast majority of his art pulling apart the motifs and structures of the High Renaissance, as Heinrich Wolfflin pointed out in his study *Principles of Art History*.[14] Tintoretto demolishes the pure geometrical schemas and triangular compositions which Raphael, for instance, had used, or Leonardo, to structure their great works of art. Tintoretto actually pulls Renaissance space to pieces: his *Last Supper* of 1594 is a chaos of squirming forms that makes a mockery out of Renaissance linearity and purity of figure.

With the art of Caravaggio, the transformation has been completed, for in his work the iconotypes no longer exist in an eternal dimension at all. They have been degraded and transformed to the level of common street people. Caravaggio essentially says: there *are* no iconotypes, for those ancients and saints whom you revere were all as dirty and thuggish as you or I. There is nothing in the least sacred about them. They have been relegated to the status of back alley criminals and everyday street thugs.

In the paintings of Leonardo, furthermore, we can actually *see* the transformation taking place; we are able to witness the disintegration of the Medieval macrosphere before our very eyes. In his *Virgin of the Rocks* of 1485, the world dome has already been reduced to a crumbling cavern in which holes and chinks are beginning to appear, through which we can catch glimpses of an infinite horizon beyond it. And indeed, this new iconotype of the Infinite Horizon irrupts into the backgrounds of Leonardo's paintings and comes ever more and more into focus as time goes by: his *Madonna of the Yarnwinder* of 1501 already features a vast and archaic landscape yawning into the murky blue distances beyond the Virgin; and by the time of his *Mona Lisa* of 1506, the transformation is complete: the Virgin of the Rocks, associated with the world dome, is here transformed into the Goddess of Infinite Space beyond whose presence a horizon of three-dimensional depth comprises the whole essence of the painting. The two-dimensional Virgin, that is to say, has become the three dimensional Mona

Lisa ("Mona," indeed, is a contraction of "Madonna," but now she is a real person). Thus, the iconotype of the real human being has now displaced the two-dimensional sacred icon; while the Infinite Horizon that becomes the basis for all subsequent landscape painting has, once and for all, pushed out the bounded world ceiling, which is now in process of collapsing and taking all the iconotypes down the drain along with it.

Indeed, the 16th century is the great century of crisis, for with the Protestant outbreak of virulent iconoclasm, the icons are wiped clean from the stage of the world picture. The Protestant churches – as depicted, for instance, in the paintings of Neef the Elder -- do not feature icons, but bare walls, for the icons by the 16th century have lost their status and been delegitimized. The whole reason they have gone down the drain is precisely because they have lost their status as ontologically convincing transcendental signifieds. The discovery of visual space, together with an attendant interest in real entities, has rendered them superfluous as revelations of awe. The Lutherans are only able to denounce them once they are no longer effective units of revelation, but now actually stand in the *way* of revelation via the power of the printed Word. Thus, Catholic Saint Peter as the patron of all images is traded out for Saint Paul who, as the author of the first Christian texts, becomes the unofficial Protestant saint.

By the middle of the 16th century, a new world picture is beginning to solidify (and it is only *then*, in 1543, that Copernicus dares to publish his world-demolishing treatise on astronomy): one in which the world is no longer bounded by a translucent macrosphere upon the walls of which iconotypes have been painted as transcendental signifieds. Infinity is now coming into being as the new grand signified that obsolesces and replaces *all* previous siginifieds.

The world dome has ruptured and spilled forth its contents. By 1600, the Medieval macrosphere has gone and a new age, Heidegger's Age of the World Picture (or, if you prefer, Foucault's Classical Age) has now come into being with an entirely different set of transcendental signifieds.

The Age of the World Picture

The second great age of Northern European art is composed of a world picture that is no longer structured by religious iconotypes. They continue, of course, for a while, out of sheer inertia, as in the art of the Catholic Counter Reformation, but it is an unconvincing art, full of Catholic kitsch and sentimentality, as in the paintings of Annibale Caracci or Zurbaran; and in order to have any effect at all, the art must be overly-theatrical and manipulative, as in the case of Bernini. The dying iconotypes are insisted upon with shouting voices that grow louder and louder in direct proportion to the lack of inspiration of the images. The Catholic Church, during the seventeenth century, was trying to bolster a world that had already become a ghost of itself.

It is, rather, in the North that the new (secularized) iconotypes are first displayed in all their beauty and grandeur: landscape paintings, still lifes and portraits of real, three-dimensional human beings. The idea of the Infinite has now come in to replace all previous transcendental signifieds: the Infinite Horizon (the horizon line now begins to replace the membrane of the ether sphere as a new boundary); Infinite Space, the infinitesimal calculus, analytical geometry: all are revelations of the new obsession with Infinity that begins to come about. God himself is a transcendental signified that carries over from the Medieval world order, but only on condition that he now be identified with the Infinite, as its primary source and ultimate vanishing point.

Thus, though the Italians are, of course -- as Panofsky has shown in his study on *Perspective and Symbolic Form*[15] -- the first to master perspective and to identify the vanishing point with the Infinite, it is the Dutch who are the great discoverers of Infinite *Space*: the sky is featured so prominently in their art that it has the quality of a new revelation of spiritual powers. In the canvases of Van Goyen, Simon Vlieger, Ruysdael or Vermeer, the heavens are revealed as a source of infinite power and expansiveness that transcends any mere Medieval macrosphere. The unbounded infinity of the heavens is a source of potential possibilities that are as yet unfathomed. This is, for perhaps the first time in history, a world picture that is *not* enclosed by boundaries of any sort. There is only space now, and the human subject (for the subject, too, is a new iconotype of this age) is the primary occupant of this space.

The creation of the transcendental subject, beginning with Descartes, is a constitutive feature of this age, for it is an age of perspectival space in which the world is looked at from the point of view of a single human individual. The bounded world of the Medieval order is now scaled down and miniaturized to the bounded self, transcendentally sealed off by God (this transcendental Ego is not apotheosized until Fichte, in his *Foundations of the Entire Science of Knowledge*, postulates it at the end of the eighteenth century); a self which confronts a realm of absolute objects whose truth value is now a function of the correspondence theory. Knowledge is "really" out there, ingrained in the book of Nature, and for one who knows how to read this book of Nature, it can be found and "acquired." The world is an objective fact, cognizable by a subject, whose vision carves out of it a single perspectival slice.

The artist, correspondingly, now becomes a sort of master optician. He is no longer the Medieval cosmocrator endlessly recreating pre-established entities and saints, but rather a master of "seeing." Hence the preoccupation with mirrors and various optical devices such as the camera obscura during this age from Van Eyck's *Arnolfini Marriage* to Velazquez's *Las Meninas*. Spinoza, lest we forget, made his living as a lens grinder, and both artist and philosopher are precisely those who are capable of "clear vision." Descartes insists that for a thing to be "true" it must be "clear and distinct," or, in other words, brought into focus.

The ontology, furthermore, is not Pentecostal, but rather Evental. The world is no longer a series of repetitions of sacred acts that took place once upon a time, but a series of singularities and unique occurrences. Every event now has its own quality and special character that must be noted down and examined by the natural scientist, the Linnaeus or the Leeuwenhoek or the Newton.

The center of the art world now shifts from Italy to the Netherlands, where a whole host of "clear seeing" Dutchmen are articulating the metaphysics of the Age of the World Picture; that age, in other words, which according to Heidegger, frames the world *as* a picture of objectively measurable entities spread out into visually connected and continuous, homogenous space. Space now is indeed, as it is for Kant, *a priori*: for the space now comes first, and only then do we consider the objects that are set inside of it. This is McLuhan's Gutenbergian Galaxy and Jean Gebser's "perspectival" phase of the mental consciousness structure.

Art is now portable, painted on movable canvases, no longer on frescoes and walls bound to specific places. Its portability gives rise to a new bourgeois art market that also simultaneously creates, for the first time ever, the impecunious artist, for with the disappearance of churchly patrons and aristocrats, the only patrons are now wealthy merchants who are interested in decorating their new homes with signs of their new wealth. The artist now has a precarious existence creating paintings for the market that might, or might not, sell. As a result, many artists must now have day jobs. Thus, as Arnold Hauser writes: "van Goyen traded in tulips, Hobbema was employed as a tax-collector, van de Velde was the proprietor of a linen business, Jan Steen and Aert van de Velde were innkeepers."[16]

The concept of intellectual property – first glimmering in the signed canvases of the High Renaissance -- is now a structural feature of the age, as well, for the artist is no longer merely a receiver of images and visions transmitted to him by God or the angels. The ontology is Evental, full of singularities, and original visions. Each artist is a unique subject who exists in three-dimensional space and who looks out upon the world as a unique entity with his own special type of ocular vision. The world is now what is seen, not what is revealed, as in the previous Pentecostal ontology.

Some of the iconotypes of the previous world age still linger, of course, as in the case of Rembrandt, who also painted Biblical themes in addition to his portrait studies and his historical images, but it is characteristic of the age that the kinds of Biblical motifs that Rembrandt painted were rather singular; iconotypes, in other words, which it had never occurred to the previous world age to represent, such as that of Samson and Delilah, or Susanna Bathing, or Bathsheba at her bath, etc. Rembrandt explores iconotypes left unearthed by the previous world age.

The aesthetic theory, then, that is proper to this second epoch of European art is that of Schopenhauer's, which he works out in his *World as Will and Idea*: according to him, art does not arouse the will but calms it, for it represents its objects in such a detached manner that the person beholding the work of art is neither moved toward nor away from it, but captured into an aesthetic stasis in which he becomes the pure, will-less Subject of the World beholding the pure Object of the world. He has no interest in the object, but only to behold it as a work of art in and of itself. This, of course, is an aesthetic transformation of the correspondence theory of truth, in which the pure subject beholds the pure, deworlded object in the mode of *Vorhandenheit*, that is to say, as a self-sufficient entity. Objects and entities are no longer, as they were in the Byzantine aesthetic, manifestations and avatars from a spiritual reality of timeless saints and heroes together with their wonder-working relics; but only ontologically deworlded entities cut from the contexts of their various worldgrounds and placed into the Cartesian x and y coordinates of three-dimensional phase space.

But this age, too, begins to cycle down toward its apocalypse long about the year 1800 when, in the art of J.M.W. Turner, there comes a new fascination with disasters and accidents. Turner is absolutely obsessed, in his art, with disasters of all kinds, and he is the first Western painter to be so preoccupied: from his *Shipwreck* of 1801 down to his famous and controversial *Slave Ship* of 1840, the world has become for Turner something of an emergency situation. (And indeed, other artists, too, at this time, such as Gericault with his famous 1819 *Raft of the Medusa*, or Delacroix with his 1824 *Massacre at Chios*, are also becoming fascinated by disasters).

The art of Turner constitutes the end-times response to the art of the discovery of Infinite Space that was apotheosized by the Dutch painters of the seventeenth century, for Turner, too, was fascinated with the atmosphere, only in his case, the atmosphere has become a threat: his paintings of storms and shipwrecks, of calamities and Biblical plagues, of Hannibal Crossing the Alps in the midst of a blizzard, is a vast portrait of the dissolution of particular forms into the very substance and fabric of the atmosphere that surrounds them and makes them possible in the first place. But that very atmosphere is now threatening and ominous, almost as though Turner as the first painter of the Industrial Revolution were already sensing the environmental catastrophes that such an age of transforming the atmosphere with the burning of fossil fuels is only now, today, bringing about. Turner does indeed, as Michel Serres insisted in his classic essay, "translate Carnot," but in such a way as to foresee the comings of an atmospheric catastrophe that begins to signal the climax of the Age of the World Picture.[17]

Turner is the first apocalyptist of that age, and it is in his art that we begin to see it approaching its crisis point, whereupon its iconotypes, too, will undergo transformation, this time at the hands of the Impressionists of the 1860s and 70s who will begin to dismantle three-dimensional space together with all its iconotypes.

The Prehistory of the Visible

What Tintoretto did to the spatial and geometrical *a priori* structuring forms of the High Renaissance – namely, according to Wolfflin, pulled them apart – the French Impressionists now proceed to do to the three-dimensional forms and secular iconotypes of the perspectival phase of European art. The epoch that extends from about the time of Manet's 1862 *Music in the Tuileries* down to Matisse's 1947 Dominican Chapel in the French Riviera, despite the many stylistic transformations that take place during this epoch, is nonetheless bound together by what the Swiss philosopher Jean Gebser termed "aperspectivity."

Gebser divided European art into the three distinct phases – and I have loosely followed him in this essay – of the preperspectival, the perspectival and the aperspectival epochs. What Gebser failed to see, however, from his vantage point of writing *The Ever-Present Origin* in 1949, was the existence of a *fourth* epoch that follows that of his integral-aperspectival consciousness structure, a sort of *post*-aperspectival period, that, namely, of contemporary art, which I have demarcated from the time of the Abstsract Expressionists down to the present moment. (It should be noted that Gebser's three phases loosely correspond to Sloterdijk's premetaphysical, metaphysical and post-metaphysical ages).

The structures and models of contemporary art simply do not fit into the period of Gebser's integral-aperspectival consciousness structure, since those models, such as they exist at all, are today in a state of continual liquefaction and disintegration that no longer follow the contours of Gebser's four-dimensional macrosphere. Instead, the characteristics of the post-World War II epoch of art have more in common with Zygmunt Bauman's "liquid modernity" or Vilem Flusser's "post-history."

Gebser sees Modernist art being painted, as it were, onto the walls of a non-Euclidean hypershpere: Cezanne, he points out, painted on curved space, the very same curved space that became the basis of the *n*-dimensional manifolds and topologies of the non-Euclidean geometries that began to surface in mathematics beginning around the year 1800 with Gauss. This hyperspheric structure of modernity is tantamount, be it noted, to the reconstruction of a new kind of macrosphere, the very same cosmos of curved space upon which Einstein painted the laws and forms of his General Relativity, in which gravity becomes a function of the curved space warped by the masses of planets and stars. Straight lines now give way to the curvatures of light rays travelling along geodesics in a sort of cosmic space that takes on the shape of a hugely expanding universe that is currently inflating like a gigantic balloon from the point of an initial singularity. Time is taken up into a four-dimensional manifold along with the previous three dimensions of space -- height, depth and width -- to become space-time: a single set of coordinates carved out by each object as it approaches the speed of light.

According to special relativity, there are three consequences to be expected from the acceleration of an object as it approaches the speed of light: the object collapses into two-dimensionality, time stops, and the mass of the object becomes infinite. It is, therefore, impossible for any object with mass to attain light speed, with the exception, of course, of those massless objects known as photons.

And indeed photons, or light particles, now become the primary fascination of Impressionist art. And it is precisely in this art that the three-dimensional space of the previous age, that of the World Picture, now begins to collapse and flatten out into two dimensions, a process that is already underway in Manet's *Le Dejeuner sur L'Herbe*, and in paintings like *Boating* or the landscapes of Pissaro and Cezanne. By the time of Van Gogh and Gauguin, space has completely flattened out and the world as they saw it has been transformed from a realm of objects spread out in space as a visual container in which light is thrown upon them by a single point of view, into a flattened, self-luminous world of objects that become, as they do especially in Van Gogh, their own light-sources, like television screens. Van Gogh transforms the landscapes of the south of France into a single luminous pane of stained glass with the light from another world -- the realm of Being -- shining through them.

The religious iconotypes have completely vanished: the art of Monet, Renoir, Pissaro, Caillebotte and Cezanne is an art that is completely shorn of mythical iconotypes, Biblical figures, historical anecdotes and legends of any kind. Indeed, the French Impressionists are the first Deconstructionists: they sweep the stage clean of all previous iconotypes, and elevate the secular iconotypes of the landscape painting and the still life to the main field of fascination. The new iconotypes are now the Baudlairean iconotypes of the *flaneur* and the City: even when an Impressionist painter is out in the countryside at Argenteuil or Bougival, he is still looking at the landscape through the eyes of the City intellect, which now sees the world entirely in terms of the present moment, a moment that is comprised of shifting patterns of light glimmering across the surfaces of things. It is an amnesic art, an art that wills to forget the past and proceeds as though there were no such thing as History. All the grand metanarratives, in other words, are already in full disintegration. The Impressionists regard them as irrelevant: the only thing that matters now is *this* present moment.

Since the transcendental signifieds of God and the Biblical saints, the soul and a metaphysical world space no longer count, a Schopenhauerian aesthetic is no longer proper to this art, since that aesthetic, as we saw, depends upon a realm of absolute, disinterested subjects beholding pure objects from a single point of view. Instead, it is a Heideggerian or Gadamerian aesthetic that now makes sense, for in a landscape painting such as that of Cezanne's *Small Houses at Auvers-sur-Oise*, it is precisely the opposition of World vs. Earth that is made evident in the tiny human habitations set back against the flattened space of the countryside.[18] According to Gadamer, who builds his aesthetic theory in *Truth and Method* off of Heidegger's aesthetics, the work of art is a sort of avatar, or emanation of Being that actually *increases* the Being of that which it represents.[19] The viewer is taken up into the feedback loop of the canvas like an actor in a play who can no longer regard himself as separate from the play, but has become entrapped inside the world erected by the play. Thus, the subject-object dichotomy of traditional aesthetics is nullified by Gadamer, for what now counts, as it does for Heidegger, is the luminous apparition of a mysterious dimension of *Being* that now begins to shine through these works, as though the light of another world were illuminating the merely transient phenomena of this one.

Heidegger's conception of Being is, of course, a kind of secularized transcendental signified: it is what Heidegger finds left of the spiritual dimension after the death of the grand metanarratives and the discrediting of the transcendental signifieds of God, soul, freedom and immortality. And it is also, correspondingly, what the Impressionists find left after they have deconstructed the grand signifieds, to which this art no longer refers. All landscapes in Impressionist art are apparitions of Heideggerian Being.

This is now an art, to use McLuhan's terminology, of light *through*, not light *on* objects, which McLuhan pointed out as especially characteristic of the pointillism of Seurat, in which each dot becomes its own light source in a way that anticipates the coming of television and electronic screens.[20]

It is also an art, at least initially, that is emphatically an art of the daytime. No Impressionist painter paints a scene at night until Van Gogh, because it is not until Van Gogh's completion and transformation of Impressionist light principles into self-radiant objects that night scenes can even be conceived. Van Gogh's *Night Café*, or his *Starry Night*, are paintings of objects that give off their own light, like bioluminescent creatures at the bottom of the sea. And Toulouse-Lautrec, who paints almost exclusively Parisian night life, does so with a cast of dream-like characters who swim about through his canvases like the day-glo colors of exotic fish in saltwater tanks. In Van Gogh and Toulouse-Lautrec, waking consciousness, in other words, is *receding* back towards the realm of dreaming consciousness.

This recession now creates a paradoxical effect that begins to inaugurate Modernist Art properly speaking: that is to say, that with the recession of Western consciousness *inwards* away from the day-world, the forms of dream and myth now begin to surface into the Clearing, and the religious iconotypes, paradoxically, begin to return, only now transformed into Jungian archetypes of the collective unconscious. It is, of course, in the artwork of Gauguin, such as in his *Yellow Christ* or *Jacob Wrestling the Angel*, that the Biblical archetypes begin to resurface, and in his later Tahitian works of the 1890s, the Tahitian gods begin to push their way up into view as they dissolve the traditional Biblical iconotypes and replace them with Jung's ethnographic elementary structures common to *all* men everywhere. Thus, the iconotypes of Modernism return as Jungian archetypes, the *a priori* structuring forms not only of the imagination, but of Modernist art, an art that is concerned, as Paul Klee put it, with a "prehistory of the visible."

This recession of consciousness inwards is simultaneously a recession down to the *a priori* structures that make the visible world possible in the first place. The great structures of Modernist art that begin with Picasso's discovery of the iconic totem of the African mask are of two kinds: mythic structures, on the one hand, and geometrical structures on the other. Of course, the two *a priori* forms are not quite as dissimilar as they might, at first glance, seem, since Plato's Forms were composed precisely of *both* geometrical and mythical forms (his Forms, as Cornford pointed out, were really the Homeric gods in disguise). What they have in common, however, is that both *a priori* kinds of forms are structuring principles that make up the very architecture of the visible world.

This becomes especially evident in the art of Paul Klee, whose entire art is based on a study of both kinds of forms. Klee was obsessed with uncovering the earth's biomorphic and geomorphic formative principles that Nature made use of in order to structure and build her vast array of morphologies: the very same forces that go into the construction of plants, for Klee, are precisely those which the artist uses to construct his paintings. Indeed, for him, the creative forces which the artist channels are precisely those incredibly archaic forces which Nature used to construct dinosaurs, amoebae and the various flora and fauna at the bottom of the ocean's depths. In his sketchbooks, he toys with the basic structuring principles for constructing not only works of art, but Creation itself. A straight line, for instance, when combined with a circle can be used to generate all sorts of forms: a lamp, a vase, a pendulum, even a heart with an arrow through it or a musical note. Solidity and fluidity are the two principles involved, and for Klee, it is of the utmost importance for the artist to know these principles in order to construct his own cosmology.

Klee's forms are, of course, self-luminous objects, as are all the forms of Modernist art. But in this art, each object is constructed out of multiple points of view: in Balla's 1912 painting *Dynamics of a Dog on a Leash*, for instance, the motion of the dog's tail and legs leaves ghosts behind it as it moves through space, but the dog as an Integral object – the construction of which is the aim of this art -- is composed by rendering *all* the phases of its motion simultaneously co-present. Therefore, as Gebser points out, time is taken up and integrated into space in Modernist art. Time is, for the first time in Western art, spatialized.

Thus, with the breakdown and disintegration of perspectival space, each object becomes a sort of hyperdimensional integral object composed of all its facets at once. Each object exists in its own space, separate from all other objects, and becomes its own self-radiant, luminous apparition, a hyper-object that is not to be found in the visual world of things located in physical space of the Age of the World Picture, but rather in the theoretical world of the artist's imagination.

And, of course, no art was ever more theoretical than Modernist Art: if the artist had been a cosmocrator in the Medieval macrosphere, and an optician in the Age of the World Picture, in Modernism, he is a theoretician par excellence. All the great artists of this epoch, from Manet to Paul Klee, are *theoreticians*, which is why it is emphatically *not* an art for the masses. Consequently, the mode of Vision for the communication of its ideas is neither Pentecostal nor Evental, but Hermetic, that is to say, as Michel Serres describes it in his book *The Parasite*, as a series of private intercommunications between the artists.[21]

It is, furthermore, an art that is enclosed on the *inside* of a greenhouse, as Monet's seven paintings of the railway station at Gare St. Lazare brilliantly demonstrate. In those paintings of 1877, the steam generated by the resting locomotive rises to fill an iron and glass structure that is the exemplary architectural structure for the age: from Walter Benjamin's arcades of the 1830s to the Crystal Palace of 1851, and on down to the various department stores and railroad stations of the age, it is a society that is now enclosed infrastructurally by a literal greenhouse. And as the smoke from Monet's locomotives is already (unconsciously on his part) suggesting, it is also the time of the first beginnings of the formation of the earth's CO_2 greenhouse as the result of the burning of fossil fuels in the external combustion of these first great steam engines.

Ontologically speaking, and as Gebser's theory of this aperspectival epoch implies, the Modernist artist paints his forms like the Paleolithic artist onto the walls of the hyperdimensional world cavern, where they float, and glow, all by themselves, as the structuring forms located in the deep recesses of the causal zones of Being that make everything in the physical world possible.

The epoch comes to its climax in 1937 with Picasso's *Guernica*, the summa of Modernism, for the image (despite its anti-war protest theme as a superficial structure) invites a certain comparison to the animal Forms painted by the Paleolithic artists of Picasso's native Spain onto the walls of their caves. The mural has a cavernous feel about it, as though we were on the *inside* of a world-space beholding the two-dimensional forms painted onto its walls. Horse, bull, fallen rider, three women: all are mythic forms. And they are illuminated by the technologized Eye of God motif that gazes down on them from above in a slot that precisely occupies the semiotic vacancy of the ancient Byzantine motif of Christ Pantocrator gazing down upon his human creation from the top of the dome of the world ceiling with his all-seeing eyes from which one cannot escape. The light bulb which Picasso has placed into the center of the God's Eye, furthermore, is already prophetically foreseeing the surrounding of the planet by today's global satellite surveillance technologies which now look down upon us at all times.

Thus, the transcendental signifieds at the end of the metaphysical age – and Modernism is its climax – are temporarily held in place by the Jungian archetypes of the collective unconscious, even though God, Soul and Freedom have been deconstructed by Nietzsche. But it is their last stand: after World War II, Gebser's Modernist Integral hypersphere collapses, and Euro-American man now finds himself shell-less and unprotected once again.

After the Death of Art

Arthur Danto, in his book, *After the Death of Art*, insists that contemporary art begins with Andy Warhol's *Brillo Boxes* in 1962. The reason for this, Danto says, is that by effacing the distinction between the traditional art object and the consumer object, art as it was traditionally practiced can now be considered to be "dead," since anything and everything can now be regarded as a work of art. The previous epoch, that of Modernism, was characterized by the issuing of manifestoes in which each group, Dadaism, Futurism, Surrealism, simultaneously anathematized each other group, insisting on the rightness of its particular understanding of art as the *only* way to practice real art. But in contemporary art, all this is over: no one can any longer anathematize anything as subject matter for art, since contemporary art welcomes all comers. Absolutely anything, practiced by anyone, can now be considered "art."[22]

However, despite Clement Greenberg's insistence that Abstract Expressionism represents the absolute pinnacle of Modernism

Art After Metaphysics

(another manifesto, in this case, Formalist), in this book I have chosen to begin my analysis of contemporary art precisely *with* the Abstract Expressionists since I see their art as representing something radically different from what the European Modernists were doing. For one thing, it begins the shifting of the art world from Paris to New York, which by itself is already enough to demarcate a new epoch, since New York becomes, at least for a couple of decades, the center of contemporary art, which then begins to become a source of anxiety for the new generations of European art that come along after World War II. Even Joseph Beuys was influenced by Abstract Expressionism, and Gerhard Richter *begins* by working through the influence of Pop Art.

But, as the following essays on Jackson Pollock and Mark Rothko should demonstrate, these two artists correspond to a structural phenomenon that takes place at the beginning of any, and every, new epoch: namely, a sweeping and clearing of the stage of all the previous structures of the earlier epoch. We have already seen how the Impressionists of the generation of Manet, Monet and Renoir swept the stage clear of all previous iconotypes by eliminating myths, legends, historical figures and Biblical settings from their art. The stage must first be cleared and deconstructed before the new forms can be generated within it. The action paintings of Jackson Pollock and the semiotic vacancies of Rothko's luminous squares, are tantamount to a structural wiping clean of the slate of Modernist iconotypes, namely geometrical structures and Jungian archetypes. Once the stage is clear, contemporary art proper begins with Andy Warhol and Land Art and Minimalism in a way that corresponds to the appearance of new forms in Van Gogh, Gauguin and Cubism during the previous epoch.

This epoch of contemporary art, furthermore, is once again, like that of the Age of the World Picture, shell-less: the Modernist hypersphere has collapsed, and Being has, as Heidegger often put it, abandoned beings in this age. The grand metanarratives are, indeed, gone, apparently for good. The transcendental signifieds, including Jungian archetypes, have vanished as ultimate anchoring terms of reference for the signifiers of the art. It is an art without narratives or structuring models of any kind. Indeed, the artist now finds himself on his own in a way that hitherto was never the case in art.

The contemporary artist must construct his own plane of signification now, with a set of meanings and signifieds that belong exclusively and idiosyncratically to *his* cosmos and to his alone. The other artists cannot illuminate his work. Each artist has to be understood now on his own terms, and in order to understand the art – which even Kenneth Clark confessed was completely "baffling" to him[23] – the artist's own private semiotics must be worked out by the beholder. There are no longer any overarching systems of meaning by which to make sense of the art, and consequently, a Gadamerian aesthetic – contrary to Gianni Vattimo's insistence[24] – simply will not do for this art, since it is not an art that increases Being or functions as emanations of Being since Being is precisely what no longer exists in this age. Being collapsed during World War II, and as Heidegger demonstrated, it was hi-jacked by technological enframing. There is no longer a single overarching understanding of Being for which the works of the contemporary artist could ever be understood as avatars.

Contemporary art is, consequently, a worldless art. It is an art that exists on its own outside of all ontological horizons. It is no longer bound to any specific place (precisely because it is no longer contained within a "world" in the Heideggerian sense) but has been dispersed across the entire planet. New York functioned only in the early stages as a center for this art, but nowadays the center is everywhere: Santa Fe, Flagstaff, London, Shanghai, Dusseldorf, Tokyo, etc.

The artist now finds himself in an exospheric mode: he is like Adam in Masaccio's painting of the *Expulsion from the Garden*, for the city no longer needs him. He has become superfluous to the endeavors of civilization, much of which has now been taken over by the technocrat and the popular artist of the comic book, the cinema, and the bestseller. The contemporary artist, like Cain, is a homeless vagabond who wanders over the surface of the earth.

Consequently, no longer tied to a specific place, the earth itself now becomes his canvas. Land Art is an art that emerges out of the age of Sputnik, in which the planet itself now becomes the field for vast works of art by Robert Smithson or James Turrell or Christo. The artist's job, ontologically speaking, is no longer to defend civilization from the impacts of the Real by constructing immunizing macrospheres, and so he finds himself on his own as an exile from civilization, carving patterns into the very soils of the earth itself.

The artist is a theoretician no longer, but rather a monadologist constructing a private semiosphere that must be puzzled out by the beholder. There is no longer a single overarching macrosphere, but rather a multiplicity of miniature spheres – as many spheres as there are artists – floating about the earth like a series of Sloterdijkian bubbles. Indeed, Sloterdijk's "foam" is a good metaphor with which to describe the ontological situation of the contemporary artist.

The artist now is a sort of spore let loose by civilization to wander across the surface of the earth. Civilization no longer needs, or wants him. He has become superfluous. Consequently, art in the posthistoric age is no longer necessary for the civilizational project.

But yet, since it persists, and is still practiced by ever-increasing numbers of artists, it must be understood, rather than dismissed, in order to fathom where civilization is at today.

The displacement of art from Paris to New York in the early 1960s corresponded to a shift of intellectual orientation in Paris to the spheres of cinema and philosophy. Indeed, it could be argued that the French thought of the 60s *is* a kind of artform transposed into the sphere of the intellect.[25] The general incomprehension of the French during this period of contemporary art, especially that of the New York variety of Jasper Johns, Robert Rauschenberg, Claes Oldenburg, etc. was more than compensated for by the dazzling brilliance of French theory which, to my satisfaction, anyway, has never been applied in an illuminating way to contemporary art. This book is an attempt, however successful it may be thought to be, to redress that gap by using the ideas of Deleuze & Guattari, Derrida, Foucault, Paul Virilio and others to opening up hidden dimensions in the art of the post-World War II epoch.

The particular artists whom I have chosen to discuss in this book seem to me to represent the best that contemporary art has to offer, although I could have chosen to elucidate the works of many,

many more artists. The names of Jackson Pollock, Mark Rothko, Joseph Beuys, Francis Bacon, Jean-Michel Basquiat, Anselm Kiefer, Gerhard Richter etc. etc. are *the* great architects of contemporary art whose work we cannot afford to overlook if we are to understand the epoch in any kind of depth. I also consider other artists to be important, as well, but for various reasons, I chose not to include them in this book. The works of Paul Thek, Andy Goldsworthy, Susan Rothenberg, James Turrell, Bill Viola, Jenny Holzer, Gottfried Helnwein, Vladimir Velickovic, Cai Guo-Qiang, Zaha Hadid etc. etc. could have been added to the mix, but then, one has to stop *somewhere* or else never finish the book.

Hopefully, the reader will find the present selection to be illuminating enough to bring out the grand lines of the epoch.

A Note on Google Images

This book does not have illustrations, for copyright issues regarding the works of currently living artists simply make such illustrations prohibitively expensive. However, thanks to the Internet, the book comes with a ready-made image search called Google Images, and the reader is advised to read the book in front of a computer with Google Images ready-to-hand. Most of the images will come up, since I have searched for them myself. There are a handful that are not to be found, but those, as I say, are only a few.

PART TWO:

GEOGRAPHICAL REGIONS

New York

Jackson Pollock - Mark Rothko - Jean-Michel Basquiat

Contemporary art, it is true, is a highly individualistic and intensely idiosyncratic kind of art in which each artist is engaged in the construction and elaboration of his or her own plane of signification. And yet, we can nevertheless discern certain distinctly regional tendencies with characteristics analogous to one of those (now outdated) Kulturkreislehre *theories of nineteenth century German anthropology, whereby entire geographical regions of the earth are noted for the spread and diffusion of a certain custom or art motif, such as the fact that, broadly considered, the X-ray style art of ancient shamanism can be found diffused from the Paleolithic caves clear across Europe and Asia and on into the New World as a single vast culture sphere, but a sphere in which this art is entirely* missing *from African art. Other motifs have much smaller geographic distributions that similarly characterize cultural zones.*

With contemporary art in New York City – which begins during the late 1940s and 50s -- there exists a twofold concern that seems to be characteristic of the artists as a grouping. On the one hand, as evidenced in the work of Jackson Pollock and Mark Rothko, there is a concern with the dissolution of form that is tantamount, as I have pointed out in the introduction, to a sweeping and clearing of the stage of the basic iconotypes of European Modernism. This is an effort on the part of the American artist to sever the ties with the European tradition in an attempt to attain his own unique identity. Pollock's art begins as an art that revolves around the Modernist archetypes of Jung – the goddess and the shaman, for instance – but eventually dismantles and dissolves those icons in favor of a flux of planetary energetic fields that is broader and wider than the scope of the Modernist forms. Pollock's drip paintings, I will argue, are the first planetary art, an art for the age of satellites orbiting the earth looking down at it as though it were one huge Pollock canvas into which specific forms had been dissolved into larger, more all-encompassing patterns of energy.

With Mark Rothko, who also begins by imitating European Modernist iconotypes, the forms are dissolved and liquefied not into dynamic fields of crackling energy, but into luminous squares and units of elementary Being as spiritual entities unto themselves, absolutely indeterminate in nature and unqualified by archetypes of any kind. Rothko discovers the absent ontological center at the Western core of Being that has come about after the collapse of the grand metanarratives and the discrediting of the transcendental signifieds of the metaphysical age.

With Andy Warhol (the reader interested in my take on him should consult my previous book Dead Celebrities, Living Icons*) and Jean-Michel Basquiat, the concern of both artists was to try to fill these new semiotic vacancies that had been opened up at the center of the West's understanding of Being with new iconotypes: celebrities, in the case of Warhol, and the two-dimensional figures of New York graffiti art in Basquiat's case. These new iconotypes are the New York equivalent of the city iconotypes of the Parisian Impressionists: the* flaneurs *and crowds of Paris correspond to Basquiat's Crown King or his spindly totemic figures; while the artist-as-celebrity finds its analogue in Warhol's cult of the two-dimensional electronic celebrity avatars of Elizabeth Taylor or Elvis Presley. Warhol and Basquiat, then, are concerned with (an ultimately abortive) attempt to create new iconotypes as the interior consciousness of the city of New York. The two artists are the prophets of the age of the Internet, into which all graffiti is poured, and YouTube (which democratizes the cult of the celebrity into the fifteen minute window of YouTube's allowed upload time that Warhol would very much have approved).*

But it is an abortive project, since New York's ascendance as the capital of the art world lasts for scarcely two or perhaps, at most, three decades. Contemporary art is a planetary phenomenon that is not tied to any particular city and so no city can any longer claim to be its center. The center is everywhere and nowhere.

Just like the Internet.

Jackson Pollock

The Superfluous Artist
In November of 1945, Jackson Pollock and his wife Lee Krasner moved from New York City to an old farm house on Fireplace Road located in a community called The Springs on Long Island. It was there, in the barn adjacent to the house, that Pollock in 1947 created his famous drip paintings that would put American Abstract Expressionism on the cultural map as a new and distinct development from the type of Modernist Art that had come into being in Europe, and especially in Paris, during the period between 1860 and 1945.

While this data is well known to the annals of art history, what is not so obvious about these events is what they imply about the ontological status of the artist, a status which, from Pollock down to our contemporary artists, has remained unchanged.

Pollock and Krasner's exile from New York City, that is to say, though self-imposed, was nonetheless tantamount to a performance of the exile of Adam and Eve from the Garden, a mythological event which Peter Sloterdijk in his book *Spheres I: Bubbles* describes as symptomatic of what he calls a "spherological crisis."[1] This is the type of ontological crisis that ensues in a civilization whenever a protective macrosphere collapses: in the case of Adam and Eve, the crisis consisted in the exile from a world of careless concern to a state of ontological anxiety in an existence of being thrown into another world in which care and concern would become, from henceforth, constitutive of the new level of human consciousness.

In the case of Pollock and Krasner, the semiotics of the two worlds are reversed, for it was the existence *within* the polisphere of New York City that compressed and constrained Pollock to a life of anxiety, worry and desperation, whereas, out on Long Island, the removal of these pressures not only allowed him to stop drinking for two years, but made possible the singularity of his own great creative explosion. Nonetheless, the *structure* shared by the historical episode with the myth is the same, namely, the crisis announced by the exile from one sphere to the next, or rather from the state of encasement *inside* a protective macrosphere – New York as the modern cosmopolis – to a state of exile and unprotected worldlessness *beyond* it.

Pollock's exile from the modern world city – like Dante's from Florence, in which case, the poet invented his own literary cosmos as a sort of Derridean "supplement" to his situation -- is an event that becomes archetypal for understanding the ontological status of the contemporary artist of today, for Pollock's exile from New York signifies that the modern world city no longer *needs* the artist, who has become entirely superfluous to its functioning.

Consider the days of sixteenth century Rome, by contrast, in which an artist like Michelangelo or Bernini was absolutely essential to the cultural project of the Renaissance, which could never have taken place without him. In seventeenth century Amsterdam, likewise, Rembrandt, together with all the other great Dutch painters, was articulating the new consciousness of a world that was then suffering the crisis of exile from another world sphere – as we have seen -- that namely, of the Copernican which, when it collapsed, took all the Christian iconotypes of Medieval art down the drain along with it. The Dutch art of the seventeenth century records the new anxieties of the ontological consequences of being out *in* space, unprotected by an immunological heavenly vault for the first time in the history of Western civilization. And the modern art articulated by the nineteenth and twentieth century painters of Paris made Paris, in Walter Benjamin's words, *the* capital of the nineteenth century.[2]

This is no longer the case with the contemporary world artist, who now finds himself perilously superfluous in the international world system created after World War II. The city no longer *needs* the artist, for it has undergone a structural transformation which has rendered him inessential to its contemporary task of building a worldless consumer cosmopolis in which art is no longer necessary because contemporary existence is no longer bounded and contained by semiotic systems of meaning that create world boundaries and membranes. World War II shattered the boundaries separating one world epoch from the next, but the traditional role of the artist had been essential in articulating such boundaries, which are defined not only by specific style formations but also by the iconotypes that confer particular meanings on these local worlds. In an international world society – a *worldless society*, in other words – art becomes irrelevant.

And so, after World War II, when the lineaments of this global world system sanctified by Bretton Woods in 1944 (together with the final withdrawals of European powers from their colonies) first began to come into being, the ontological status of the artist shifted from that of an immunologist defending the particular boundaries of a local world sphere to that of a monadologist creating his *own* self-enclosed system of meaning in the manner of a *bricoleur* using scraps of whatever happens to be at hand.

The artist, in other words, as Robinson Crusoe, the first figure in Western literature to be imagined in an *exospheric* mode, that is to say, as an outcast from civilization who must remake his own microsphere as a world island unto itself.

Hence, the exile of Pollock from the world city of New York illustrates a *rupture* in art history demarcating the existential status of the artist from henceforth as an exile from a world horizon who must suffer the agon, *not* of competing and dialoguing with the Old Masters in an effort to find – as Andre Malraux described in his *Voices of Silence* – his own voice (those days are long gone) but rather to create his own monadologically self-contained world island of meaning that may – or may not – have any kind of semiological dialogue with the masters of the now vanished metaphysical age. Hence, the impression that strikes anyone who glances at contemporary art for the first time and sees mostly vacant nihilism.

Art that is created *outside* a World may very well not have any meaning at all since, as Heidegger was the first to warn, the creation of a globalized cosmopolis that is based upon the elimination of distance only results in an effacing of meaning and significance from the local horizon.³ Meaning, on the cultural plane, cannot be exported in the same way as gas stations, parking lots and shopping malls which have a universal applicability precisely because such non-places *have* no meaning. An art that would have cross-cultural universal appeal is almost a contradiction in terms.

So the task of the contemporary artist is a different one from any that has gone before, because it is no longer that of dialoguing with the Old Masters, but rather demarcating decisive *ruptures* with them and wrestling out idiosyncratic systems of meaning against the ever-persistent threat of meaninglessness. The wrestle is not with the Old Masters anymore, but with meaning itself.

Pollock's exile from Manhattan – in which the artist is excreted from the city as a new kind of entropy in order to ensure the smooth functioning of the city as a dissipative structure -- is the annunciation of this whole development. Which also explains why his work, beginning with the drip paintings, struck many of his contemporaries as nihilistic and pointless.

Planetary Artist

But Pollock's work also opens up another window, for he is the first *planetary artist*, the first artist, that is – in the Western tradition, anyway – to enlist the powers of the earth in the creation of his images. In this respect, he is the forerunner of later artists like Christo, Robert Smithson, James Turrell, Andy Goldsworthy, Michael Heizer, et. al.: artists, in other words, who presuppose the earth itself as their canvas. In the global ecumene, art likewise expands to planetary scale.

Pollock, though not, technically speaking, the first to lay his canvases flat on the ground and dispense with the easel, was nevertheless the first to make this practice his trademark signature. In doing so, he also eliminated the brush and instead used a stick dipped into a can of house paint -- thus also eschewing the palette – to create his vortical cosmoses by leaning over the canvas and utilizing gravity – in place of the brush – to apply the paint to the canvas. In doing so, gravity itself, for the first time, becomes a tool in the artist's repertoire. Pollock, in other words, allies himself with the *very curvature of the space surrounding the earth* in order to bring forth his images. The images, therefore, are not random at all, but follow the contours of the earth's gravitational field – which, according to Einstein's General Theory of Relativity, is a function of curved space warped by the mass of the planet inside it. In his drip paintings, then, Pollock was visualizing curved space, allowing his stick to follow the concavities surrounding the earth, rather than any particular objects upon it.

Pollock himself pointed out in interviews that Navajo and Tibetan sand painters also painted their images on the ground and therefore utilized gravity as a tool, but what he did *not* remark upon was that these traditional artists were not capable of painting curved space, since the conventions of their iconotypes that structured their *seeing* allowed them to paint only mythological images. By the time of Pollock's art, such iconotypes, as we have seen already in this book's Introduction, had by then largely disappeared.

Pollock, as French theoretician Paul Virilio has pointed out, orbited his canvases like a Landsat satellite looking down at the abstract topologies of the earth from outer space, and in this respect, too, he foreshadows the coming epoch of the encompassing of the planet by human technologies.[4] Pollock's first drip paintings in 1947 prefigure the launch of Sputnik in 1957 by a decade. Thus, though it is a truism to say it, the artist always anticipates what's coming over the horizon before it ever actually arrives.

And in painting the curvature surrounding the earth – *all* of his lines are curved; nowhere in Pollock do we find the rectilinear lines of Barnet Newman or Mark Rothko -- he is also prophetically looking ahead to the surrounding of the planet not only by satellites – and hence, its transformation into a giant art object – but by the cocoon of electromagnetic white noise that would soon engulf it in beams of radiation that compose a vast, satellized network of competing transmission signals, all combining – invisibly – to create a mesh of interference patterns densely woven around the earth like the fibers of a moth's cocoon.

Indeed, Pollock was painting the white noise that surrounds the earth's curvature just as Karlheinz Stockhausen, at about the same time in Germany, was composing his first electronic compositions built out of the degradation of white noise into colored sounds. Stockhausen's *Electronic Studies* of 1953 – 54 are the auditory equivalent of Pollock's drip paintings.

Thus, Pollock was already making visible in his art the invisible environment that would slowly begin to close around the planet in subsequent decades.

He is, therefore, the first truly planetary artist, and as such, his drip paintings constitute a complete singularity, a total rupture, from everything that had taken place in art history before him. In Alain Badiou's event ontology, Pollock's work corresponds to what Badiou describes as the irruption of a singularity into a status quo situation. An Event, in other words, that changes the subsequent history of the situation.[5]

For after Pollock, as is well known, art would never be the same again.

Modernist Iconotypes: the Shaman and the Great Mother

But in order to understand this development, we must look at the evolution of Pollock's images, for they *do* follow the lines of a development, a transformation of growth and form that follows the laws of its own inner logic.

There are, to begin with, two figures, and *only* two figures that form the protagonists of his figurative art up until the 1947 drip paintings, and they are first announced in two of his earliest paintings, both of which date from about 1930. This is the painting that is variously titled *Woman* or *Mother*, and which shows a pendulous-breasted woman surrounded by five mysterious beings, probably male, looming up from behind her. This painting has been interpreted by Ellen Landau and others as an autobiographical portrait of Pollock's mother and her five sons, and on the literal level, this is probably correct.[6] However, she is rendered in such a way as to suggest an unmistakable comparison to ancient images of the archetypal Neolithic Great Mother, who will form one of the major Figures that will undergo transformation throughout the evolution of his images.

The other Figure appears in a self portrait painted about the same time as *Woman*, which shows Pollock himself as an eerie two-faced being, half of whose face is in shadow and apparently undergoing transformation into a mask. This mask is, of course, the masked shamanic apparition that will appear in his totemic paintings of the late 1930s and early 1940s. That apparition is simply a transformation of himself as alter ego, the masked shaman being whose consort is the Great Mother, just as in Paleolithic iconography mammoth ivory sculptures of the Great Mother appear in tandem with shaman beings, such as the 30,000 year old standing shaman lion-man found at Hohlenstein-Stadel in Eastern Europe.[7]

This masked shaman being makes its actual debut in his 1938 painting *Birth* – his first masterpiece, incidentally – which shows a series of masked faces all tumbling in disarray as they fall downward, as though they were spilling forth from some kind of cosmic womb (like the vaginal cleft of *The Deep*, one of his last paintings). It has been said that this series of apparitions, with its vertical orientation, suggests the totem pole of the Native Americans of the Northwest Pacific Coast, an image which I think Pollock probably did have in mind when he composed it. The masks, as is well known, are modeled from carved Eskimo shaman masks, but they also represent the birth of his mature style (Phase I, as it were) the paintings of which now begin to tumble forth – after a long struggle down the false path of Thomas Hart Benton pastiches throughout the 1930s -- with ever-increasing rapidity from here onward. The downward gravitational pull of the falling faces, moreover, already foreshadows his later use of gravity in the construction of the drip paintings.

These masked apparitions continue to appear in the series of paintings from this period, including *Naked Man, Masqued Image, Bird* and *Magic Mirror*. Pollock was, in actuality, a displaced Southwestern artist – he traded places with Georgia O'Keefe, who migrated from New York to Santa Fe at just about the time Pollock migrated from Arizona to New York in 1929-30-- since his early influences, as is well known, were mostly Mexican mural artists and Native American art. This perfectly suited him for the Modernist project of painting tribal icons on the walls of the Modernist world sphere, a sphere that had first begun to configure itself with the rupture of Impressionism.

The iconotypes of Modernist Art, with its tribal world cavern, are precisely the Jungian archetypes, and so it is apropos that Jungian theory and mythology interested Pollock in these early paintings. With the advent, then, of his drip paintings would come, not only the death of Modernist Art, but also the death of tribal icons as its primary structuring Forms. Pollock's art is a recapitulation in miniature of the shift from Modernist iconotypes to the worldless visions of contemporary art which *have* no iconotypes.

Hyperspheric Goddess

In the 1942 painting entitled *Stenographic Woman*, we have his second great masterpiece, although it is a masterpiece thoroughly dominated by the influence of European Modernism, and most especially, Picasso. This was the painting that confounded Peggy Guggenheim and caused a stir at her exhibition because it is, at first, so difficult to read. Initially it looks like an image of two separate figures – a mistake made by Steven Naifeh in his massive Pollock biography – but upon closer inspection it is seen to be, as Ellen Landau correctly remarks, a type of the reclining female nude first crystallized by Titian's and Giorgione's various Venus paintings. She is lying horizontally across the surface of the canvas, with legs spread apart like a Playboy centerfold, and surrounded by stenographic figures that are evocative of mathematical equations.

This is, in fact, Pollock's Great Mother archetype, only now she has been placed *inside* the hypersphere of the Modernist world cavern. Just as Lewis Carroll's Alice was the first character in Western literature to be placed inside the universe of non-Euclidean geometry, where she undergoes various spatial distortions, so Pollock's goddess archetype is distorted by the Modernist n-dimensional hypersphere, which has the effect of breaking her up into multiple spaces and frames of reference. Pollock has here painted the goddess of Einsteinian space, as it were, the goddess of the hypersphere whose curved anatomy follows the contours of its topology. Whereas Newtonian visual space had been rectilinear, optically correct and masculine, in Einsteinian space, light travels along the geodesics of the various spaces curved and warped by planets, stars and galaxies. Likewise, in the painting, a yellow light ray passes through the central figure along a curved geodesic while the equations surrounding her track the transformations of this Minkowskian world line through spacetime. The image is thus an X-ray of the female anatomy of the Modernist hypersphere itself upon which all the paintings of European art were then in process of being executed.

It is this very cosmos, identified with the body of his Great Mother, that Pollock will soon cut apart in order to create the abstract cosmos of his later drip paintings.

Becoming Animal

In the 1943 painting known as *She-Wolf*, meanwhile, the shaman avatar from the earlier masked apparition paintings reappears, only now he is transformed into his animal avatar. Shamans are beings capable of transformation into animal totems, and the image on this canvas shows Pollock's alter ego, combined and blended with the female identity of his Goddess, in his becoming-animal form, as Deleuze and Guattari would put it.[8]

The central horizontal stripe that resembles an arrow and which follows the axis of the animal's vertebral column already looks ahead to the becoming-animal of Pollock himself, for with the axial shift of his canvases from upright to supine, so too, the spinal column of the painter, erect for centuries (like an evolved *Homo sapien*) will shift to a nearly horizontal (and hence animal-like) orientation. Thus, Pollock himself, with his drip paintings, will undergo metamorphosis into a human-animal-planet assemblage: a new, and strange, kind of artistic being that evokes a certain comparison with the painters of the Paleolithic and their obsession with animal Forms, like the totemic She-Wolf of this painting which was directly inspired by Paleolithic art.

This new human-animal-planet assemblage of the artist is a function of Pollock's relation to the earth which, with the vertical skyscrapers of Manhattan now behind him, becomes suddenly, and spectacularly visible in his horizontal art. Like the myth of Antaeus, Pollock too derives his strength from contact with the earth.

The Rupture

But now with the 1943 painting known as *Pasiphae*, the sacrifice begins to take place: the goddess that he had transformed into the Great Mother of the Modernist Hypersphere in *Stenographic Figure* will now be slain, cut up and completely torn to pieces. With the debris of her body, Pollock will then proceed to construct his abstract cosmos.

Pasiphae was originally entitled *Moby Dick*, which evokes the myth of the hunt of the great beast, for the canvas features a central creature, obviously female, that is flailing around in what looks like water while several armed beings stand around her, ready to thrust their spears into her in a performance of the Babylonian myth of the sacrifice of the goddess Tiamat, whose body was cut apart by Marduk to make the heavens and the earth out of it.[9] In an Aztec equivalent of this same myth, the earth goddess Tlaltecuhtli is torn in half by the creator gods Qetzalcoatl and Tezcatlipoca who each grab one half of her body and pull it apart, then use the pieces to construct the cosmos.[10]

It is significant that *Pasiphae* is one of Pollock's last figurative paintings before the leap into pure abstraction that is signified by the Guggenheim mural which he painted in January of 1944. That painting had begun as the image of a series of stampeding horses, bisons, bulls and cows all slamming into one another – as though chased over a cliff by Native Americans – which Pollock kept reworking and reworking beneath a latticework of vertical curves until the animal forms were completely dissolved beneath the abstract designs. The creation of the Guggenheim mural shows that he was, in fact, involved in an elaborate process of sacrificing Form to create a new, densely interwoven cosmos out of the bodies – in this case, animals – of living beings.

In the 1943 painting *Guardians of the Secret*, this new cosmos is already foretold in the rectangle that occupies the center of the composition that is flanked by two threshold guardians, one on either side of it, as though unveiling a revelation. The rectangle in the center painting is full of abstract, totally non-figurative forms, as though Pollock's next development, the creation of an abstract cosmos out of his Great Mother and her animal familiars, was already being clearly foreseen.

And that is, in fact, what begins to appear, as the next paintings like *Conflict* and *Night Mist* are abstract paintings – though not yet drip paintings – in which he has disassembled his Great Mother and created a new kind of cosmos out of the pieces of her body, a non-figurative, non-spatial cosmos that is as densely woven together as a Persian textile.

The very first drip paintings begin to appear at this time, too, in 1943, with *Composition With Pouring I* and *II* and also *Water Birds*, but they are only tentative steps toward what will later become the new revelation of his art.

Cosmos

One of the other constitutive features of Aztec myth was the idea that blood was the fuel upon which civilization depended – just the way we depend upon oil – for its operation. In the myth of the sacrifice of the goddess Tlaltecuhtli, blood must be offered back to the earth goddess in order for her to grow the plants and various vegetables, such as maize and corn, upon which the human being depends for his survival. Blood, too, is offered up to the sun god and makes him continue to shine and travel his course on a chariot pulled by fire serpents across the earth. *Nothing* can happen in Mesoamerican civilization without the offering of blood.

The Mesoamerican priest, consequently, was normally required to offer his own blood in order to summon the ancestral beings to do his will for him. He had to slice his genitals or perforate his tongue and then perform a whirling dervish dance that splattered the blood from his genitals onto sheets of paper that surrounded him, and this splattered blood would cause a Vision Serpent to appear and open its mouth, whereupon an ancestor being would peep forth and ask him what he wanted.[11]

We have seen that the fate of Pollock's Great Mother was to be cut up and torn apart to form an abstract cosmos out of pieces of her body carefully woven together to create a dense textile of anti-Form. But now we must inquire into the fate of Pollock's alter ego, the masked shaman whose last appearance in his art are the *Totem Lessons* from 1944 and 45. After that, the masked apparition does not appear again until the black and white canvases that follow his action paintings.

The drip paintings that he proceeds to create on Long Island, then, represent the spattered blood of this shamanic being, which he now offers up to the sacrificed remains of his Great Mother, which are together united – drips along with forms – to create the cosmos of his abstract drip paintings. They are a synthetic fusion of the blood of his shaman protagonist mixed together with chunks of the Great Mother's body, and so both Figures *are* still present, therefore, in his later paintings.

The universe that he creates out of the body of his Great Mother is based upon the revelation – soon to be taken up by Systems Theory during the 1950s -- of self-organization from noise. His drip paintings, created by using vortical motions of his hand, are dense vortices that evoke ancient creation myths in which the cosmos spontaneously brought itself into being from out of its own swirling vortices, like the atoms of Lucretius that swirl the cosmos into being (note that it is Venus, a goddess, whom Lucretius evokes in the opening lines of his text).

This myth of the autopoietic – or self-making cosmos – is very much opposed to the poietic myth of the maker in which Yahweh or else Plato's demiurge fashion the universe into being along the lines of an artist craftsman who uses a material like clay or bricks to create a manufactured artifact. The creation of the universe out of the body of Tiamat by Marduk or Tlaltecuhtli by Qetzalcoatl and Tezcatlipoca are also cosmogonic myths of this kind.

But the myth of self-organization, which is a much older myth, still preserved in the opening lines of Hesiod's *Theogony* in which Gaia gives birth parthenogenically (i.e. without insemination by a male) to her husband Ouranos, survives from the ancient Neolithic plant world in which the Great Mother as goddess of the earth gave rise from out of her own substance to the plants whose spiral growth, twisting slowly up out of the soil, imitate the spiral patterns of the motions of the heavenly bodies.

This mythology, as I have written about elsewhere, later resurfaces in complex dynamical systems theory, in which autopoietic systems that self-organize from noise become the primary revelation. Pollock, in his drip paintings, is already pointing ahead to the discovery of noise as a revelation, of the pre-cosmic Chaos from out of which cosmoses swirl themselves into being.

Thus, Pollock in his artistic technique, unconsciously imitates the myth of the maker who cuts up the body of the goddess to create a cosmos out of her, but yet the cosmos that he invents is precisely that of the swirling motions of the power of the goddess to self-organize. His work, therefore, is something of a paradox and defies facile readings that try to compress it into one or another category.

His drip paintings are not merely "energy made visible" as the cliché goes; rather, they are an instance of *both / and*: they image both the curvature of the earth together with the electromagnetic noise that surrounds it; *and* they also retrieve the body of the sacrificed goddess whose power of self-organization from noise *is* the very myth that underlies information and complexity theories.

Pollock's art is great art, and great art is great precisely because it always evades complete capture by any one semiotic system of meaning. Multiple semiotic systems are required to illuminate it from various angles.

But the one idea underlying *all* of these systems – whether mythological or technological – is the revelation that the Noise prior to the formation of the system *is* the revelation from out of which the system, be it cosmos or signal, arises.

World Island

Pollock, then, creates his own world-island in the barn on Fireplace Road, transforming the barn into a microspheric cavern upon the walls of which he paints, not animal Forms as in the case of the Paleolithic caves, but the vortical motions of the body of the Great Mother (who is also simultaneously the curvature of the space around the earth) which brings form into being through the process of morphogenesis. Pollock's paintings, then, envision morphogenesis itself *in the very moments in which it first begins to take place,* like the Benard cells that first appear when a pot of water on the stove is just on the point of boiling. (To confirm this, all one needs to do is imagine the evolution of Pollock's paintings in reverse: beginning with the drip paintings and going backward in time, one can see the gradual emergence of forms and figures from out of the self-organizing fields of pure intensities, stage by stage. Pollock's drip paintings are, therefore, visualizations of what the philosopher Gilles Deleuze called the realm of intensivities, or the virtual flows, energy potentials and differential relations that give rise to the concrete world of extensivities).[12]

As an exile from the great world city, Pollock is washed ashore along with so much civilizational effluvia, like Robinson Crusoe, from out of which he must build and shape the spaces of his own world island as a microsphere surrounding him. In doing so, his unique world island splinters itself off from the Modernist project as a whole, to which it no longer bears any relation. His drip paintings, though cosmological – they remind one of the Japanese myth of the creator god Izanagi who drips saltwater from the tip of his spear onto the earth in order to create the world -- are no longer images painted upon the walls of the Modernist world cavern as his early tribal art had been; rather, they are images whose semiotics are completely divorced from the realm of that world cavern, from which they have broken off into a private island of meaning all their own. The meanings are, of course, universal, as all great myths are: but they are no longer specifically Modernist, having shed their tribalism and dismantled their mythic figuration.

If Modernist Art had been about the shift from the waking consciousness of European space to the level of dreaming consciousness and the realm of Jungian myth formations, then Pollock's work represents a scission from *that* level and a dropping down to one level further, what the Hindus in the *Upanishads* call the level of deep dreamless sleep, where *no* forms exist at all, only the causal zones of energy that give rise to such forms.

This is not a cavern world, like that of the Modernist hypersphere upon which tribal forms were painted, for spacetime does not exist at this level of consciousness. Rather, spacetime is *constructed* at this level out of what the Hindus term *akasha*, a kind of living ether from out of which forms crackle and hum into being. The Hindus have no word that corresponds to our Western perspectival idea of empty space, for *akasha* is not empty space, it is *living* space which spontaneously, through self-organization, gives rise to living forms, including the gods and goddesses of the realm of subtle matter.

Pollock's art, therefore, does not belong *in* or *to* the Modernist project. It is a completely new development, a shift into the aniconism and worldlessness of contemporary art, which is an art that takes place, as I have said, *outside* the containing bounds of any World whatsoever. The artist, in this development, does not contribute art *to* a World equipped with a semiotic system that pre-exists him, as Modernist art did; rather, the contemporary artist *makes his own world from scratch*.

World-making, as an endless series of monadological projects – there are as many Worlds in contemporary art as there are artists – is the essence of post World War II art, whose prophetic visionary was Jackson Pollock.

Media Catastrophe

But now these private microspherological worlds are very fragile and so they *can* be damaged, especially by electronic media, which is another reason why contemporary art is in such a perilous situation. Pollock's decline as an artist is a proverbial example of how such small and independently floating world bubbles no longer connected to a functioning World can collapse beneath the impact of new mediatic forms.

Pollock's last great year of productivity as an artist was the summer of 1950, during which he created his largest and also his finest canvases, such as the gigantic *Lavender Mist* and the magnificent *Autumn Rhythm*. But the moment of his decline can be marked very precisely: this was in September 1950, when Hans Namuth pointed a movie camera at him and, over the next few months, filmed him in action.

In 1949, *Life* magazine had already created the Jackson Pollock icon: in the famous image of him standing in front of his painting with arms crossed defiantly, cigarette dangling from his mouth, Pollock's second self was created as a two-dimensional avatar. This mediatic Pollock was mass produced through the circulation of the magazine, whereupon his cloned and replicated image was sent, via subscription, to the homes of the average domestic American, instantly transforming him into America's first celebrity painter. The article not only made Pollock famous overnight, it created a *second* Jackson Pollock, a flattened and caricatured version of him which corresponded only vaguely to the complexities of the real, three dimensional Pollock, the Pollock who drank obsessively and who always showed up at the party to ruin everyone's good time with outbursts of venomous anger and physical assaults. *This* Pollock, the bisexual Pollock who suffered from a mother fixation and who insisted, wherever he went, on not only being the greatest American painter, but the greatest living painter on the planet, had very little in common with the simplified flattening of him that appeared in the *Life* magazine article by shearing away his complexities and reducing him to a mere hieroglyph.

The existence of this image golem of Pollock began to destabilize the *real* Jackson Pollock by taking root in his brain and haunting every action that he did, no matter how trivial. Now it was no longer important to *be* a great painter, it became important to him to be *seen* as a great painter, and so he was soon overcome with a great deal of worry and anxiety about how best to match up to the image that *Life* magazine had created of him.

When Hans Namuth then came along a year later and filmed him creating his paintings, it wasn't, as Steven Naifeh points out, Pollock as a great artist that he was interested in constructing, but rather Jackson Pollock as a celebrity. Consequently, the artificiality of the staging – showing Pollock painting outdoors, when in fact, he always painted in the barn (his Polyphemus cavern, as it were) – and directing him to take off his shoes in a certain way, to stand in a way that was properly cinematic, and so forth – created so much cognitive dissonance in Pollock's psyche that the moment the filming was done he walked straight inside the house and started pouring himself stiff drinks for the first time in two years. Electric media were already beginning the slow, gradual process of killing this modern incarnation of the delicate dying and reviving flower god, only Pollock didn't realize what was happening to him.

The problem was, in reality, a matter of colliding media, with their different image dynamics. Pollock's canvases, over the years, had been getting larger and larger, and also more and more accomplished artistically until they culminated, just before Namuth's arrival at Fireplace Road, with his best work. The gigantifying of his canvases, however, actually had the inverse effect of shrinking Pollock *the man* down as a person. In direct proportion to the growing scale of his work, Pollock himself began to shrink, like Richard Matheson's *Incredible Shrinking Man*, as his mighty canvases dwarfed him.

With the creation of his mediatized icon, however, beginning with the *Life* magazine article and becoming more and more pronounced with the Namuth film and all the other media attention, it was Pollock's *image avatar* that now began to grow larger and larger. Before long, the shadow cast over him by his mediatic avatar was huge, and stood over him and his art like Michelangelo's David. The growing size of this avatar began to leech energy and vitality from the canvases, and as a result, when he returned to paint them after the Namuth film was made, he was now larger – in effect – than the canvases he had previously created. His mediatic shadow loomed over *them* now, and they seemed to him small and paltry by comparison.

Thus, when he started painting again, the images that appeared were the inferior black and white canvases that were now leeched of color, as though Namuth's creation of his movie avatar in color had drained the color from his own imagination. The color was gone, but color – not drawing – was precisely what had been his strength as a painter all along. Pollock knew how colors fit together and it could almost be said that his knowledge of the precise ways in which they fit together was the linchpin that had composed all his canvases and given them the wholeness and harmony as works of art that they had possessed.

But now the color was gone from his canvases and his mediatized avatar was, like the giant Alice in Lewis Carroll's book, out of all proportion to their scale. The avatar, consequently, due to its heavy gravitational pull, curved the space around it and so brought people into its orbit to see his exhibitions, but not because they were interested in the art, which they didn't understand anyway, but rather because they wanted to see what the infamous Jackson Pollock celebrity icon would do, what type of antic he would pull, who he would insult, what garbage can or fireplace he would urinate into.[13]

In other words, the creation of his mediatized avatar destroyed Pollock's microworld, causing it to collapse and implode in upon itself.

Thus, in the conditions of electronic society, art cannot thrive because electronic media are at cross purposes with the process of making traditional art. They are completely incompatible with the kinds of image modes, with the *ways of seeing* as John Berger once put it, that are innate to such traditional media as painting and sculpture. They cast image shadows that interfere with and distort the processes of these traditional ways of seeing and as a result, they often have the effect of rupturing their ability to function properly.

The only thing left, then, for Jackson to do in order to compete with his own image avatar was precisely what James Dean had done, and what later Marilyn Monroe and Elvis Presley would be forced to do when caught in similar agons with their own image avatars: destroy his physical self.[14]

Thus, in running his car off the road in 1956, Pollock succeeded in derailing his physical self from reality so that his image avatar could be left behind to continue thriving in his place where it has, in fact, done so ever since. The image avatar created by the celebrity stands like a zero where a number should be. It is a place holder signifying the *absence* of a human being, like the images of a foot or a handprint in early Buddhist art signifying that the Enlightened One had once been here but due to his attainment of nirvana could no longer be pictured in corporeal form.

In the end, only Pollock's avatar remained behind in the world, where it continued living on without him to trouble it, and was later brought forth from its cave like Lazarus in Ed Harris's faulty reconstruction of him in his film *Pollock* in which Harris *very* selectively constructs a narrative from Naifeh's biography that is consistent *only* with the myth of the lonely romantic artist who is doomed by his own visions to commit suicide. Harris, conspicuously, leaves out the complexities of Pollock's real self, such as his mean streak, his cruelty to friends and neighbors whose property he was always willfully destroying, his misogyny or his bisexuality. Harris's film is not a portrait of the real Pollock, but it *is* consistent with the image avatar of him first constructed by *Life* magazine and then manipulated by Hans Namuth as the Hemingway of the American art world.

But let's face it: in the end, the avatar *always* wins.

Mark Rothko

Singularity

In a series of paintings executed in 1946, Mark Rothko, for the first time in his art, began to create a unique, signature style. For twenty years, he had been trying, and mostly failing, to discover a vision that persistently eluded him through a series of pastiches, first, of nineteenth century Impressionist masters like Cezanne, and then, from about 1940, of Modernist giants like Picasso, Miro and Matta. These early works, however, while sometimes brilliant, were almost never original, and it wasn't until he began to melt down the Modernist iconotypes in those 1946 paintings which have become known as "multiforms" that he began to articulate something truly new. Indeed, *these* paintings are tantamount to a complete singularity, a rupture, not only with all his previous work, but with the history of twentieth century art, as well. For these canvases function like X-rays to reveal the collapse and dissolution of Modernist art, an art that, by the time of World War II, had largely run its course.

But since Rothko's art is all about the fate of the West's understanding of Being, it will be necessary, at the start, to briefly review the history of that understanding.

A Brief History of Being

According to Martin Heidegger, Being in the West has gone through a series of epochs in which it has been understood differently in each age (this is not a Progress model of the Hegelian sort, in which Being has gotten "better and better," but rather a series of metaphysical "turnings" in which it has undergone transformations analogous to what the Swiss philosopher Jean Gebser has termed "structures of consciousness"). In the pre-Socratic period, for instance, Being was understood as *physis*, not in the sense of "nature" as it is often translated, but nature as seen in a particular metaphysical *way*, that namely, in which entities arise, unconceal themselves as numinous mysteries, and then withdraw back into the self-secluding primordial darkness.[1] There were also specific understandings of Being, such as that of Heraclitus with his Logos, which is a cosmic ordering principle that shapes, gathers and organizes entities in a meaningful way. And of course, as any reader of even the most basic of Heidegger's writings knows, he regarded Being as having been divorced from Becoming by Plato's scission of the intellect from the senses, in which Being is understood as *eidos*, that is to say, as the ultimate Forms upon which the merely ephemeral shadows of the physical world are but imperfect copies.

With Christianity, though, the Heraclitean Logos which had been, for him, a general cosmic principle by way of which *all* beings could be understood, became incarnate in a *single* being, Jesus Christ, who was an avatar of the Mind of God. From the church fathers to the Scholastics, then, Being was understood as truth in the mind of God, from which the lives and imperfect intellects of sin-laden and wayward human beings were, to one degree or another, measured up.[2]

In the Age of the World Picture, which attained its full clarity during the seventeenth century, Being was understood as a realm of Absolute Subjects contemplating Pure Objects in an abstract – and deworlded – three dimensional phase space.[3] *To be* was to be an individuated subject in a visually connected and rational space inside which objects were situated. This was the essence of the metaphysical age, which Heidegger insisted came to its end in the latter half of the nineteenth century, with Nietzsche as its last great philosopher.

After the metaphysical age, beings lost contact with Being. They became mere objects rather than Things laden with significance, while subjects became mere entities fallen into the mode of average everydayness. The age lost contact with Being, which became forgotten, although, with the rise of industrialization, a revised – and trivialized – understanding of Being as *Gestell*, or Enframing, was brought about by technology, in which Being became merely the technological extraction of resources from the earth, which were stored up and held on demand for future use.[4] For Heidegger, Being, in the modern age, was no longer shaped by poets and philosophers, but by science and technology, and a gradual impoverishment of Western society was the result.

But it is clear that Heidegger, like his contemporary Oswald Spengler, neither sympathized with, nor understood, Modernity. It was left up to the Swiss philosopher Jean Gebser who, in his 1949 book *The Ever-Present Origin*, had to confer, as it were, synthetic unity on the manifold of the various phenomena of Modernity with his idea of the integral consciousness structure, which Gebser saw as the sequel to the rational consciousness structure that had characterized the metaphysical age.[5] Gebser envisioned this structure of consciousness coming into being in the middle of the nineteenth century at precisely the point where Heidegger and Spengler saw only a decline and disintegration into a "destitute time." Gebser characterized this consciousness structure as having the shape of an "integral sphere" of curved space upon which all the artists, from Cezanne to Picasso, painted their forms (like cave men inscribing animal icons on the walls of their caves). The understanding of Being during this epoch, that of the Modernist age, was not just technological Enframing, but rather Multiplicity: the Modernist cosmos is a spherical world of multiple times, multiple spaces, and multiple consciousness structures that could be accessed by any thinker, poet or artist gifted with a type of visionary mind which Gebser termed "veristic." Such a mind could render all contemporary phenomena – paintings, buildings, literature, etc. -- "diaphanous" to transcendent spiritual energies.

But of course, Modernist art, as we know, was an art primarily characterized by mythic and magical iconotypes – the Jungian archetypes, more or less – painted on the curved walls of non-Euclidean space, the Modernist hypersphere. It is *these* consciousness structures, rather than the rational consciousness structure, which predominated in Modernist art, and so, despite Gebser's insistence on *all* structures being present in the integral sphere which integrated and united them, they didn't all play an equally important role in the composition of its world space. But it was precisely the Jungian iconotypes – masked apparitions, tribal visions, myths, gods and heroes – that Mark Rothko was busy, in his 1946 multiforms, wiping out of existence.

The Collapse of Gebser's Integral Sphere

Gebser's integral sphere, however, was already in process of deflating at just the time in 1949 when he was writing about it as the unifying cosmology of Modernism. (He saw it functioning in a way similar to one of Peter Sloterdijk's macrospheres, the last one of which Sloterdijk sees as collapsing in the time of Copernicus).[6] The period of its dissolution took place precisely during World War II: Hiroshima and Nagasaki were not only physically devastating, but they were *ontologically* devastating as well, since their white-hot clouds flattened not only those two Japanese cities, but also Gebser's integral sphere right along with them. The implosion of that sphere, together with its liquefying mythic iconotypes, can be seen taking place in 1946 – one year after the detonation of the bombs – on Rothko's canvases. One only needs to flip through the pages of his catalogue raisonne to watch it happen, step by step.

In doing so, one sees a sequence of untitled paintings from the years between 1946-48, in which Rothko's previous forms, which had been borrowed largely from Modernist iconotypes – gods, heroes and mythic entities – are melted down into the visual slag of blurred, indistinct chunks of color, light and indeterminate forms.[7] In the multiforms of these canvases, the iconotypes shift and settle into blobs of glowing color that gradually give way to the cohesion and organization of squares and rectangles that begin sorting them out. It is a world of light and dissolution that perfectly documents the shift out of the Modernist world sphere into that second Modernity which Zygmunt Bauman has called "liquid modernity," in which no forms can crystallize or remain stable for very long.[8] These blurry fragments of previous myth-figures are forms of light; they are no longer forms of entities and mysterious beings out of the collective unconscious.

So by 1946, the Modernist world sphere was collapsing, together with all its structuring forms, and the West's understanding of Being as composed out of multiple times and multiple spaces, together with multiple consciousness structures – all articulated in the language of big philosophical metanarratives like Gebser's or Hegel's – had been liquidated and the slate, as Rothko once put it, "wiped clean." Lacking not only grand metanarratives, but structuring forms with which to build them, the Modernist project, by the late 1940s, was over. Gebser's *Ever-Present Origin*, then – one of the century's last grand metanarratives -- suffers from what McLuhan called "the rearview mirror effect," that is to say that while the culture moves forward, the mind looks nostalgically backward and sees the present in terms of a past that has already vanished.

Contemporary art – which, as I have pointed out in this book's introduction, I see beginning immediately after World War II, and not, as most art scholars, assume, with Pop Art in the early 1960s[9] – from henceforth will be about the quest for new forms (and not forms, that is, recycled from ancient civilizations). Rothko's art, in particular, shows the wiping clean of the slate of the West's understanding of Being, and his famous rectangles of light, which he would discover in 1949, not only document the semiotic vacancy left behind in the wake of the collapse of Being, but also, like a Hebrew prophet, provide us with a glimpse of the understanding of Being in terms of self-luminous surfaces that was then on the way.

Rothko's Cosmology of Light

At just the time, then, when nuclear physics was splitting the atom open in order to release the enormous quantities of energy bound up inside of it, so too, Rothko was cracking open his earlier material (both physical *and* subtle) forms in order to liberate the light trapped inside them. This began in 1949 when his cosmos stabilized and crystallized into a world of glowing, incandescent rectangles arranged into stacked tiers, beginning with painting *No. 15*[10] which depicts a single large rectangle of purple framed by a greenish border which hovers in the upper half of the painting beneath a stratified series of blurred, indistinct lines.

In paintings like *No. 30*,[11] in which a short burning rectangle rests, like a candle flame, atop a slender gold column; or *White Center*[12] of 1950, in which a vanilla-colored slab rests in between a mauve rectangle and a yellowish-red rectangle that rests atop it; or in *Untitled* of 1954,[13] in which a cream white square floats, disembodied, against a deep crimson ground; in all of these works, Rothko has created a realm of dematerialized light forms, a universe of limpid, serene and healing visions of light from another world that calms and reassures one of the reality of the Spirit. Indeed, Rothko's cosmos – despite his insistence on being a materialist -- evokes images of the disembodied soul in the Afterlife beholding a world of subtle forms made only out of delicate skins of light.

These paintings also function as difference engines that power the machine of Rothko's art: in this metaphor, Rothko himself becomes a sort of Maxwellian demon who reverses entropy by separating realms of light into regions of potential energy. His ever more firmly developing horizon lines perform this primordial act of Gathering and Separation, in this case, not of material forms – like Yahweh separating an archaic Pangaea from an oceanic Tethys – but of light forms. The *Untitled* of 1950,[14] for instance, is the first of these paintings to evidence such a firmly chiseled horizon line that differentiates a yellow top half from a darker, sedimentary bottom half. Another *Untitled* of 1950,[15] likewise, shows a solid line in the center dividing an emerald green upper rectangle from a coffee brown lower one. Indeed, the evolution of these horizon lines is more and more suggestive of primordial cosmic activities, of separations of regions of light from one another, as though some demiurge were organizing them in order to begin the first phases of his process of world formation.

Thus, after the implosion of Gebser's integral sphere as chronicled by the multiforms of 1946-48, Rothko's light forms evince the earliest morphological stages of cosmic formation of a *new* world that is to come but one which Rothko never actually managed to finish, since he didn't return to the material world in his work again. Just as the formation of light precedes the material cosmos, so Rothko sets about organizing light into cosmological patterns as though in preparation for the formation of a new cosmos that he intends to construct in order to fill the semiotic vacancy left by the dissolution of the previous world sphere.

This parallels the collapse of the Christian macrosphere at the end of the sixteenth century—in which all the iconotypes of Nativity, Ascension, Last Supper, Crucifixion, etc. ceased to function in a world building manner -- which was followed by an opening up of space in the discovery of vast expanses of the sky with the Dutch canvases of the seventeenth century; in Rothko's case, with the collapse of the Modernist world sphere, his canvases unveil a sudden and unexpected world of light that opens up and unfolds around the viewer, expanding and surrounding him with glowing forms of photoluminescent energy: burning reds and searing oranges; cool greens and ice blues and frozen slabs of white. Just as the Dutch world was a realm of three-dimensional space that lay *beyond* and *outside of* the Christian cosmos, so Rothko's cosmos is an expansive realm of pure forms of light *beyond* the Modernist world sphere.

These rectangles and squares are what I would term "elementary units of Being," and they begin to shift and drift and reorganize in the wake of the collapse of a world horizon, just as ice floes shift to accommodate the sudden collapse of glaciers into the sea. They are images of the semiotic vacancy that is left at the center of the West's understanding of Being after that particular understanding has collapsed, but *before* a new one has taken its place. (A similar sort of disorientation and anxiety is evident in the paintings of Caravaggio, where the issue is one of forms of *darkness*, rather than forms of light, that are shifting around in the wake of the collapse of the Christian macrosphere).

But, as I have said, Rothko's paintings *do* foreshadow the coming of a new, postwar conception of Being, one which Heidegger, with his understanding of technology as *industrial* technology, completely missed. This cosmos of self-luminous squares and rectangles already points like a vector to the world of electronic video screens, *also* composed of self-luminous squares and rectangles, that currently surround us today, and which have shaped a completely new understanding of Being, for in the age of liquid modernity, *to be* is to be an avatar on a luminous video screen. Today, you are nothing if you are not a phantom in the electronic universe of video surfaces. It is difficult to look at a painting like the *Untitled* of 1949,[16] which resembles a television screen with the power turned off; or *Light Over Gray* of 1956,[17] which resembles a cell phone, and *not* be reminded of the swarm of video screens that currently surround us.

Artists, as McLuhan always said, function as the Distant Early Warning System of a society, and Rothko is a classic case of that sort of visionary *pre*-vision in which coming cultural developments are already glimpsed on their way over the horizon before they are seen by anybody else. This should be contrasted with the rear-view mirror orientation of the philosopher, such as Gebser, who is always one generation *behind* the current developments.

And so, Rothko's light paintings chronicle the semiotic vacancy left by the collapse of one understanding of Being as it is wiped clean off the walls of the vanishing Modernist macrosphere, but also simultaneously point the way to the coming shift from *texts* to *surfaces*, as Vilem Flusser has described it, in the subsequent epoch.[18]

The Seagram Murals

In 1957, Rothko's art begins to be infected with an element of darkening from which it never recovers. It is at this time that his color palette shifts to dark browns and blacks and maroons; earth tones, in other words, which represent the missing material element in his cosmos of light. Indeed, black rectangles begin to appear with a sudden frequency in works like *Black in Deep Red*,[19] *Deep Red and Black*,[20] *Black on Red*[21] or *Light Red Over Black*.[22] It is an ominous sign, indicating the invasion of his cosmos by an alien and intrusive element that begins slowly, ever so slowly, to destabilize his world of elementary units of Being.

In the famous Seagram murals that he was hired to do for Philip Johnson's Four Seasons restaurant (and which were never used, ultimately, due to Rothko's withdrawing of them, fearing their degradation into the visual equivalent of Muzak), this new element of darkening becomes pervasive: murals such as *Black on Maroon*[23] depict single, or sometimes double, forms of empty rectangles outlined in sinister black bands, or else dark maroon bands which highlight a central, vacant square that no longer presses against the borders of the canvas, pushing out *toward* the viewer as the light forms had done, but begin rather to act with gravitational force to pull him *into* and *toward* the canvas, irresistibly. A different sort of cosmos is beginning to surface in these murals, an *anti*-cosmos that reacts against his earlier light cosmos with a sucking and dissolving effect that pulls it centripetally toward its disintegration as though these new semiotic vacancies – and they are now, indeed, vacancies, rather than pulsing, throbbing cells of living light -- were acting as basins of attraction rather than fields of radiant energy.

And indeed, these central rectangles with their curved sides, such as *Red on Maroon*,[24] are negative – and not, like the earlier rectangles, positive spaces -- vacancies, inside which, in the past, one would have expected to find a Western iconotype: a Crucifixion, say, in the time of the Medieval cosmos, or a portrait study of some aristocrat in the metaphysical age. But in the *post*-metaphysical age, those iconotypes are gone, and before new ones have come to take their place, Rothko manages to capture the semiotic void left at the heart of Western Being, a void that will soon be filled in with the idiosyncratic images of contemporary art as broken signifiers unplugged, like Heidegger's mere objects, from all systems of Being whatsoever.

The earlier black rectangles that had begun to appear in the midst of his light rectangles in 1957, however, now begin to invade these canvases as *borders*, surrounding and encompassing their central vacancies with a hostile and alien black nothingness, as though they threatened to swallow his rectangles completely. Indeed, in *Maroon on Blue*,[25] this darkening spreads across the entire canvas, leaving only a thin burning rectangle at the lower center that glows like a coal inside of a furnace.

That Rothko senses some kind of an impending threat to his cosmos is evident in the Harvard murals of 1962, in which he begins to connect these elementary units of Being together into chains, like polymers: in *Panel Two*,[26] for instance, or *Panel Four*,[27] dark Stonehenge-like rectangles are linked together in series by connecting filaments that make chains out of them. Polymerization is a sign that a membrane is beginning to form, as in the case of the polymerization of lipids joining together to form a bilayer in cellular evolution that constructs the cell wall which keeps alien molecules *out*. Rothko, in these Harvard murals, is joining his elementary units of Being together to form an ontological bilayer, as it were, in order to keep out the Black elements that have, since 1957, begun to infect his cosmology like a virus.

The Black is of course the ancient and primordial enemy of Light; it is the Nothing that is opposed to, and threatens the very existence of Being itself.

Rothko's art has now become a desperate battle to keep his cosmos from being swallowed up by the Nothing.

The Rothko Chapel in Houston

As Heidegger points out in his *Introduction to Metaphysics*, the Nothing introduces an oscillation into Being; it destabilizes Being by factoring into it the possibility that an entity that *is* might not, at some point, *be* any longer. Being can no longer be taken for granted, since everything that *is* will eventually be *not*.[28]

And so it is with Rothko's cosmology: in the years between 1964-67, when he was commissioned by the de Menils to paint a series of murals for a chapel dedicated to his art in Houston, Texas, he produced a series of completely black canvases in which the Nothing has, at last, triumphed over his cosmology of Light. These canvases are tantamount to a confession that the Nothing has won: for the black element that emerged in the 1957 canvases as a stain, more or less, had grown steadily larger over the years, becoming ever more pervasive, and despite his abortive attempts in the Harvard murals to construct a membrane defending his cosmos from assault by the Nothing, the Nothing, nonetheless, had by this time completely overtaken it. Rothko's cosmos, in these canvases, has vanished, and been replaced by the empty signifier of the Void, for what he has painted is not the semiotic vacancy left behind by the vanishing of older ideas of Being in the Western tradition, as had been the case in his Seagram murals, but the vacancy left behind by the vanishing of *his own* cosmos. The Houston murals are images of the semiotic vacancy left behind by the complete dissolution of *his* cosmos into the Nothing.

In the art of early Indian Buddhism, the Buddha could not be represented directly: one could only indicate the semiotic vacancy left behind by his *absence*, his vanishing into Nirvana, with a chakra or a footprint. Rothko, likewise, at the end of his development as an artist, leaves behind the signifier of a black monolith which has drained, like a black hole sucking light from a star, his cosmos of light away into nothingness.

Rothko's art, at this point, had entered into a *pralaya*, that is to say, the interim of chaos between World Ages in ancient mythology into which one age has disintegrated and from out of which the age to come remains as yet unborn.

As an artist, it would have made perfect sense for him to stop painting at this point, since the evolution of his art, like Pollock's with the later drip paintings, had exhausted its possibilities. But he wasn't quite finished.

Yet.

The Blacks on Grays

Instead, after an aneurism that nearly killed him, he resorted to a series of acrylic paintings in which Being, once again, begins to reassert itself against the Nothing. These final canvases feature a cosmos that is more or less directly bisected into two halves: an upper half of dark black and a lower half of grayish-white that pushes *upward* – rather than outward or sucking inward – against the void of nothingness hanging oppressively above it.

In these canvases, Rothko has returned to his difference engine, retrieving the horizon line that first appeared in 1950, but using it in a more final, absolutist manner. These canvases are equivalent to a Manichaean vision that captures the contending forces of Being and Nothing that have been struggling for possession over his cosmos all along, and distills them from the actual protagonist color squares so that they become reified as powers of Light and Darkness unto themselves.

According to Manichaean cosmology, the world began with a pair of two completely separated zones: a Kingdom of Light up above, and a Realm of Darkness down below. The two began to intermix when the Lord of Darkness decided to attack the Kingdom of Light, and the Kingdom of Light attempted to forestall this attack by sending a being known as the Anthropos, garbed in an armor of light, down into the world of matter to do battle with the devils and demons. The demons, however, tore off his armor of light and ate it, and that is how Light fell, and became trapped, in matter. The entirety of world history ever since is composed of an intermingling of darkness and light, of matter and energy, but the world will end, according to Manichaean eschatology, when these two principles become absolutely separated again in the formation of a single statue of Light, gathered from all of the liberated light particles that will be used to recompose the original armor of light. The Light will then triumph over the Darkness by sealing it away into a pit of blackness for all eternity. The cosmos thus ends where it began, with two completely opposed principles.

And so, likewise, Rothko's cosmos ends with a complete and final separation of the powers of Being and Nothing, of Light and Darkness, from one another. It is uncertain, though, which of the two has won, despite the victory of the Nothing in the Houston murals. These final canvases, made not long before Rothko committed suicide by slicing into his arms with a double bladed razor at the kitchen sink, could just as well represent the beginnings of a new cosmos as the ending of one, especially since the myth of the Separation of the World Parents, of the heavens from the earth, is primordial and marks the start of the cosmogonies of all the high civilizations.

The two powers remain poised in these paintings, in direct opposition, neither one nor the other prevailing.

They are like the momentary equilibrium, immediately after World War II, of Heavy Modernity and Light Modernity: the Heavy Modernity of industrial technologies – of Heidegger's Enframing – which has conquered the earth; and the Light Modernity of self-luminous electronic technologies that, in Rothko's time, was just about to be unleashed, a technology that will saturate the surface of the earth and its outer spheres, clear on up to the Exosphere, with pulsing signals of light that will completely transform human existence and melt down all previous forms of media. (Rothko's lunar-looking landscapes in these final paintings even look ahead to this shifting of technology to the outer spheres around the earth).

Who can say at this point, in the battle between technologies of Matter vs. technologies of Light, which one will prevail?

Jean-Michel Basquiat

Apparatuses of Semiotic Capture
The central anxiety of Basquiat's art – and it is an anxiety that runs through every single painting he ever did – is the *absence* of an apparatus of semiotic capture. In an age of semiotic overload when all the signifiers have been torn free from the previous apparatuses that once captured and bound them into ordered systems of meaning and significance (i.e. Heidegger's various epochs of Being; Sloterdijk's macrospheres, etc.) the precise problem now for the artist who finds himself on the *outside* of Everything is to find and construct new apparatuses that will capture and collect the signifiers, assigning them new places of fixity and meaning, thus neutralizing the dangers of information overload (which tends to have a hollowing effect on the human subject).

Indeed, ever since the collapse of Gebser's Integral Sphere – the equivalent, more or less, for Modernist Art of Derrida's "transcendental signified"[1] – signifiers have been running around loose all throughout our society: across billboards, sliding as graffiti across the surfaces of buildings, glaring with neon luminescence as islands in the dark amongst deserted gas stations and poorly lit convenience stores. Everywhere we go nowadays, we are bombarded by signifiers that have escaped from their transcendental apparatuses to assault and overwhelm the human psyche on a constant basis. Television screens; video monitors on gas pumps; electronic billboards; entire buildings with ad logos crawling across them, torn loose from their surfaces of inscription in the pages of printed books.

It is an age of signifier overload, and the artist is vitally necessary – now more than ever before, in fact – to create new apparatuses of capture that trap and code these signifiers into systems of patterned order and meaning. It is, of course, ironic that the artist is now regarded as superfluous to the project of contemporary hypermodernity as a whole, for it is an age in which, precisely due to the lack of such artists, individuals are drowning in signifier overload. The psychological effects of such overload are not hard to figure out: paranoia, public violence, spree killings, drugs and cognitive disorientation. Indeed, far from being superfluous, the artist is *essential* to the health and functioning of *any* and *every* society. Without him, what Peter Sloterdijk calls, in his essay "Rules for the Human Zoo," "disinhibiting media" take his place, media such as popular films and comic books which tend to *feed* rather than *inhibit* the regression of the human personality to the status of neo-Roman bestiality.[2]

But it wasn't, of course, always like this: one is therefore forced to ask, what was the status of the signifier in the metaphysical or the Medieval ages prior to the disintegration of the apparatuses which held them in place and kept them from running around like escaped zoo animals?

Why, in other words, wasn't there any graffiti on the walls of Medieval churches and towns (graffiti that is, on the scale of today's dense meshwork of scrawls)?

And the answer is because all the signifiers were locked and held into place by the apparatus of semiotic capture of the cathedral, and the transcendent cosmology that the cathedral realized in physical space. The Medieval signifiers – saints, let's say, or the various myths and legends of Christian folklore – were organized into the niches and portals and windows of the art surrounding the cathedral, which acted as a sort of giant exoskeleton for holding them in place. The cathedral was normally laid out on an east-west axis, with the altar to the east and apocalyptic imagery adorning the west portals, while the stained glass of the windows transformed their interiors into the bejeweled radiance of the New Jerusalem which each cathedral was thought, from about the time of Abott Suger on, to symbolize. The image of Christ nailed to the Cosmic Tree was the master signifier that held the whole apparatus together: nothing random, and everything, as the Radiohead song goes, in its right place.

In the Age of the World Picture that followed and to some extent overlapped the Medieval age, the apparatus of semiotic capture that displaced the cathedral, together with its organization of space as a sacred revelation, was Cartesian phase space, which, along with its *x* and *y* axes, organized three dimensional physical space as an objectively measurable realm of subjects confronting objects in motion. The master signifier of that age was the Cartesian *cogito*, for the human subject, in the form of the portrait study, soon began to displace Christ and his various iconic representations as *the* central image of Western art. Mathematics, especially analytical geometry and the infinitesimal calculus, captured and bound all the signifiers, locking them into place as Transcendental Objects suitable for scientific analysis.

But, as Derrida has pointed out in his essay on "Structure, Sign and Play in the Discourse of the Human Sciences,"[3] the transcendental signifieds disappeared during the time of Modernity, leaving behind an absent ontological center to which signifiers no longer referred. And, in doing so, the signifiers, now let loose from their traditional modes of capture by various surfaces of inscription, began to tear themselves free from their various media and run riot over the walls of the culture. With the deauthorization of the grand metanarrative by French thought, on the one hand, and the assault on the Gutenbergian media of the printed book by the rise of various electronic media, on the other, a Crisis of Surfaces came about, in which signifiers, like Yeats's circus animals, no longer had anyone to tame them. So they began migrating, crawling, swarming and shifting across the walls of public space in quest of new surfaces of inscription.

And contemporary graffiti, which originated in Philadelphia around 1967, was one of the new manifestations of floating signifiers shifting and drifting across the walls of public space. Like Jenny Holzer's floating lines of text crawling up the sides of buildings, graffiti signs were largely composed of words, and not so much images, torn free from traditional surfaces of inscription and looking for new surfaces. In the absence of properly functioning apparatuses of semiotic capture, they had no place else to go, and so they started entering into public space as codes indicating the fragmentation and disruption of the social fabric into internal tribal hordes of city proletariat not taken into account by the overcoding of the capitalist consumer society. Corporate advertising on public signs and billboards is simply *legal* graffiti; *illegal* graffiti is regarded as a form of vandalism and, as such, is perceived and targeted by the immune system of the city for erasure.

Which brings us (back) to Jean-Michel Basquiat who, though not *technically* a graffiti artist, nonetheless *began* as a graffiti artist in the late 1970s, spray-painting lines of his own made up texts throughout the East Village in New York City, and signing them with the tag of "SAMO." Basquiat's graffiti was largely imageless, but his art on the other hand, while incorporating words within it, was largely about images. This is one of the reasons why his art cannot be dismissed merely as graffiti art, since it *isn't* graffiti art, which (at least in America) is dominated primarily by *words* rather than *images* (whereas with body tattoos the situation is reversed).

Basquiat, then, appropriated *some* of the semiotics of graffiti art in bringing it *inside* the world of New York art museums and galleries. In doing so, he "deterritorialized" – to borrow from Deleuze and Guattari – graffiti art from its origins in the streets and then "reterritorialized" it for the museums. But this problem, then, of taking the *outside* (as Andy Warhol once put it) and putting it on the *inside* brings us back to Basquiat's central anxiety, that, namely, of creating new apparatuses of capture with which to harness the semiotic overload of the streets.

Ontological Canvas

Basquiat, though, is always on the Outside. The central conceit of his art, the *Ur-phanomen*, if you will, is the crumbling, abandoned City Wall that one, in beholding his canvases, is presumed to be standing in front of. Basquiat, as a painter, is as it were the archetypal graffiti artist painting his images on the surface of this crumbling outer wall on some vacant side street of the City. But take note that this conceit always exiles him, no matter where he finds himself in the real world, to the Outside of Things. He is *always* on the outside inscribing images onto the surfaces of a simulated public façade. This is consistent with the ontological status of the artist in contemporary society, which is that of an outcaste: he paints on the *exteriors* of the city, which has turned its back to him and is no longer interested in his fate. (In the metaphysical age, by contrast, the artist was always on the Inside, whether he was Michelangelo painting on the ceiling of the Sistine Chapel or Rembrandt painting canvases in his atelier which were destined to be hung in bourgeois or aristocratic homes).

And this was the whole problem of Basquiat's agon as an artist since, no matter where he was at in his life, or how far *inside* the art world he managed to penetrate, the very conceit of his art always placed him on the Outside. Hence, the increasing use of the drugs to create a *faux* interior, an intrauterine state, in which his consciousness could be captured, bound and held to an Inside even while he painted on the exo-surfaces of simulated city walls.

The Totem vs. the City

Basquiat's first paintings, dating from about 1980-81, are images of cityscapes and urban techno-forms, such as the 1981 *Cadillac Moon*,[4] which depicts a stack of television sets beside two automobiles; or the car crashes of *Untitled* 1980,[5] or the cityscape of *Untitled* 1981.[6] These early paintings are cityscapes devoid of people, and they become very quickly overcrowded with floating signifiers, such as his famous Crown King signature or the notary seal that often figures in his canvases, or the letter "A" that is reiterated across the surface of *Cadillac Moon*. The first signs of a human presence appear in the *Untitled (Red Man)* of 1981,[7] in which a mysterious reddish-yellow figure with its right arm pointing up into the air surfaces on the left side of the canvas, while the right half is overcrowded with cars, planes and scrawled words. It is significant that the figure (the first of Basquiat's totemic Presences) is leaning *against* the right half of the canvas, as though it were pushing back the crowd of city signifiers in an effort to repel them.

And indeed, it is. In subsequent *Untitled* paintings of 1981, strange and mysterious totem figures suddenly emerge and dominate the canvas, towering over the city signifiers which have begun to recede into the background surrounding them. These beings, such as the archetypal Fisherman,[8] are rendered in the so-called X-ray style of art that is characteristic worldwide of shamanic art.[9] They appear early in Basquiat's canvases as invocations of totemic Presences which begin pushing back against the semiotic overload of the city, and they are rendered in an X-ray style in which we can see their skeletons and internal organs because it is precisely his fascination with the *interior* of the human body as an antidote to the perennial Outside of the city wall, which will become his main fascination.

It is the Human Body which Basquiat will begin to experiment with as a possible apparatus of semiotic capture *inside* which the escaped signifiers will be swallowed up, just as in the Medieval Age, the mystical body of Christ functioned as an apparatus of semiotic capture inside which all of his believers were gathered as cells.

This becomes especially clear in Basquiat's *Self-Portrait* of 1982,[10] in which he depicts himself scaled up to the size of a giant, a huge and solid shadow body, with an arrow in his left hand that seems to function like an eraser, for the various smears all across the surface of this canvas indicate *erased* signifiers which this giant, pharaoh-sized shadow body has wiped clean from the surface of inscription that he stands before. The human body as totemic, ancestral Presence will become the new semiotic machine that not only captures and attempts to neutralize the signifier overload, but will be precisely pitted *against* Basquiat's cityscapes.

In the famous *Untitled (Skull)* of 1981,[11] Basquiat places a patchwork version of his cityscape on the *inside* of this ancestral-looking skull. Indeed, if one compares the cityscape of *Untitled,* 1981[12] with the jumbled contents which Basquiat depicts, using his X-ray style, on the inside of this skull, then it becomes clear that he is beginning to experiment with the human body as a possible substitute for traditional apparatuses of semiotic capture. Whereas, in his earlier canvases, the City had swallowed up every trace of the human being, in this case, the human Presence has swallowed the City entire.

In the art of the ancient Egyptians, the signifier of the pharaoh was always scaled up to gigantic size in order to indicate his spiritual importance as the master signifier of the art.[13] In these early canvases, Basquiat, in similar fashion, proceeds to invoke and enlist the aid of a series of mythical totem beings, scaled up to giant size, to assist him

Art After Metaphysics

in the endeavor of capturing and neutralizing the semiotic overload. The *Untitled* of 1982[14] is a classic example of this.

The problem, however, soon becomes evident in paintings like the *Untitled (Black Skull)* of 1982,[15] which depicts a floating skull above a pair of scales, with an arrow and a thigh bone as disconnected entities on the surface of the canvas. Basquiat's totemic Presences, that is to say, have a tendency to explode apart and destructure themselves under the impacts of the signifiers that Basquiat tries to stuff inside them. There are too many signifiers – this is the age of information overload, after all – and his totem beings are unable to successfully contain them. They burst such beings apart, rupturing them into pieces, so that city signifiers are constantly spilling across the surfaces of his canvases from henceforth. By the time of such canvases as *Leonardo da Vinci's Greatest Hits*[16] and *Portrait of the Artist as a Young Derelict*[17] (both from 1982), it becomes clear that the signifiers are winning the battle, for they have exploded across the surfaces of the canvases in rich, dense profusion. Bits and pieces of the anatomy of his ruptured Human Presence dot these canvases with their effluvia: the floating head in *Portrait of the Artist*; the detached leg and the various feet and limbs in *Leonardo da Vinci*, etc.

In spectacular paintings like *Charles the First* (1982)[18] and *Horn Players* (1983),[19] the signifiers are completely free-floating once again and run rampant across the abandoned City Wall of his canvases. The body-as-apparatus-of-semiotic-capture is almost completely gone, and the signifiers have broken free once more, flooding the human subject with dizzying waves of information overload as city signifiers beam at him at the speed of light from all directions simultaneously. The internal anatomy that is visible in *Anybody Speaking Words*[20] is a momentary relapse of his earlier attempts to use the human body as a kind of fisherman's net for capturing the signifiers; but the *Self-Portrait as a Heel, Part Two* of 1982[21] shows the results, in which he depicts himself as an exploded and ruptured entity, a destructured being, like one of the Armani suits that he loved to wear while painting.

The problem is that, without an apparatus of semiotic capture – like one of Bacon's hermeneutic cubes – Basquiat as a philosophical subject, (and he is, himself, the subject of his own art), fails to develop a protective membrane in order to allow it to function. Canvases like *The Italian Version of Popeye Has no Pork in His Diet* (1982)[22] and *Untitled (Hand Anatomy)*,[23] also from 1982, demonstrate the signifier overload, the invasion, that is, from every quarter, of his psyche by crowds of signifiers. And this, of course, is also the problem of the contemporary self in general, for it is a self which, differing vastly from the Cartesian *cogito* or the Husserlian Transcendental Ego, is often unable to develop proper defense mechanisms against the information overload of electronic society, which beams so much information at the self, that in many cases it simply wilts under their impact like a tank under the green deathray of one of George Pal's *War of the Worlds* spaceships.

Basquiat's signifiers, as evident, for instance in *LNAPRK* (1982),[24] are a chaotic wilderness of disorganized forms that look as though they had been scrawled like graffiti upon a city wall by *multiple* hands. With graffiti art, there is no subject of enunciation, as in the case of the production of a classical novel or work of art, precisely because graffiti art is produced by a *collective* assemblage of enunciation; multiple artists, in other words. The subject is a We, not an I.

And so the problem in Basquiat's art is the very same: he is not an "I," but a "We." A stable self never crystallizes in Basquiat's art, as is made clear in the painting entitled *Jesse* of 1983,[25] which shows a central circle drawn over a collection of pages of diagrams and objects that look as though they had been ripped from the spine of a sketchbook. The circle is, of course, the traditional symbol of the self, and in Basquiat's case, it is a permeable self that fails to produce a solid interior that would provide him with a safe hollow inside which he might escape from the semiotic overload of the contemporary city. But as the image makes clear, there is no interior for Basquiat, no inside into which he could escape, since the images flood the inside just as much as the outside. Hence, the need for the drugs, to provide him with a safe, but temporary, inside to escape from the overload.

Technological Substitute

Basquiat's attempts at constructing new semiotic machines for processing and rewiring the various disconnected elements of his fragmented cosmos were largely failures. But the central point of his art, namely, the *need* for a new machine of semiotic capture to supplement the lack of the traditional apparatuses that once organized our signifiers and created cognitive coherence, was not only correct, but also prophetic.

Supposing one were to take one of his later canvases, such as the 1984 *Sienna*[26] or the *Melting Point of Ice*[27] from the same year and plug them in and turn them "on," sending electric current racing through the canvases. What would we have then?

Something very much resembling, I think, William Gibson's vision of cyberspace, which he was articulating in his science fiction novels at just about the same time as Basquiat was painting his art, for Gibson's cyberspace, too, is a realm of disconnected signifiers, corporate logos and Voodoo gods. Gibson's vision of cyberspace, furthermore, was a clear foreshadowing of the coming of the Internet, that recent technological substitute for all traditional semiotic apparatuses. The Internet is an electronic apparatus of capture that takes up all the floating signifiers from public space – ad logos, corporate symbols, graffiti both legal and illegal – and scoops them up into a world space that becomes the interior consciousness of the city itself.

It is a truism to say that artists are often prophetic of future developments, but in the art of Jean-Michel Basquiat, with its wilderness of floating signifiers divorced from any material substrates in any traditional media whatsoever, the coming of the Internet as a new apparatus of capture of public signifiers is clearly foreseen. Unlike all previous apparatuses, however, it does not organize and give meaning to these signifiers; it merely swallows them up and gathers them all into the Inside of a new world interior.

Consequently, just as Basquiat's art took the outside and put it on the inside; that is to say, captured the semiotics of the city wall and folded it inward into the New York art world; so too, the Internet captured *all* forms of public graffiti and folded it up to become the new Inside of city consciousness. The Internet is the Within of the city, its interior nervous system and the self-luminous correlate to its exterior nighttime luminescence.

Basquiat's various endeavors were clear intuitions that all these signifiers would eventually have to be gathered up into the same space in some way. In his case, he was gathering them onto the surface of a mythical abandoned city wall, while in the case of the Internet, they have been dematerialized from all their substrates in previous media. Nevertheless, the effort, in both cases, to build new systems of semiotic capture, are directly parallel to one another.

The Problem with Warhol

This is especially the case with Basquiat's collaborations with Andy Warhol, which are dress rehearsals, as it were, for the coming of this development. This series of paintings, done between 1984-85, when Basquiat and Warhol were hanging out together, performs the graffiti myth perfectly: Warhol's clean corporate logos and bits and pieces from advertisements were "defaced" by Basquiat, who would come along and paint little graffiti cartoons over them, as though he were an actual graffiti artist painting his tags over public walls.

But then, of course, this is precisely what the Internet is composed of: corporate logos and websites (electronic billboards, in other words, made portable) together with such forms of (now legal) vandalism as Customer Reviews on Amazon or the various Comments left on blogs and websites or even the websites of private individuals themselves. Together, Warhol and Basquiat are foreseeing the coming technological developments (as Warhol so often did in other cases) that lay just around the corner from them. Basquiat's "comments" on Warhol's ad logos are the equivalent of the various "comments" and "customer reviews" on today's official websites.

But there is another problem posed by these collaborations, one that involves an entirely different set of considerations. In rendering Basquiat's art a mere commentary on Warhol's, the collaborations tended to reduce his art to the status of a mere supplement (in Derrida's sense). Basquiat's art becomes *supplemental* to Warhol's, an ontological status which it had never possessed before, and this introduced a perturbation into Basquiat's art that he never recovered from. Hitherto, his art had been perfectly confident in the metaphysics of its own presence. But now, with his very high esteem of Warhol, whom he looked up to, it was suddenly reduced to the status of a supplement to the Master, a phenomenon not uncommon amongst traditional artists at the *beginning* of their careers (Leonardo painting the folds of the angel's robe on Verocchio's canvas as a supplement to the Master whom he was only apprenticing at the time being a classic example). But Basquiat was not at the *start* of his career; in fact, his best art already lay behind him. So for him to be *supplementing* the works of a Master like Andy Warhol at this point in his career proved to be disastrous for him.

From this point on, Basquiat's canvases grow ever less sophisticated, ever less sure of themselves; they become sketchier and less and less authoritative as metaphysical Presences. A new, and fatal, tentativity begins to set in, which is evident, for instance, in canvases like *To Be Titled* of 1987,[28] or *Riddle Me This Batman*[29] from the same year. A cartoony, sketchbook-like quality begins to dominate these later works, such as *Glassnose* of 1987[30] or *Victor 25448*.[31] Their ontological model is no longer that of the abandoned City Wall, but that of the Sketchbook. They are more like doodles drawn by a bored man on the pages of his notebook than works of the master that Basquiat had once been. Even his final great (and one of the very few in these years) painting *Riding With Death*[32] has a cartoon character quality about it that renders its status as great art questionable.

In these last couple of years, then, the semiotics of graffiti no longer provided Basquiat with his inspiration, but rather the images of cartoon characters and comic books. With the shifting of his ontological canvas from that of the abandoned City Wall to the sketchbooks of a cartoonist, the central Vision that had always "animated" his art for nearly seven years, was, by that point, gone.

And along with it, Basquiat's art.

The End

The commonplace observation, of course, is that the drugs were at fault. But the drugs had been there all along. Basquiat had been a hardcore heroin user right from the start, and he had enjoyed the peace of mind and ability to slow time down that it gave him, allowing him to focus intensely enough to produce the minute details of his early canvases. The drug usage, it is true, had grown gradually worse, especially as the result of his becoming one of the richest artists alive. Cash was never a problem for him, as Phoebe Hoban, in her biography, makes clear.[33]

And the fame hit him hard, too, as it did Jackson Pollock and many, many other celebrities.

However, nothing hit him as hard as Andy Warhol, the Master Signifier whose Factory had always represented for Basquiat the ultimate Inside of Art. If, like Kafka's K. in *The Castle*, he could ever manage to wend his way into Warhol's inner sanctum, then he would finally find himself on the Inside of the art world where he had always so longed to be. But, once he had befriended Warhol, who had a crush on him, finding himself on the Inside did nothing for him, since, as I have pointed out, Basquiat was, as a city wall painter, *always* on the Outside and always would be. There was no Inside for him ever to get *into*.

Warhol was the great master that he most admired, and the collaborations with him had the unfortunate effect of regressing him to the status of an apprentice, paradoxically while already having achieved the status of a Master on his own *first*. (In electronic society, effects, nowadays, often come before the causes).

But it was, of course, Warhol's death in February of 1987 that created a sucking vortex on the *Inside* that finally pulled him down, since Warhol was the symbol that anchored his cosmos, the axial center around which he had revolved. Warhol was the great Magus of Pop Art who had opened all the doors, and Basquiat would have been nothing without his admiration for him.

In the end, he had been reduced from the status of a Master to that of an Apprentice, and it was this ontological shrinkage of his status *in his own eyes* that permanently disabled him as an artist. There would be no more Visions from henceforth, and he knew it.

And so, in August of 1988, about a year and a half after Warhol's death, Basquiat died of a combined heroin-cocaine overdose.

By then, he was finally, and permanently, on the Inside.

The Greater German Grouping

Joseph Beuys - Gerhard Richter - Odd Nerdrum - Zdzislaw Beksinski - Anselm Kiefer

The Greater German Grouping which extends from Oslo to Warsaw includes the work of five contemporary artists: Joseph Beuys, Gerhard Richter, Anselm Kiefer, Zdzislaw Beksinski and Odd Nerdrum. All five artists, it seems to me, despite the diversity of the various media they use, constitute a grouping in that all are in permanent post-traumatic stress mode. These artists are attempting to recover from a catastrophe that has so badly damaged and mangled their culture that it is nearly impossible to come to grips with it.

The work of Joseph Beuys is concerned with an attempt to recode and reterritorialize objects that, like a piano or a record player, had completely different meanings under the conditions of a previous world age. The objects themselves have a tendency in his work to withdraw into seclusion, to break off into private spaces of ruptured meaning which form a damaged cosmos of silent entities no longer capable of communicating with each other. Indeed, for Beuys, the West's morphic art field has become so injured by catastrophe that it is no longer capable of producing anything but ruptured objects. Baudrillard, in his book The Conspiracy of Art, *insists that one of the main problems with contemporary art is that it is composed of a scrap heap of broken objects, since much of its content consists of removing objects from their normal functioning and simply putting them into museums. This does seem to be a major characteristic of Beuys's art, for it is filled with objects that no longer work or communicate in the way they are supposed to, bringing into question their very useability.*

Gerhard Richter, on the other hand, is concerned in his work with the scars and semiotic vacancies of the Western semiosphere that have been left behind like the residue of posters removed from city walls: his work is obsessed with erasing and effacing signifiers which are no longer anchored to their controlling signifieds. It is motivated by a kind of aniconic phobia, like that of the pharaoh Akhenaten, who spent his life crossing out the earlier works of Egyptian art.

Anselm Kiefer, meanwhile, has been engaged with building a cosmology of ruins and destruction out of the collapsed middenheap of the metaphysical age. If objects have withdrawn into silence in the work of Joseph Beuys, in Kiefer they have been reduced to the status of shells and piles of rubble: deconstructed texts, discarded ideas, broken icons. It is difficult to see how any sort of a functioning cosmology could ever again arise from this middenheap of shattered vessels and fallen stars.

The surrealist painter Zdzislaw Beksinki's entire oeuvre was tantamount to an apocalyptic confrontation with the armies of the dead and the Underworld, pouring themselves forth through the mouth of Hell and entering into the crumbling post-war streets of contemporary Warsaw. His work is a chronicle of the invasion of the World War II dead, who haunt his canvases like an occupying army.

In Oslo, Odd Nerdrum has tried to construct his own micro-cosmology to fill the void left by the collapse of the signifieds of Western Being. He has evolved in his paintings a private world of myths and visions which have no signifieds and refer to nothing beyond themselves. It is an expanding universe with which, like the iconotypes of Basquiat and Warhol, he attempts to fill the empty void of Western cosmology. But it remains unuseable as an overarching cosmology for the age precisely because History has ended and there are no longer any means for the creation of foundational stress events that would make sense out of his images. Instead, they drift and float in a void around the earth, homeless signifiers looking for signifieds which they will never find.

The art of these contemporary Germans – using the designation only figuratively for Beksinski and Nerdrum -- is the art of a shattered people who are still attempting to process the post-traumatic grief of a catastrophic Event that has decimated their meaning systems. It is as though all semiotic connections have been removed from objects on their cognitive maps which are drifting away from each other into a space of potential nihilism. It is no longer clear what "imaginary significations" still guide their culture, for the value of all the previous significations has now been called into question.

It is an art of beings abandoned by Being.

Joseph Beuys

The Crisis of Meaning
Whenever an Age collapses – whether by natural catastrophe, barbarian invasion, or gigantic war makes no difference – the collapse itself generates a crisis of meaning. Things, that is to say, in a broken age, no longer mean what they used to mean. A piano, for instance, in the Classical Age, was an instrument, especially in the hands of a Beethoven, for sounding out the cosmic architecture of the creator's Infinite Spaces. In the art of a post-metaphysical age, however, it becomes a suspect instrument, an object of rupture and communication breakdown, a sign that objects are withdrawing from each other into their own innermost recesses as each fractures away from the other into its own private world of silence. Hence, a felt-wrapped piano in a post-metaphysical age is an object that has been reterritorialized to perform a different function *within* a different age.

Inside a functioning macrosphere things have meaning that is ascribed to them by transcendental signifieds that give them their place in the cosmic order and prevent them from sliding along the Chain of Being, coming loose and bumping into other objects that may, or may not, have any relevance to them. The problem of an age when a functioning macrosphere no longer exists – as, for instance, has been the case since World War II – is that the meaning of things is now uncertain; indeed, a creeping suspicion begins to dawn that they *might not* have any meaning anymore at all. Another larger, more ominous suspicion, too, begins to arise, namely, that the artist might no longer even *matter*, since it was with the bricks of his very Ideas that the entire edifice of the metaphysical age had been built in the first place. What need, then, for his Ideas, in an age when all macrospheres have broken down, and society seems to function on its own as a machine *outside* of all Worlds whatsoever. Is he, indeed, necessary at all anymore to the functioning of such a society?

Hence, the crisis of contemporary art, a crisis which no artist epitomizes more than Joseph Beuys. In a post-metaphysical age, the job of the artist is an entirely different one than it had been before, when his Ideas were used to construct the actual fabric of the functioning cosmology. Now his job is not to build the cosmology of an entire age, but rather to *reterritorialize* once familiar objects, to recode them so that they perform strange and new functions that rupture all traditional categories once ascribed to them. In doing so, a new cosmology does not -- indeed, cannot -- any longer come into being. Instead, what happens is that the objects reveal strange new abysses of meaning hitherto never before suspected, abysses that bring into question the very idea of *meaning* itself.

What does it mean for this or that object to *signify*? It means that it has been given a function to perform by an artist, one that the population of a given society may take and accept as a whole (in a functional Age) or may not. And if not, we arrive at the situation today, in which artists can no longer construct semiospheres for the society as a whole, but must instead create private microspheres for their ever smaller, and more remote, cults of the elite, those who, as in the various Mystery cults that flourished in the ruins of the Hellenistic Age, must be initiated into its private mysteries.

Nowadays, the artist is closer in function to the priest of a private mystery cult into which one must be initiated, for art no longer functions in a way that builds up an entire World for an entire population. It is a broken world now, and each artist is the priest of his own mysteries.

How to Reterritorialize an Object

But then, what does it mean, precisely, to *reterritorialize* something?

Deleuze and Guattari have, in their various books together, introduced us to this idea, especially in *A Thousand Plateaus*, in which they say that the hand, for instance, is a deterritorialized paw; the human face, likewise, is a deterritorialized snout; but more specifically, lips, teeth and tongue have been deterritorialized from their original function as organs of nourishment and then *reterritorialized* to their Anthropogenic function of building language as the House of Being.[1] A reterritorialized organ is an organ that has been recoded to perform a function that is altogether different from what it was originally designed to do. The human being, Deleuze and Guattari point out, is the animal of reterritorialization par excellence.

But with art we are dealing with signifiers and their relationship to various signifieds. If the signifieds – especially the transcendental ones like God or the soul or Heaven – have broken down, then the signifiers have to be recoded to refer to different, and perhaps even, brand new signifieds invented by the artist himself. Conversely, however, it may be the case that the artist wants to retain the old signifieds, but has to invent entirely new signifiers as fresh clothing with which to reincarnate them, as it were. This is precisely the case with Beuys, who differs from most other contemporary artists in this respect (Warhol, by contrast, invents entirely new signifiers *and* new signifieds to go along with them).

Take Beuys's *Virgin* of 1952,[2] one of his early works, as an example: here the ancient signified of the goddess as an archetype has been retained, not scrapped. However, the outer vestments of her signifiers have been completely redrawn, for in Beuys's sculpture, she appears in schematic form (as in the ancient Neolithic) in which her legs have been spread apart to reveal her world-generating vagina. But the form, strangely, has been wrapped in gauze bandages and it has been given to us on a dirty, used pillow. The bandages signify that the situation with this ancient archetype has now taken on the status of a medical emergency: something urgent is involved. And the dirty pillow indicates that the grand formality of a previous age has passed, and now all that is left with which to present Her is this pillow salvaged from the ruins of some catastrophe or other. In other words, She has been reterritorialized to suit the semiology of a post-catastrophic society, a society that is locked into a post-traumatic stress mode in which it is still recovering from the prior disaster that has wrecked its integral hypersphere.

This, then, is the premise from which Beuys begins his work: all the traditional signifieds are recovering from war wounds and exist now in damaged form. Beuys, then, is working with a *damaged cosmology*, a cosmology in which the form-generating aesthetic fields are no longer functioning properly and so can only produce broken, frayed, warped, torn or otherwise damaged aesthetic objects. All of Beuys's work, without exception, is painted and sculpted, inscribed, that is, on damaged surfaces: water stained canvases; used sheets of notebook paper; broken, non-functional machinery, etc. All this implies that the form-producing field of Western art *has itself been damaged* by the catastrophe. It is no longer capable of producing clean, symmetrical and beautiful forms. It can only produce mangled forms, just as though genetic defects had interfered with the morphic field of an organism, enabling it to actualize itself in space-time only as a deformed organism.

The entirety of Beuys's work, then, taken as a whole, tells us that the morphic field of Western art can *only* produce damaged forms. The Catastrophe, in other words, was so profound, that it actually affected the West all the way down into its ontological recesses where art forms themselves are shaped and produced.

Cosmology A

The first phase of Beuys's work, then, which extends from about 1948 to 1960, has its own, quite distinct structural features which demarcate it like a geological epoch from the epoch which follows it beginning in 1960 (and which itself lasts until somewhere into the mid-70s).[3] Long about 1960, his cosmology will undergo a complete restructuring into *another*, second, and very different cosmology from the one with which he started out.

That first cosmology is one in which Beuys hangs on to the basic signifieds of Modernism (as was the case with the early Pollock), drawing his inspiration, as is well-known, from shamanism and the cosmology of Rudolf Steiner. In the various plant and animal drawings from 1947-48, and the goddess sculptures of 1949, Beuys operates out of an essentially Modernist and mythically-inspired worldview: plants, animals, goddesses, and a fascination with the Steinerian etheric and astral forces which animate such phenomena. A masterpiece such as the 1949 painting entitled

"Sheep's Skeleton,"[4] or the bronze sculpture "Animal Woman"[5] with its clear Paleolithic inspiration, are emblematic of this epoch.

But the primary Image of this phase, its Ur-symbol as it were, is that of the human body, specifically in its mode as that of Cosmic Man, or rather Cosmic Woman since, in his case, it is the ancient signified of the Goddess that he is most concerned with at this time. A great deal of the art of this period is devoted to tracking the transformations of Goethe's *Ewige Weibliche*: she is plugged into various cosmic circuits (*Three Women* of 1948)[6]; shuttled back and forth between the human and animal strata (*Frau* of 1957,[7] where she is in the mode of the Queen Bee, or the various interactions with the Swan from this period); and inserted into diverse social personae, as well (such as *Aktrice* of 1956[8] or *Judith* of 1957[9]). She is the central figure, the surface of inscription, as it were, for all his musings.

The human body, too, taken as a whole, is involved with all of this, especially in its spiritualized Steinerian form as etheric and astral bodies open to cosmic influences, such as the drawing from 1957, *Girl astronaut*,[10] in which the top of her skull is left uncompleted in order to signify her receptivity to cosmic influences. Even the various bee sculptures and paintings from this time are but analogues of the human body, for Beuys directly analogized the bees a la Steiner to human blood cells building the honey-comb-like vortices of the bones just the way bees build their hives. The human body, during this period, is the constant pre-occupation of Beuys and everything in the cosmos is, in some way, always referred back to it. The human figure is rarely absent from his art, either sculpted or painted, of this early period.

Thus, woman, man (the brilliant sculpture *Deadman* of 1955,[11] of clay lumps wrapped in bandages, is the counterpart to his 1952 *Virgin*), and their various becomings-animal as they interact with goats, cows, swans and bees, form the basic cosmos of Beuys Cosmology A. It is not too dissimilar, in this respect, from the early Modernist cosmology of Jackson Pollock, which was also concerned with the Goddess, the Shaman and their becomings-animal before he liquefied them into his abstract canvases.

But: long about 1958 or so, this cosmology begins to disintegrate. It was, significantly enough, in that very year that Beuys constructed his Auschwitz installation, the harbinger of which was the 1957 painting, *Death and the Maiden*,[12] which depicts the shadows of two skeletons in an intimate embrace upon the back of a manila envelope stamped ominously with the address of "Auschwitz." This painting foreshadows the transformation of his goddess muse into a figure of disgust and repulsion, for in the paintings of 1958, she turns up almost exclusively as what Marija Gimbutas once called "the stiff nude death goddess" of the Neolithic.[13] She is already there in the 1957 painting *Madchen*,[14] in which the bony body of his muse now has band-aids in place of legs; and in various other paintings of 1957, such as the *Untitled* in which she appears in the form of a repulsive spidery creature;[15] or the bony figure of *Salamander II* (1958);[16] or the reworking of his *Virgin* sculpture as a line drawing in the 1958 *Frauenakt* in which the vaginal orifice reappears as a creepy, well-shaped hole.[17] The fire-spewing females of *Hexen Feuer* of 1959[18] are of the essence of this transformation.

In the Auschwitz installation, however, we notice that the human body is conspicuous precisely by its *absence*. In these vitrines, there are blocks of fat on warming plates; decayed rolls of sausage; a mummified rat on a bed of straw; chunks of rusting metal; disused string; and other such objects. Nowhere do we find the human body, but only the traces which it has left behind in the wake of its disappearance into the ovens and gas chambers. For the Holocaust was tantamount to an eschatology of the human body, a vast and sinister apocalypse of the human being as incarnational vessel which could be disarranged, pulled apart and disarticulated like the processing of pigs and cattle at a meat-packing factory. The Holocaust is, in essence, the *anathema* of the human form, an assault on the very ontological conditions of its presence in the world and a vision of the systematic liquidation of its structure and form.

But it is precisely the human body which, after 1958, begins to disappear from the art of Joseph Beuys. Instead, the paintings of 1959 are almost Abstract Expressionist in their deliberate disintegration of Form. In place of the human body, or indeed, of anything definitively formal at all, we see the pure red cloud of *Filter* (1959);[19] the brown and gray smears of *Hubert Troost* (1959);[20] the earth-like strata of *Was am Hirschhorn gerschah* (1959);[21] or the notebook page covered with black paint and a small square of red smears in the left corner of *Gulo Borealis* (1959).[22] The paintings of this year are the closest that Beuys ever came to Abstract Expressionism, but, as with the multiforms of Mark Rothko, they signify a similar kind of meltdown and dissolution of the artist's previous cosmology.

When the cosmology begins to recrystallize in 1960, what emerges in such sculptural works as *Bathtub*,[23] *Horns*,[24] or *Eisbar*[25] is a world that is *void* of human presence and which, like the haunting piles of clothing and suitcases and teeth left behind by the victims of the gas chambers, signify only the *traces* of a once present human being who is now conspicuous precisely by his *absence*.

Cosmology B

Art, after Auschwitz, must now become post-humanist. Just as Heidegger, in his 1946 *Letter on Humanism* argued that it was precisely the humanistic tradition as such that led to the atrocities of the twentieth century, and that a post-humanist vision would be one that would be attentive to Being,[26] so too, with Beuys's middle period – that of the grand apogee of his art – the human being has vanished into an impersonal cosmos in which the primary protagonists now are *physico-chemical forces* rather than human beings themselves.

The key work that signifies the shift into Beuys's Cosmology B is the 1960 sculpture entitled simply *Bathtub*. This work is the gateway, as it were, by means of which the new cosmology is born (indeed, Beuys says it was the bathtub in which he was born from his mother).[27] In this work, the human being has been replaced by a trace of his once-functioning world, a world in which this displaced object once made a certain kind of sense but has now been reterritorialized by Beuys in a post-catastrophic world to make another kind of sense altogether. For Beuys, the bathtub is an object of renewal and rebirth, no longer merely a place for washing the now non-existent human physical body. It is a displaced object, like an organ without a body, torn from the anatomy of the world inside which it had once functioned.

In the same year, his sculpture *Horns* represents the fate of his earlier animal protagonists, for they, too, have now vanished (at least temporarily) and left behind only these traces of their presence, a pair of horns connected to tubes through which hare's blood has been sent circulating. Beuys has said that it is a vision of the mystery of the circulation of the blood through the animal that produces its horns on an annual basis,[28] but it is precisely the animal itself as a Figure that is now *missing*. It is a syncopated image: the viewer has to fill in the rest of the animal on his own, just as with the *Bathtub*, he had had to supply the entirety of the missing human world inside which the tub had once functioned.

Beuys's famous *Fat Chair* of 1964[29] is even more to the point, for in this case we have a signifier that is left behind by the vanished human being in the form of yet another trace, in this case of a chair, but a chair that is no longer occupied by a human being. In its former use, in another world (such as the metaphysical age of Van Gogh), it would have provided the human being with a place to sit, but now the object has been reterritorialized to perform an altogether different function, namely, to illustrate a metaphysical process of morphogenesis, for the slab of fat on the chair represents the principle of the Indeterminate which has now been given Form by placing it into the chair's right angle, thus conferring on unshaped matter a metabolic Form. Thus, the chair has been reterritorialized to perform a metaphysical and distinctly *non-human* process that now becomes of the essence of Beuysian cosmology.

The Pack, too, from 1969,[30] illustrates the features of this new cosmology, for neither the human, nor even the animal is anywhere to be found, but instead only their traces and stand-ins: for the image of all the sleds being disgorged from the back of the VW van is itself a deliberate reversal of the traditional image of the single sled being pulled by a pack of dogs. Now the dogs are gone and a multitude of sleds stands in for them, but each sled contains an emergency survival kit – a hunk of fat, a flashlight and a roll of felt – designed for the survival of the now ontologically "homeless" human being. The human being who, today, finds himself in exile from Being, as Heidegger put it, finds himself washed ashore like Crusoe with no macrosphere to protect him, and so Beuys provides such a nomadic human with an emergency kit for survival.

When the human form does turn up at all in this new cosmology, it has been pulled apart and destructured: its various astral, etheric and physical sheaths have been pulled away from each other, and Beuys illustrates one or the other of them, but never the human being himself. For example, in *Grauballe Man* of 1962,[31] Beuys has substituted for the human form a cosmic process illustrating him: the work is composed of a series of concentric circular copper tubes, for just as copper conducts electricity, so the human etheric body, a la Steiner, conducts spiritual forces. The actual human is nowhere to be found here in this mock grave, but only the signifier of his etheric body, an impersonal and cosmic force. The human being *as human being* is no longer involved, for he has been swallowed up into a larger cosmic picture.

This process was already clearly foreshadowed in a drawing entitled *Nude*, from 1957,[32] in which the body of a naked human female has blurred and blended into a landscape, becoming identical with it. Thus, in sculptural works like the 1961 *Virgin*[33] and the *Mountain King*[34] of the same year, the sculpted forms become visually identical with entire landscapes: the body of the Virgin is made from a chopped up log of teak wood, while the sculpted Mountain King represents the actual physical landscape itself (like HCE in *Finnegans Wake*), with the central hollow tube where his spinal column would have been now a metaphor for the human processes of mining and digging tunnels into the earth. The human body has now, in Cosmology B, been absorbed into the cosmos, as in Eastern myth and mysticism. Cosmic forces, that is, as in Cosmology A, no longer illustrate the operations of the human body, but rather the other way round: the human body is now but a localized illustration of vast cosmic forces that have absorbed it.

This *is* an evolutionary cosmology, though, as it was inspired by and based upon some of Steiner's core ideas, for Beuys's new fascination in Cosmology B with substances such as fat and felt, copper and iron, wax and wood, are meant to be illustrative of spiritual processes of human transformation and potential. However, the problem is the same as with that of Eastern mysticism: the cosmic forces have now won out, and they have swallowed up the human being who has now become enmeshed within them as a helpless prisoner of processes that are vast and ancient, and impossible for him to harness or control.

Thus, in the great cosmology of Beuys's middle period, the human being disappears into the processual matrix, having become its prisoner, and it is doubtful whether Beuys could ever have rescued him from his precipitous fall into these abstract networks of self-organizing forces that gobbled him up.

An Opposed Tendency

But now another tendency, or rather structural feature, of this second cosmology begins to become evident from as early as 1962, when he produced a series of sculptures called *Silent Gramophones*.[35] These are images of LP records that are sometimes coated in red paint and stuck up vertically or laid horizontally with, in place of a needle, an animal bone. These are examples of ruptured objects, in which the normal function of the object has not only been reterritorialized but also ruptured so that it is completely inoperative. These gramophones are silent precisely because they can no longer give forth any sound at all. They are therefore illustrations of an opposed cosmological tendency in this second epoch of Beuys's work, namely, an entropic tendency in which objects recede, break down or cease to function.

This middle period is also, of course, the great period of Beuys's famous Actions, which first began in 1963 when he associated with the so-called Fluxus Group. These actions continued all through the 1960s and on into the middle 70s, and despite their bewildering diversity and puzzling content, they all have precisely *one theme* in common, namely, communication breakdown. They are like four-dimensional illustrations of his ruptured objects (indeed, Beuys's art in its broad strokes had moved from two dimensions, with his early paintings, to three dimensions with his sculptures and to the fourth dimension of Time with his Actions).

Art After Metaphysics

In December of 1964, for instance, Beuys performed an Action entitled "The Chief," in which he wrapped himself in a felt blanket and lay on the floor for nine hours croaking primeval animal sounds into a microphone that he kept inside the felt blanket with him. At either end of him lay a dead hare, and a speaker on the wall amplified his animal croakings. By way of explanation, Beuys tells us that he was trying to rupture his own species' range of semantics in order to open up forms of communication with other animal species.[36] But this, then, is precisely the theme of another Action, this one performed in November of 1965, entitled "How to Explain Pictures to a Dead Hare," in which Beuys sat in a chair in a booth behind glass with a dead hare in his lap and whispered explanations to it of various drawings that he had hung on the walls around him. His head was covered with honey and gold leaf like a mask, and one foot was anchored with an iron sole, while the other was insulated with a felt sole. Beneath his chair lay a primitive "radio," namely, an animal bone with electrical wire wrapped around it.[37] The anxiety here is precisely that of opening up portals between the human and animal worlds, and between human thinking and earlier, more archaic forms of instinctual, intuitive thought.

In the February, 1967 Action entitled "Eurasian Staff Action," Beuys performed the ritual of erecting four felt-wrapped metal pillars inside of a large room. Then he took the "Eurasian staff," a long copper pole bent back on itself in a U-shape and used it to touch the ceiling as a means of conducting spiritual energy into the room. The square shape made by the four pillars was left open in order to receive these spiritual energies. Beuys himself was, once again, anchored by an iron sole and insulated by a felt sole.[38]

In the famous "Coyote" Action of 1974 – which more or less wraps up this epoch of Actions – he spent a few days with a live coyote in a room in a building in New York, trying to open up portals of connection in shamanic fashion with the animal, a now forgotten mode of conversing with the animals, obscured and paved over, like Heidegger's Being, by modern scientific – industrial rational thinking.

Thus, the theme of the Actions is always communication breakdown of one sort or another: either between the human and the animal worlds; or between and amongst Objects themselves. The famous felt-wrapped piano, for instance, was a relic of a 1966 Action entitled "Infiltration-Homogen for grand piano, the great contemporary composer is the thalidomide child."[39] Felt, in the Beuysian cosmology, always signifies insulation, warmth, and isolation. The piano that is completely wrapped in felt can, of course, no longer emit sound and so its traditional function is thereby ruptured. It has withdrawn away from the universe of Other Things into a private space of broken lines of communication along with all the other ruptured objects that Beuys produced in this period as examples of the Entropic counter theme of his evolutionary cosmology: the various Silent Gramophones; the tuning fork on a felt pad;[40] the half-crosses made of felt (the missing half being the ruptured completion of a traditional cross), etc. etc.

The Actions feed back into his cosmology, where they reinforce the production of these felt-suffocated objects and illustrate the opposed cosmic force which gives to the cosmology of his great period all its tension: that namely between Evolution and Entropy, precisely as Teilhard de Chardin described it in *The Phenomenon of Man*. In Beuysian cosmology, copper, with its electricity-conducting potential, and fat, with its form-receptive potential are the opposed double articulation of his Evolutionary theme (for whereas, according to Beuys, electricity is associated with the cold, mineralogical principle, fat is associated with the principle of organic warmth); while felt, with its suffocating but insulating properties tends to be associated with his various Entropic objects, such as the *Felt Suit* that he made which has no buttons or zippers and so cannot function properly.[41]

In Cosmology B, then, objects either illustrate vast spiritual energies that are at work in processes of formation and transformation, such as the various copper batteries that he built in his "Fond" series; or they are objects that have broken off from all cosmologies whatsoever into their own private spaces, such as the Silent Gramophones and Felt Pianos, which illustrate a decaying universe of ruptured and fragmented lines of communication in which objects can no longer organize and gather to form a World anymore precisely because they lack the force of the necessary cosmic reciprocity (as in Kant) that would make them intercommunicate and therefore render the cosmology functional.

It is as though Beuys's cosmology were working at cross-purposes with itself, and it is this basic conflict at the core of Cosmology B which gives his work such a fragmented, broken and semiotically bewildering array of meanings to the puzzled viewer who stands before it. It is, in other words, a cosmology struggling to be born, but which, since it cannot eject the necessary entropy to enable it to function as a dissipative structure, never coheres into a stable world Image.

Beuys's cosmology, then, is a *damaged cosmology*, one that never really emerges into full and clear definition.

The Victory of the Mineralogical

In Beuysian cosmology, then, as we have said, copper is normally linked with the evolutionary forces, whereas felt tends to be associated with entropic ones. (*Snowfall*, a 1965 sculpture,[42] perfectly illustrates this latter tendency, with its image of three bare tree branches suffocated by layers of felt as stand ins for snow). But in the various "batteries" that Beuys began to produce in the latter years of this middle cosmology, such as *Fond II* of 1965[43] or *Site* of 1967,[44] the two substances, and hence also, the two cosmic forces, tend to merge and interpenetrate. In *Site*, for instance, a flat sheet of copper is laid on the floor to represent the "site" of some unspecified future energy transformation, while it is surrounded by scraps of felt. But by the time of the great "batteries" of spiritual energy with *Fond III* of 1979,[45] the felt and the copper have been mutually interpenetrated, for this large sculpture is made of interleaved rectangles of felt and copper sheets in nine large stacks. It is a battery of spiritual energy for social transformation, one which completely reverses and absorbs entropy, a battery which grows larger with *Fond IV*[46] and eventually in 1985 reaches monumental proportions in *Fond VII*.[47]

In Beuys's third and final period, as a result, which extends from about 1974 to 1985, entropic objects and tendencies are, for the most part, noticeably absent (with a few exceptions, of course, such as *Plight* of 1985). The Actions, during this period, have also largely ceased and given way instead to ever larger and more comprehensive installations and environments which tend to surround and engulf the viewer with a kind of *Gesamtkunstwerk* totality. But the absence of the entropic tendency in the art (apparently gobbled up by the "batteries") causes the brilliance of the art to lose much of its tension and as a result, Beuys's Late Period is a typical example of the Late Period of any great artist, for it is mostly concerned with monumentalizing previous works and repeating his earlier themes.

The huge *Tallow*, for instance, of 1977,[48] represents Beuys's monumentalization of his earlier brilliant "Fat corners" from the 1960s.[49] The point of creating triangle-shaped corners of fat in rooms was a means of neutralizing the right-angularity of Western masculinist, scientific thinking with the soft and organic contours of fat. Indeed, Beuys often began his actions by creating such fat corners as a means of reterritorializing rectangular rooms, and rounding off their corners, as it were, to introduce more warming, organic and feminine-spiritual geometries. But *Tallow* is a huge sculpture made of fat that was used to fill in a mold taken from a pedestrian underpass in the city of Munster. It was, in other words, a means of extracting a tooth, as Caroline Tisdall puts it,[50] to show its decay, in this case, the sterility and ennui of the kinds of concrete gigantism that have blighted our cities. But this is not a new point in Beuys, merely a monumental version of his fat corners.

The 1985 environment entitled *Plight* is one of the few entropic objects from this later period: it is a series of rooms in which the walls have been soundproofed with huge rolls of felt while a piano stands by itself in the middle of the room. The piano's capacity to produce sound has therefore been ruptured by the fact that the felt will absorb it all, and so what we have is merely a monumentalized version of Beuys's earlier brilliant felt-wrapped pianos. It makes precisely the same point as the previous sculptures.

Honey Pump at the Workplace from 1977,[51] in which a machine connected to tubes filled with honey as stand-in for blood travel up and down a stairwell of the Museum Fridericianum, re-makes the same point as his 1960 *Horns*, only it substitutes its syncopated imagery for the human body instead of animal anatomy.

The gigantification of art is a tendency that is universally characteristic of decadent periods, such as for example in the case of New Kingdom Egypt when, under Rameses II, its art underwent a scaling up to truly inhuman proportions with his various tombs. The enormous ziggurats from the time of Ur-Nammu in Mesopotamia are, of course, the largest ever built and come in at the end of that civilization as it is reaching its twilight. And the same goes for the gigantic Forums and gladiatorial arenas of the Roman Empire.

Colossification is a sign that something in the art is beginning to disappear, and so the art must insist upon itself with ever larger and more grandiose gestures in order to have any effect upon the beholder at all. The point is the same, but now it is made on a scale that is designed to intimidate the beholder by capturing him in the shadow cast by all-encompassing and totalitarian forms.

Thus, when the entropic theme largely, though not entirely, disappeared from the art of Beuys's third period, something else went out of the art, too, for it lost much of its brilliance and inventiveness and descended into a repetition of a fixed stock of forms. And the stark grandeur of his vast and impersonal cosmology, in which there was no longer any room for the human being as such, tended to cancel out much of its point, namely, that these forces are available to the human being to use for personal and social transformation.

But, of course, they cannot be used when they are inaccessible and impersonal, too gigantic and cosmic to reach, and so no longer touch the central warmth aspect, as Beuys would put it, at the heart of the human being. Thus, the very cold principle of the stiffening and rigidification of form that had been symbolized in many of Beuys's earlier works – such as the brilliant bronze landscape sculpture *Val* of 1961[52] – and which he had opposed to his "warming" principles of fat and felt and wax (themselves privileged over the cold pole of his cosmic dichotomy) eventually won the field in his art, which, in the end, petrified and stiffened up, while the warmth principle faded out altogether.

One of his final environments, *The End of the Twentieth Century* of 1985[53] says it all: a museum room filled with a pile of overturned and featureless basalt blocks.

The complete triumph of the stiffened mineralogical principle.

Gerhard Richter

Erasures

Whenever the transcendental signifieds of a particular world age cease to have any relevance for subsequent ages, then the signifiers of the previous age have to be crossed out, effaced, erased and overcoded with new signifiers that point to a different set of signifieds. Hence, Heidegger in his essay "On the Question of Being" crosses out the word "Being" in order to neutralize it as a signifier referring to a metaphysics of presence in favor of his own more dynamic understanding of Being-as-event.[1] Derrida, in his own work *Of Grammatology*, does something similar in deliberate evocation of Heidegger when he crosses out the word "is" as part of his deconstruction of the logocentrism of the metaphysical age.[2]

But this is not a new tactic in the history of civilization: the Egyptian pharaoh Akhenaten did exactly the same thing when he sent armies of men with chisels out across the land to efface and erase the signifiers of the Theban macrosphere, which he himself was busy deconstructing, by scratching out the names of all the previous astral deities like Osiris, Amun, Sokar, Ptah, etc. The plural signifier for "gods" was crossed out, since in his own new macrosphere there was only room for *one* god, the Aten. All the signifiers of the previous Theban macrosphere had to be scrapped and replaced with his own metaphysics of the one true solar god. Akhenaten was the Derrida of his age.

And since, in our own tradition, with the collapse of the metaphysical age – finally laid to rest during World War II – the signifieds of that age, together with its logocentrism, its phonocentrism and its metaphysics of presence, no longer have relevance in a time of "soft ontologies" and "hermeneutics," then new signifiers must be constructed, while old ones are chiseled away from the surface of Being, as it were.

And so, with the first official painting of Gerhard Richter's catalogue raisonne, the 1962 *Table*,[3] we have just such an example of a crossing out, for in this painting Richter took an illustration for an expanding Gardella table from an Italian architectural magazine, painted a canvas-sized version of it and then, feeling that the painting was not working, crossed it out with a circular blur of his paintbrush.[4] Feeling that the painting was now somehow "right," Richter let it stand as the first of his new work list after having relocated to West Germany from East Germany.

But this was not an atypical action for Richter: for from *Table* to his most recent abstract paintings, in which the image is deliberately effaced by dragging a long plastic squeegee across its surface, the act of creation through destruction has been the whole point of his oeuvre from the beginning. *All* of Richter's paintings, as we shall see, proceed by means of this deconstructive method of effacing and erasing previously extant images.

The Ontology of the Photopaintings

Richter's first period of work, which extends from 1962 to about 1968 or so, is composed of canvases which Richter terms "photopaintings," which is to say that they are based on previously extant photographs that Richter has cut from various magazines, newspapers and advertisements – or else they are personal photographs from his family albums, etc. – and blown up to canvas scale and then overpainted. The image is normally blurred by Richter in various ways, usually by dragging the paintbrush across the surface of the image, so that it is no longer a photograph properly speaking but rather a "painting" of a photograph. The original photograph, however, is often creatively altered, so that it is not simply a matter of transferring the photo to the canvas, but of creatively reconstructing it. All of Richter's canvases from this period, however (save the color palettes) are based upon preexistent images.

The days, in other words, of the artist directly painting the Real, like Cezanne sitting outdoors and painting imaginary reconstructions of the French countryside, are over. As Baudrillard famously put it, the Real has vanished. It no longer exists, for it has long since disappeared inside the matrix of mediated images. The Real has been replaced by a mediatized simulacrum beneath which it has disappeared like a palimpsest. What it has left behind are only traces of the once existing signifieds that had composed its ontology.

Richter's entire ontology -- during this first period, anyway -- as his famous *Atlas* reveals, is based upon the construction of a plane of signification that is composed entirely out of the cellular matrix of photographs. Indeed, he is one of those rare artists who has actually made his ontology visible for us in book form as the *Atlas*, which is composed of all the photos he used as source material: pages and pages of raw photos, advertisements, newspaper clippings, magazine photos, each one of them the *potential* subject of a painting.[5] This book composes Richter's ontology of the Real as a cellular matrix of mediatized images in which the actual Real, reality itself, is nowhere to be found.

But, of course, as Vilem Flusser has pointed out, a journalistic photograph is not simply a naïve recording of the Real, an "objective" image of what's "out there," but rather an image of a *theory* about the Real, a chemical theory in fact (later, a digitized theory) about the Real.[6] Cameras are mechanical equivalents of German Idealist philosophy: they actually refute naïve British theories about the mind as a *tabula rasa* recording representations received through the senses that fill it up like a data storage bank, for the black and white photograph is a chemical construction of a non-existent Manichean reality of a gray world we never actually *see*. And even the color photograph is a similar theoretical construction of the Real, based upon concepts, for the green of the field that I have just photographed is not the actual green *out there*, but rather a chemical theory about green that has been programmed into my camera. My camera, just like my mind according to the German idealists, is recording a pre-programmed *construct* of the Real, never the Real itself.

The photograph, in other words, has *crossed out* the Real, which has disappeared into the trace left behind by the emulsive surface of the photo, crossed it out and replaced it with another stratum of theorized reality that has been chemically laid on top of it, like a second stratum.

Nevertheless, the photograph itself has the effect of deworlding a chunk of the Real, to use Heidegger's terminology from *Being and Time*, by divorcing it from its context in the actual world and putting it into this frozen, theoretical mode that I now have before me. *All photographs are in the mode of Heidegger's broken hammer, for they are all in the Vorhandenheit mode of theoretical, problematized reality*, a reality that is no longer part of a lifeworld context that is living and flowing through time.

As an artist, however, Richter has removed these journalistic images from their objective, theoretical mode, and put them into another mode of Being entirely, namely, Being-as-an-art-object. By deliberately blurring the image – a process which he has called *Vermalung*, or "inpainting" – Richter has increased the ambiguity of it, and therefore multiplied the semiotic complexity of the image. It has lost the clarity and distinctness of a reportorial photograph in the "objective" mode in direct proportion to the degree that it has gained ambiguity and complexity as an art object.

Take the 1964 painting, *Administrative Building*:[7] the blurred effect Richter has given to the photo of this building makes it seem as though the viewer were in a speeding car, perhaps, moving rapidly past it, thus giving it the phenomenological properties that Paul Virilio has termed "dromoscopic," and which refer to the blurred features that a landscape takes on through my windshield as I move past it at high speeds.[8] Of course, this same type of blurring of an image will result if my subject happens to move at the moment I click the shutter of the camera, or if I happen to move at that moment. With Richter's *Vermalung*, we are no longer certain *what* the precise semiotics of the image are, but it is this increase in ambiguity that transforms the photo into a work of art. It is now polysemic.

With his 1965 photopainting of one of his relatives, entitled *Aunt Marianne*,[9] the blurring of this private family photo does not so much suggest physical motion through space, but rather emotional distance through time, for early childhood memories also have a similar blurring effect. Such memories are rarely clear: faces in them are blurred; circumstances but dimly recalled; people only vaguely and sketchily filled in. So in this case, Richter's blurring effect is suggestive of dimly recalled memories, and this adds yet another layer of semiotic ambiguity to these images.

But in taking them out of their objective *Vorhandenheit* modes, and transforming these photographs into works of art by increasing their ambiguities, Richter is essentially also *crossing them out* as photographs and adding another semiotic stratum over them, just as the photograph itself crosses out the Real by adding a theoretical stratum on top of it. The Real is now thrice removed from Richter's painting: it has been occluded by multiple layers of technological and artistic semiotics.

A Second Plane of Signification

Long about 1968 or so, Richter was beginning to feel restless with his identity as a photopainter. For one thing, American minimalism had pronounced the death of painting as a viable art form, but he was also feeling confined by adhering to the construction of his work on a single plane of signification. He had already attempted, in the 1966 color palettes, to take another vector of approach, but it was the commission from the Siemens corporation to do a large townscape painting for them that proved to open up another line of creative flight. This resulted in the *Cathedral Square, Milan*[10] of 1968, another typical photopainting, but this time of a townscape seen from ground level like an Impressionist painting, with tiny zigzags painted in tediously by hand to provide the painting's *Vermalung* effect.

Richter then proceeded to attempt another large townscape without using a photo as underlayer, but when this didn't work, he broke the image up into nine smaller canvases.[11] This then proved to be the basis for a new series of townscapes of European cities seen from the air, as though they were bombing targets. These townscapes are not photopaintings, but paintings that are *modeled* after aerial photographs, and they are painted in ashen, charcoal, gray and white tones so that, while they are not exactly images of ruins, the semiotics nevertheless *convey* ruins, especially when one approaches the paintings close up on a gallery wall and sees their topologies as cityscapes disappear into an abstract painting of smeared brush strokes. *Townscape Paris*[12] in particular has a smudged, broken quality about it, and the painting *Townscape PL*,[13] seen from very high up, invites a clear comparison to rubble and ruins.

The key thing, though, about these paintings is how they provide a line of flight that leads him to evade capture by the totalizing overcoding of the photopaintings and on into the construction of a new, and second, plane of signification. The townscapes are clear bridges – especially *Townscape PX*,[14] which is completely unrecognizable as a city -- to the abstract paintings that he first began to paint during that same year. These paintings are a complete rupture with everything Richter had done before: *Untitled (Stroke)*,[15] *Grey Beams*,[16] *Colored Grey*,[17] *Grey Streaks*,[18] *Grid Streaks*,[19] and *Untitled (Green)*[20] constitute a German response to American Abstract Expressionism. They are abstract images of strictly formal properties, intensities, flows and energy gradients: the very plane of consistency which Deleuze and Guattari had insisted underlay the plane of organization of stratified, law-bound forms.

Thus, from henceforth, Richter will be a bipolar artist who oscillates from one plane of signification to the other: the opposition between his figurative photopaintings and his abstract art is one that is analogous not only to Nietzsche's distinction between Apollonian (or form-giving) and Dionysian (or form-destroying) tendencies, but it is also structurally analogous to Deleuze and Guattari's plane of organization vs. the plane of consistency. The one plane is ruled by form and law, multiplicities that are locked into place along the various strata of the geological, animal, plant or human worlds; while the other, the plane of consistency, is really a plane of formative energies that have destratified and broken loose from all forms, but from out of which all forms inevitably arise: energy gradients, morphogenetic chreodes, thermal properties, and intensivities as pure potential for form.[21]

In creating a second plane of signification for himself, then, with his abstract canvases, Richter destratified from his figurative world of recognizable forms and traced a line of flight out onto the plane of energies, which gives him room to think and explore and palpate the contours for the evolution of new forms.

As the result of this opening up of his cognitive landscape, two transformations take place in his art: on the figurative plane, a series of landscapes and seascapes on the one hand; and then a series of anti-portraits of great Western men on the other; while on the plane of formative energies, new paintings like the *Details* series of the early 1970s emerge.

Landscapes and Portraits

The great landscape paintings that emerge beginning with *Corsica* in 1968[22] and then in 1969 with *Bridge (by the Sea)*[23] and *Landscape near Hubblerath*,[24] and which are then followed by the various seascapes such as *Seascape (Cloudy)* (1969),[25] and *Sea-Sea* (1970),[26] along with the *Clouds* (also of 1970)[27] constitute, as it were, a recapitulation of the great seventeenth century explosion of Dutch art, in which the sky and the sea were really discovered in art for the first time as wide open space after the collapse of the Copernican macrosphere that had previously sealed, and also immunized, Western man against its disintegrative effects. The earlier photopaintings had functioned for Richter in a way analogous to the Copernican macrosphere in that they had erected a boundary around him, composed out of photographic images behind which the Real had disappeared and ceased to trouble him. But with the creation of a second plane of signification in 1968 with the abstract canvases, this had a kind of tectonic shifting and rupturing effect on his first plane of signification that opened it up and out to the outer world, first with the townscapes, then with the landscape paintings.

Richter was accused by some critics of simply returning to the kitsch of German Romantic landscapes, but what such critics invariably failed to take into account was that these were *photopaintings* of landscapes, not unmediated constructions of the Real.[28] Richter's landscapes are all based upon photographs, and their mediated gazes thus suggest the impossibility of ever experiencing "Nature" in any pure, Romantic sense ever again. Nature, too, like the Real, has also vanished into the mediatized matrix and now can only be experienced by means of the prosthetic extension of the Vision Machine. There is no way in which, with such an apparatus in the way, the human can ever blend and merge with the sublime landscapes of Nature ever again, since such a Nature no longer exists. *That* was the point of Richter's landscape paintings of the early 1970s.

With Richter's famous *48 Portraits* of 1971,[29] meanwhile, he returned to the world of the human being with an attempt to reverse and deconstruct the traditional Western metaphysical portrait study. The portrait study, as practiced during the metaphysical age, had been about the capturing of the Subject, the *cogito*, as a metaphysical presence unto itself. But by taking the portraits of famous men and painting over each one in exactly the same brush stroke-less style and then arranging them all on the wall in serialized fashion, he de-subjectivized these Great Men and re-embedded them back into anonymity. They are no longer Great Men but individuals who have been placed back into a collective assemblage of enunciation, three dimensional subjects of enunciation no more.

But this is all part of Richter's aniconism, his tendency to cross out and efface the metaphysics of presence: he is drawing a line here through the Subject as an entity, and flattening out its three dimensionality as Absolute Subject in Cartesian phase space. He is placing these Subjects *back* into the ontological grid of squares and rectangles where they can no longer self-presence as unique entities, but simply blend back in with all the other images in the *Atlas* to become images among other images without distinction. These icons are icons no longer, for they have been effaced and depotentiated, leveled off back onto Richter's own original plane of signification.

Meanwhile, on the plane of formative energies, Richter painted the famous *Detail* paintings of 1970: *Detail (Red-Blue)*[30] and *Detail (Grey-Lilac)*.[31] These paintings, unlike the first abstract paintings of 1968, are no longer directionless and tentative probings of a pure world of formative energies and impulses, for now the energies are pictured as *doing something*: they are squirming, writhing, convulsing; they are in motion *towards* something, as though these detached and loose signifiers were on the way toward the formation of a cosmos all their own. Something is struggling to come into being here with these images, a new cosmos, perhaps, in which the signifiers will be able to birth their own brand new signifieds, signifieds that will become the structural features of a new cosmology.

But in fact, this proves to be an abortive cosmology, one which, as with all his paintings, Richter will proceed to *cross out*.

Scars of Being

By about 1977, this cosmology begins to become more insistent: in the abstract paintings from this time, such as the various *Abstract Pictures*, a spatial world of vectors, floating grids, and hovering lines begins to configure itself, like a proto-cosmology. But it is the great 1980 horizontal painting, composed of multiple canvases aligned side by side, entitled *Stroke (on Red)*[32] in which we see the great gesture of the cosmic demiurge begin to prepare for his creative act: an incandescent yellow line hovers against a red background speckled with bluish-green dots. This is a cosmic Mark, tantamount to the drawing of a boundary, like the kind of Boundary Act that takes place in the great cosmogonies in which the World Parents, Father Sky and Mother Earth are separated by some cosmic demarcator: in Egyptian cosmology, the air god Shu, for instance, cuts his sky mother Nut away from her earth consort Geb; in Greek mythology, it is Gaia who is separated from Uranus by the sickle which Chronos uses to separate them. But such an act is also similar to the same sorts of boundaries and membranes that surface in evolutionary narratives, such as the first cellular membranes that enabled the archaic proto-bacteria to emerge in thermal vents on the sea floors. Or the first walls built around Mesopotamian cities. And so forth.

Richter's glowing yellow line, in any event, is the first act of a cosmic demarcation, the drawing of a Mark that will refer to the creation of new signifieds. And indeed, this cosmology does begin to shape-shift its way into its preliminary stages in the abstract paintings of the 1980s, such as *Hedge* of 1982,[33] or *Abstract Painting* of 1983,[34] in which a Cosmic Separation is taking place: globs of color are beginning to separate as floating blue hyphens cut into this blue-green void where red begins to separate from yellow and green from blue as primordial, Goethean colors. In *Clouds* of 1982,[35] an abstract world of the Heavens, composed of archaic meteorological phenomena, begins to separate from the earth, which is itself then depicted in *Abstract Picture* of 1984[36] and *Bush* of 1985,[37] abstract images of primordial chthonic energies and serpentine movements of tectonic plates and earthly forces. A World is clearly beginning to open up and form in these paintings of the 1980s, but it is a world which is brought to a halt by the application of Richter's squeegee to the images: the first such painting in which he had erased the image with a squeegee was the *Abstract Painting* of 1980,[38] which appears as an anomaly, but after about 1987 becomes the norm for the abstract works.

Beginning with works like the *Abstrract Painting* of 1987,[39] or *A.B. St. John* of 1988,[40] the entire canvas is effaced by Richter's destructive act of using a long squeegee loaded with paint that is then carefully drawn across the canvas from left to right, or sometimes from top to bottom (the directions in which we read in the West, significantly) which has the effect of completely effacing the image into an abstract non-painting. The act, which will be characteristic of all of Richter's paintings from henceforth, is one of erasure: the proto-cosmology that had been organizing into form on the plane of abstract energies is frozen, arrested and halted in its tracks. Instead, an image of erasure is left behind as a trace of this now vanished cosmology.

Thus, Richter's later abstract paintings are all images of erasure; images, that is to say, of scars and traces left behind by the absence of signifieds that have disappeared from the walls of Being, as it were, and left behind only these Marks, iterable to infinity, on Richter's canvases. His proto-cosmology has transformed from eo-signifiers to traces of signifiers, like Derrida's iterable marks that are no longer controlled by transcendental signifieds, and so can be repeated via the processes of citation and intertextuality to infinity. Richter's late abstract work is composed, similarly, of iterable traces that can be repeated in any number of variations from canvas to canvas since they no longer refer to anything beyond or outside them. No signifieds exist to control their iterability, which now begins to proceed in viral fashion to reiterate themselves as scars of Being in an endless chain of paintings that rehearse the same myth of deconstruction by drawing the squeegee across the image from left to right, top to bottom in an act that bears the traces of the older metaphysical act of Western reading from left to right, top to bottom on the page. Richter's art is an art of traces only, never signifieds.

But this process of erasure with the squeegee bears yet another trace of its own, that namely of Richter's earlier practice from his photopaintings of blurring the image by tracing the paintbrush from left to right across its surface. Thus, the techniques from one plane of signification are beginning to be transferred onto another: the blurring of his photopaintings now begins to influence and transfer onto the plane of his formative energies as the blurring and erasure of the signifiers altogether. The two planes are beginning to cross-fertilize each other, which is precisely what takes place from this point on.

The fifteen canvases that Richter painted, for example, during 1988 of the Baader-Meinhof group, known as *October 18, 1977*,[41] are so severely blurred, that they are beginning, more and more, to resemble his abstract paintings. *Arrest 1*[42] and *Arrest 2*[43] are extremely low definition images that can scarcely be made out, while *Hanged*[44] and *Cel*[45] are also severely blurred. But this extreme blurring, or effacing, rather, of the image, is tantamount to an increase in noise in the image, a noise that begins to build up like static in his canvases from this point on, rendering them noisier and noisier.

The 1995 series *S. with Child*,[46] for example, is composed of figurative images of a mother with her infant that evoke the iconotype of the Madonna. But the image is shown devolving through the series as coming apart at the seams into five horizontal strips that discompose, and badly degrade it, so that it can almost no longer be recognized. In the paintings *16 Nov 99*[47] and *17 Nov 99*[48] the photographs of Richter's wife with her child are badly eroded by overlayers of abstract painting, suggesting a clear fusion of the two planes of signification that is now taking place in Richter's art.

The Dissolution of the Clearing

What has fascinated Richter during this most recent phase of his art has been precisely works which depict the *absence* of an image, such as the *Pane of Glass* of 2002,[49] or the *11 Panes* of 2003,[50] which are simply glass rectangles mounted on wood or metal blocks, depicting precisely, *nothing.* The *Pane of Glass* of 2002 or the *Eight Gray* of 2001[51] are likewise literal realizations of the complaint which Baudrillard always leveled at contemporary art, which is composed, as he put it, of "images in which there is precisely *nothing* to see."

The abstract paintings from about this time come increasingly to resemble vacant walls and the scarred places left on the sides of buildings after posters have been taken down, where scars and traces of previous images have been left, such as *Abstract Picture, Kine*, of 1995,[52] or *Abstract Picture* of 2000,[53] which are images of nearly completely effaced images, signifiers that have been wiped clean from the walls of Being.

The increase in noise in Richter's paintings as they go along invites a certain comparison of the images to the kinds of low resolution images produced on old black and white TV sets. Indeed, the *Vermalung* process, when he had first introduced it back in the 1960s, tended to give his photopaintings of that time the quality of images as seen on the black and white television sets of that time: grainy, fuzzy images that were difficult to make out. The later abstract paintings, on the other hand, with their complete drowning of the signal ("signifier") by noise and feedback come more and more to resemble electronic image screens tuned to dead channels.

In direct opposition, however, to this process of gradual degradation of the image by entropy, Western electronic technology has developed in such a way as to considerably increase the resolution and clarity of its images with High Definition movies, Blu Ray DVDs, digital photographs and faster Internet speeds, all of which have had the effect of *increasing*, rather than decreasing, the information content of the signal.

The degradation of the image in Richter's art, by contrast, which has increased over time, tends to point the images not so much to the electronic world but rather to the truth process itself, as first articulated by Heidegger in *Being and Time* as the process of uncovering of entities.[54] The entities in the clearing of Truth, Richter's art implies, are unconcealing themselves more and more imperfectly over time. The entity in the Heideggerian clearing, that is to say, is not coming more and more into focus, but going more and more *out* of focus as cognitive noise invades the West's semiosphere. The age of soft ontologies, hermeneutics, the death of the grand metanarratives, and deconstruction have all conspired to render truth an ever fuzzier and fuzzier process in which clarity has decreased and noise in the semiosphere has decidedly increased. The entities of the clearing now are so badly eroded that we can scarcely make them out at all anymore. The *aletheia* process of unconcealment *is itself disintegrating*, as Richter's art suggests, in direct proportion to the increase of clarity in the realm of electronic images.

It is the technical image which now holds the floor today. The age of discursive thought, of conceptual discourse with its matching theory of truth as correspondence, has begun to vanish over the horizon along with the disappearing metaphysical age, and even *aletheia* itself is no longer much of a process of unconcealmeant, as Truth disappears into truths (paralleling the disappearance of the Real into the mediatized matrix). With the breakdown of the axial relationship of Being and its transcendental signifieds to the control of meaning, no one knows any longer for certain *what* is true and what isn't. Being has broken down and its signifieds have disappeared. Technically produced images have now replaced those signifieds, a fact that is perfectly illustrated in Richter's art by the stained glass work that he did for Cologne cathedral in 2007 in which, instead of the legends of saints and Biblical myths depicted in the glass, a purely digitized realm of colored boxes and pixels now fills the frame of the windows.[55]

Richter, I think, here gets it just right: Being has been replaced by digital Simulation. The signifieds have disappeared and their place has now been taken by digitized pixels of fabricated images which *might* be real, or they might not be.

Who knows?

Anselm Kiefer

Anselm Kiefer's transformation of an abandoned silk factory at La Ribaute – located near the town of Barjac in France – into a monumental work of contemporary art is perhaps the summa of his entire career as an artist. As chronicled by Sophie Fiennes in her excellent documentary entitled *Over Your Cities Grass Will Grow*, we see Kiefer at work constructing his monumental opus out of the ruins of 47 buildings strewn with paintings, broken pottery vessels, fallen meteorites, stacks of sculptured books, layers of shattered glass and a haunting series of enigmatic pillars built out of concrete slabs stacked with precarious incertitude atop sculptures of books with splayed open pages, spines broken, and contents ruptured like innards exposed to the heavens.

As we watch Kiefer apply a blowtorch to melt liquid metal in a cauldron which he then spills out across a dirt mound; or throw panes of glass which shatter across the floor of an installation composed of burnt-out, ashy-looking books; or dump cans of paint and dust across huge canvases laid out on the floor, we begin to realize that something strange is happening – indeed, *has* already happened – to the ontological status of the Western artist. He is no longer, that is to say, a creator of forms, but rather an *unmaker* of them: a builder not of cosmologies but rather a chronicler of their decimation. This is a complete overturning of the traditional role of the artist, who was always, in the ancient world, the great man who became deified as the result of creating radically new technological breakthroughs.

Daedalus was the larger than life engineer who invented the possibility of flight; Prometheus domesticated fire; Cain built the first cities; Vulcan made the various tools and implements with which the gods of Mount Olympus adorned themselves. The Medieval artist, furthermore, as we have seen, was always a cosmocrator, imitating in miniature Yahweh's feats of designing the cosmos like a draughtsman. Indeed the artist, clear down to the Modernists, was a builder of *worlds*.

But Kiefer's installation at La Ribaute is no longer tantamount to the construction of a world, but is rather an apotheosis of a three-dimensional middenheap composed out of the shattered forms and discarded signifiers that, once upon a time, served as the building blocks for the construction of the metaphysical age. The middenheap, as Marshall McLuhan was fond of pointing out, is what results from the technological innovations that come along to construct new environments and cosmologies, but in the process, simultaneously scrap the previous environment into a junk-heap.[1] Here, the previous environment of the industrial city is retrieved and scaled down to become a work of art in the new environment of the digital age that has rendered it superfluous.

It was Plato, as McLuhan points out, who created the first middenheap by junking the world of Becoming and tossing it into his cave as a disused artifact, together with the entire Paleolithic-tribal world of shadow forms on the walls. The Hebrews of the Old Testament, nearly simultaneously – both Jews and Greeks are the inceptual founders of the metaphysical age – scrapped the technologies of the Mesopotamians and the Egyptians in the Old Testament, for just as the alphabet junked Egyptian hieroglyphs – when Moses comes down the mountain he orders the shattering of the iconic Golden Calf – so too the Mesopotamian ziggurat was delegitimized precisely through the process of caricaturizing it as the Tower of Babel.

The Christians, too, tossed the entire pagan world onto the scrap heap during the fourth century AD when, under the edicts of the emperor Theodosius, the cessation of the pagan holidays, the stopping of the Olympic Games and the closing of the Temple of the Vestal Virgins took place. The Christians, meanwhile, elevated the codex as the new technology of the book that tossed both the Jewish as well as the Greek scrolls onto the junk heap.

But it was the Renaissance humanists who began to retrieve from the scrap heap the basic archetypal forms which they used to construct their new age: the Laocoon was dug up in 1506 and became the great influence on Michelangelo's later works, just as Botticelli,

Titian and the other great artists began to retrieve humanistic themes to become the building blocks for the Age of the World Picture. The Renaissance was an essentially *negentropic* undertaking, in which the rubbish heap bequeathed to Europe by antiquity was, for the first time, raided and pillaged for ideas and works of art to be used as constitutive features for a new civilization.

Carl Jung, too, created a middenheap out of the desacraclized gods of antiquity when he placed all the world's great religious forms into the debris pile of his collective unconscious from whence literary theoreticians like Joseph Campbell and Erich Neumann retrieved the gods to be used under the ontologically reduced status of mere symbols and metaphors. And, as we have seen, the great artists of Modernism – such as Marc Chagall and Paul Klee – retrieved these archetypal forms to become the structuring iconotypes of Modernist Art.

Even a work like Derrida's *Of Grammatology* is essentially one vast reduction of the great texts of the metaphysical age to a single middenheap. Derrida, in deconstructing all the great metaphysical systems, essentially tosses them into his textual junkyard of deconstructed signifieds. Once the transcendental signifieds are out of the way, they free up for him the endless *differance* of the play of signification in which meaning can be deferred to infinity.[2]

But now note that it is not traditionally the artist, but rather the thinker, who reduces previous world ages to middenheaps. Plato, the Hebrew prophets, the Christian church fathers, Jung and Derrida are all thinkers, not artists; thinkers, moreover, who at a stroke reduced previous world ages to piles of debris and discarded signifiers. The artist, on the other hand, is the one who, like Daedalus or Prometheus, initiates new technologies and creates new worlds by building forms up, or else retrieving older forms from previous middenheaps generated by the entropic processes of cultural evolution.

With the art of Anselm Kiefer at La Ribaute, however, it is clear that the traditional semiotics of these processes have now been turned upside down. In scene after scene of Sophie Fiennes's film, we witness Kiefer breaking forms down, melting them into slagheaps and reducing them to piles of rubble. The contemporary artist is a cosmocrator no longer, but a builder of junk heaps. The central concern of Kiefer's art has shifted from that of the future to the past; from the construction of cosmologies to an interest in the entropic processes generated by the dissipative structures of such cosmologies.

Kiefer's work is a monument to the discarded forms and deconstructed metanarratives of the metaphysical age. As the eye roams across La Ribaute, it discovers abandoned and broken signifiers everywhere. A painting full of U-boats, a technology that once functioned as an extension of the forces of destruction that led to the apocalypse of World War II; or his sculpted texts that look as if they had survived the burning down of some vast library, lining the shelves of crumbling archives surrounded by broken glass. The great textual narratives that once functioned as the warp and the weft of the construction of ideas in the metaphysical age are here reduced to a slagheap, just as for Gadamer, in his *Truth and Method*, the text – as opposed to the work of art which, for Gadamer, *gains* being – actually suffers a reduction in ontological status as it *loses* being. For Gadamer, the text can never be "objectively" reconstructed; it is always only a product of the biases and prejudices of its age, and so it recedes and diminishes its ontological status nearly to zero.[3] The texts that once built Western civilization are no longer, for either Kiefer or Gadamer, grand transcendental signifieds functioning as orienting constellations in the night sky of the Western imagination, but rather burned, shriveled, ragged and ashy forms that look as though they had survived an apocalypse, and are about as useful.

The huge canvases upon which Kiefer and his assistant are shown in the film gluing over-sized teeth into a cracked and parched earth are, of course, Cadmus's dragon's teeth as symbols of the alphabet, those linealized units of *pars pro toto* that carved up the two-dimensional images of the mythical age and reduced them to one-dimensional lines of text on the printed page. The teeth are the alphabet which Cadmus was said to have imported to Greece from Phoenicia, and they are the seeds of abstract visual linearity from out of which the text as Christian codex grew, the very texts at the dawn of the metaphysical age that anathematized the pagan deities. In another scene, we see these teeth strewn randomly across stacks of large, oversized sculpted books, as the very seeds of the Western tradition from out of which the books as flowers took form.

Kiefer's towers of Babel that he has constructed out of a series of slabs of concrete and erected upon platforms containing his sculpted, processed and acidified books, are the delegitimized ziggurats of the Old Testament. The towers, in other words, are *growing* out of the books as their foundations, for indeed, the Tower of Babel was constructed out of the teeth of the Hebrew alphabet which they used, like chips broken from the jaw of Moses, to deauthorize the technologies of the entire first generation of human civilization in Mesopotamia. The Biblical image of the Tower of Babel is a vision of the collapse of an entire plane of organization, together with all its various strata – star gods above, infernal gods below, human cities in between – into one vast desert plane of roving Bedouins and limestone cliffs where lizards dart across rocks.

Everywhere at La Ribaute, we find the ruins of the metaphysical age: paintings with maps of constellations, those patterns that once organized and built entire civilizations in the ancient Near East; melted slag heaps of liquid metal processed over mounds of dirt; abandoned rooms littered with brittle stacks of discarded palm fronds (the palm of Palm Sunday that Christ took with him on the ride into Jerusalem?); and a whole underground labyrinth of tunnels full of broken pottery vessels and fallen meteorites as artifacts of the Neolithic: pottery made from earthly clay, just as the meteorites became the foundation for the great megalith cults of Cybele and the Ka'aba.

La Ribaute is a veritable Foucauldian heterotopia, a space of otherness in which we are witness to the collapse of the West's entire plane of organization, once organized arborescently into linear tiers and strata erected all the way to the heavens. But in the post-metaphysical age, this plane of organization, like the Old Testament Tower of Babel, has collapsed, stratum on top of stratum, into a vast plane of consistency littered with destratified forms and crushed signifiers. This is not an art that is pregnant with the future, but an art that is entirely directed back toward the past, a cross-sectional analysis of the collapse of the entire skeleton of the Western mind, vertebra imploded into vertebra, pulled down by its own gravitational inertia.

The artist of such a heterotopia is a fashioner of ruins who reveals to us what has become of the metaphysical age; he is no longer, however, in process on the way to a discovery of new forms, as was initiated during the Carolingian era when the Irish monks imported into the court at Aix-la-Chapelle began the process of sifting out signifiers from the middenheap of antiquity: Greek, Latin and Hebrew as languages dusted off from the scrap pile to begin the cult of historical scholarship that would eventually lead to the Renaissance. But Kiefer's middenheap is a vision of the Omega Point of Western history as a collapsed, rusted and broken edifice like one of those shattered cathedrals in a Caspar David Friedrich painting. It is, indeed, an art that comes *after* Auschwitz, for the metaphysical certainties of that age – racial degeneracy, ethnic cleansing, Indo-Aryanism – made the camps possible in the first place, and these grim articulations of the Western mind were unfolded and illuminated to men's minds from out of the pages of the metaphysically-certain printed book.

Thus, the very books that began European history at one end with their revelations of the Three Ages of the Father, the Son and the Holy Spirit eventually culminate via the back alleys of philology into the climax of history as a Third Reich with various Final Solutions applied towards the management of its End. Indeed, the bombings of cities from the air – Dresden and Hamburg, Hiroshima and Nagasaki – were extreme events that ultimately were made possible by the pages of books. Hence, the landscape at La Ribaute is littered with the shattered and blackened shells of their remains. The metaphysically certain book can be trusted no longer, for we have seen what sorts of atrocities it can lead to.

But then the film's final closing image of those haunting, slender towers of Babel, inhabited by the ghost of Lilith, might also be read as vectors pointing into the future, for some day, some band of wandering nomads might stumble upon the ruins of our Western metropolises, and they may, indeed, resemble nothing so much as a skyline of abandoned and multiplicitous towers of Babel, towering over the wreck of a once mighty civilization sunken into the cracked red earth and covered with dust and windblown detritus.

It is, perhaps, an art of the future after all.

Zdzislaw Beksinski

Master Signifier

In 1975, the great Polish artist Zdzislaw Beksinski created a painting that I wish to consider here as a sort of master signifier, or key to understanding his work as a whole. The painting is untitled, as in fact, were all of Beksinski's paintings since, like the untitled chapters of *Finnegans Wake*, Beksinski did not wish to confer on his images any specific meanings. "Meaning is meaningless to me," he is famous for saying;[1] but then, Beksinski's profession was not that of a semiotician. His paintings most certainly *do* have meaning in them, if one knows where, and how, to look at them.

The painting in question shows an image of a sort of man-creature crawling along the ground on all fours while apparently fleeing from the ruins of a burning city behind him.[2] The man-thing's head is completely wrapped in white gauze bandages, which are marked with a crimson stain precisely where his facial features would be, so it does not appear that he could see very well. And this is perhaps why he is using his right hand as a sort of blind man's cane for palpating the ground in front of him, using fingertips as though reading Braille. The man-thing's body is dark and possibly furry: in any event, his legs and arms resemble those of a quadruped. In the background, flames light up the windows of the tall buildings like thousands of burning candles. Rubble and wreckage are strewn everywhere. The colors are infernal, as though we were peering down into a crack in the earth which had opened up to reveal streams of molten lava flowing with orange, red and yellow incandescence through the earth's interior.

Thus, the image.

Now, the question: namely, whence comes this mysterious figure crawling its way along the ground in search of who knows what? The figure itself vaguely resembles a question mark turned over onto its side, with the bandaged head serving as punctuation point.

The bandaged head recalls Grunewald's 1504 depiction of *The Mocking of Christ*, in which Christ is shown being humiliated on his way to the cross, the top half of his head covered by a white bandage. Indeed, Francis Bacon alluded to this painting in his 1944 *Three Studies for Figures at the Base of a Crucifixion*. And, as it turns out, the image of the crucifix is one of the master signifiers of Beksinski's art, reiterated over and over again from about 1968 all the way down to the late 1990s.

In one of his early crucifixion studies, furthermore, dating from 1969, Beksinski painted an image of the crucified Christ with a crumbling, dessicated body that is falling apart.[3] The body has separated away from one of the arms, which remains dangling on its own from the cross, while the rotting carcass is angled so that the head is turned away from the viewer. But when one takes a closer look at the legs of this figure, one notices that they are not those of a human being: they are far too long for that, and indeed they are articulated in such a way as to recall those of a bird. In fact, these legs are sufficiently similar to the quadruped legs of the crawling figure in the 1975 composition that we could even say, without sounding too rash, that the crawling figure *is* Beksinski's half-human, half-animal Christ-being who has slid down from his perch at the center of the Western tradition, and gone scurrying away in search of clues to its fate.

The 1969 crucifixion is a kind of Lacanian *point de capiton*, that is to say, a stitch point in his theory of the psyche that marks a stable intersection of a signifier and its signified. A sufficient number of such stitch points, where signifiers are anchored firmly to their signifieds, is necessary, in Lacanian theory, for mental health and confers stability on the patient's world view. But when one of these stitch points comes undone, the signifiers come unattached from their signifieds and begin to slide around in the psyche, where they become floating signifiers looking for new signifieds to attach to them.[4] Beksinski's 1969 crucifixion, then, is equivalent to a Lacanian *point de capiton* that has come undone, for the image of the crucifix was, of course, *the* great master signifier of Western civilization that anchored meaning and gave form and purpose to the entire society. It was a signifier that was attached to a transcendental signified, namely, the Idea of the Descent of God to earth.

But in the posthistoric civilization which we now inhabit, all such transcendental signifieds have been deconstructed and dismantled. They no longer function as they once did, as master signifiers to organize an entire civilization. The metaphysical age, as Beksinski shows in his 1975 painting, has gone up in flames all around us.

Posthistoric Civilization

Our present civilization is not so much postmodern, as it is posthistoric.[5] As Vilem Flusser has pointed out, history proper began with *texts* (in the sense of textiles as weaves that held and stitched the signifiers of Western civilization together with their signifieds). Writing, especially in its alphabetic phase, originated as a criticism of the images of the mythical consciousness structure, for both Plato and the Hebrew prophets have in common a shared antipathy to mythical images. Writing is a criticism of such images, a criticism that flattens out the two-dimensional surfaces of mythic icons into the one dimensional lines of written texts. But with the advent of the techno-images of the Vision Machine that began with photography in the nineteenth century, and which has accelerated since then into the dizzying unfolding of ever more and more elaborate Vision Machines, it is the two-dimensional image surfaces of the mass media that have come to displace writing and hence, along with it, historical consciousness. Writing creates history. To live in a civilization in which writing becomes secondary, or even tertiary, to images, is to live in a posthistoric civilization. Thus Vilem Flusser.[6]

In a posthistoric civilization, the texts that once acted as weaves stitching together signifiers with their signifieds have all come undone, and so now we are faced with a proliferation of free-floating signifiers looking for new signifieds. The signifiers have come sliding free, just as in Lacanian theory when a Borromean knot that weds the three orders of the imaginary, the symbolic and the real together comes unraveled, the result is semiotic chaos, and hence, a psychosis. We are now living in the midst of a civilizational psychosis.

Hence, the creature in Beksinski's 1975 painting, who palpates the ground with his right hand – the hand that once upon a time wielded the pen – as though searching amongst the middenheap that surrounds him for some new signified to which this formerly transcendent crucified man could reattach himself. He is Flusser's posthistoric man, desubjectivized and destratified, unplugged, that is, from all previous sign regimes. Deleuze and Guattari's signifying and post-signifying sign regimes (as discussed in *A Thousand Plateaus*),[7] which together constructed Western civilization, have ceased to function for posthistoric man, who has been desubjectivized and stripped clean of his signifying identity. In fact, he has been destratified from the sign regimes into which he had once been firmly locked in place on the plane of organization, and has now come disattached, a floating signifier drifting out onto the (horizontal) plane of consistency, where all previous forms of signification liquefy into an asignifying regime. (Hence, when Beksinski says, "meaning has no meaning for me," it is precisely because his central figures have come unplugged from all previous sign regimes, especially the signifying sign regime that locked them into systems of transcendent meaning. The signifying (paranoid) and post-signifying (or subjectifying) sign regimes which Deleuze and Guattari discuss in *A Thousand Plateaus* are equivalent, more or less, to Jean Gebser's mental consciousness structure and to Heidegger's metaphysical age. All such ages, together with their accompanying sign regimes, have now collapsed.)

The ruins of the burning buildings in the background of Beksinski's painting have not only folded into them Auschwitz, Hiroshima and the firebombing of Dresden (the planetary war in which all systems of meaning and their grand metanarratives were melted down into the posthistoric slag heap), but also the backgrounds of the burning buildings in the paintings of Hieronymous Bosch, especially in works like *The Temptations of Saint Anthony*, the Hell panel of the *Garden of Earthly Delights* and *Tondal's Vision*. These works were painted in the sixteenth century, and they too, signify a time of collapse and disintegration, for they are stress reaction images of the meltdown of the Medieval macrosphere and its shift into what was then a new age, the age, namely, of Heidegger's World Picture and Spengler's Infinite Space into which the Medieval iconotypes, with their naïve and quaint view of man as God's gardener on earth, dissolved into perspectival space.

At that time, as Marshall McLuhan has pointed out, the media were shifting from orality and illuminated manuscripts to the new kind of literacy configured by the printing press, a kind of literacy in which visual space was favored, and the sense of sight stepped up at the expense of the other senses, especially those of hearing and touch. The collapse of the Medieval sensorium, with its highly tactile and involving nature, was registered by painters like Bosch and Bruegel, and literary artists like Shakespeare and Cervantes, as a catastrophe. Hence, Bruegel's *Triumph of Death* as the triumph of visual, three-dimensional space *inside which* objects exist, as opposed to the Medieval order where they glow with their own self-luminous energies like the newborn infant Christ in Geertgen Sin Jans's 1490 *Birth of Jesus*. But ever since the nineteenth century, and coinciding both with the rise of Paul Virilio's Vision Machine[8] and the twilight of Flusser's historic mentality, the sense of sight has been gradually stepped down to allow the senses of touch and hearing to configure acoustic space, which is spherical rather than box-like, while melting down visual space, as reflected in the shift from three dimensional painting to aperspectival Modernist Art.

Beksinski's mysterious creature reminds us of this shift, too, for he cannot *see*: that is to say, his sense of sight has been stepped down as the world of visuality dissolves into ruins behind him, while he uses the sense of touch to palpate his way along like the blind men in Bruegel's painting *The Blind Leading the Blind*. We must *feel* our way, nowadays, through the ruins of the middenheap, using other senses than that of the merely visual, to orientate ourselves in posthistoric society. The sense of touch is discontinuous rather than linear, while acoustic space is spherical and, as it were, all-at-once. Surrounding the planet with electromagnetic pulse signals melts down visual space and configures an all-round space of simultaneity, enabling everyone to be everywhere, and anywhere, at all times via iconic and electronic avatars. Point of view, which presupposes location on a Cartesian grid with precise coordinates in space and time, simply vanishes under such conditions.

The crawling figure who feels his way through the ruins of the middenheap is in quest of new signs that will make sense out of his essentially *a*-signifying existence. He is Christ, the master signifier of the metaphysical age, *recoded* as the desubjectivized entity each one of us has now become in posthistoric society, who is on his own and must sift through the ruins of the imploded metaphysical age that now lies behind us, where systems of meaning had been preestablished and fixed for us in advance, like the discourse of Lacan's Big Other. Now, with the liquefaction of all semiotic systems and sign regimes, each of us is washed ashore on his own world island where he must act as a *bricoleur* to retrieve from the middenheap whatever signifiers will make sense out of the path he must create for himself as he lays it out. Private, as opposed to public, semiotics, in other words.

Indeed, in Beksinski's art as a whole, the theme of the middenheap is a recurring motif. In painting after painting, his image of the crucifix presides over a ruined heap of broken forms, as in the 1983 painting which shows the cross with a pile of bones in place of Christ upon it, standing atop a heap of wreckage: discarded bottles, broken chairs, ruined furniture, empty washbasins, etc.[9] A ladder extends from the middenheap to the cross, as though to suggest the construction of a subject out of whatever signs lay ready to hand, like the Lacanian Subject that is constructed out of scraps of signifiers from the discourse of the Other. This once mighty master signifier that shaped and built the metaphysical age has formative power no more. It has come unglued from all sign regimes and now remains only as the ghost of a vanished world, presiding over ruins.

Indeed, the Underworld generally speaking, is a sort of societal scrap heap where all the repressed and discarded signifiers, regarded as incompatible with the prevailing episteme, are tossed. In Beksinski's art, especially with his paintings beginning around 1970, he depicts an invasion of armies of the dead from the Underworld, who come pouring into the cityscapes of Poland, as though he were foreshadowing our own present pop cultural preoccupation with zombies and the undead. And this astral invasion that is depicted on his canvases all throughout the 1970s is made possible precisely by the decline of the Cross as a master signifier which, together with the Fichtean membrane that surrounds and protects the Ego with a transcendental immune system, has collapsed and rendered the psyche prey to astral invasion. (The cult of the ancestral dead, too, was tossed onto the middenheap of the Western Underworld as being incompatible with its cult of the Wonder Child and the new, *always* new thing that has propelled the forward motion of technological innovation).

And so, the cross today can preside only over the middenheap of the collapsed metaphysical age, where all its archetypes, signifiers, signifieds, metanarratives and machinic assemblages have been tossed into the rubble to be found by some future civilization who will retrieve from it the various bits and pieces which they will use, during some *Volkerwanderung*, to construct a new civilization.

That is precisely what the palpating right hand of Beksinski's creature is looking for: signifieds from the middenheap of the collapsed metaphysical age that will recode it and plug it into a new assemblage of enunciation. But that future assemblage, whatever it will be, remains too far off for us to see what its lineaments might look like. Each individual today must become his own semiotic machine who constructs his own personal assemblages.

Civilization as an Anthropogenic container, to borrow a term from Peter Sloterdijk, is a thing of the past, for now each individual is stranded upon his or her own semiotic world island, like the various colonies of isolated people sitting around camp fires in one of Beksinski's 1975 paintings, each gathered atop a kind of geological precipice that is separate from all others.[10]

Subhuman Christ

So, in Beksinski's untitled 1975 painting, we have seen how his sub-human Christ figure has come down from its once exalted place on the cross, where it once formed a *point de capiton* to hold meaning in place, to crawl upon the surface of the earth in quest of new significance. Thus, the Christ image that was once held up toward the sky to signify the descent of God to earth has shifted to a more chthonic, earth bound image, of a sub-human and bestial Christ figure that has demorphosized and destratified to the status of a becoming-animal. Note that in Deleuze and Guattari's pre-signifying regime of signs (or, if you prefer, Gebser's magical consciousness structure) the destratification of the human into a becoming-animal was regarded as a positive thing, indicating the ability of shamans to slip in and out of communion with pre-human animal spirits and totemic beings. But Beksinski's image of the Last Man at the End of History is more troubling: its devolved and dismantled humaneity, if we may put it that way, indicates the ontological status of the human being *after* Auschwitz and Hiroshima. The human being, that is to say, has become a posthuman, bestial creature who has lost his once exalted status. In the age of humanism, Christ on the cross was the great symbol of a drawing *upward* of the gaze of the human spirit towards a higher ideal, that namely, of the Man-God who had descended to earth to lead the human entity to the heavens. In the posthistoric age configured in Beksinski's painting, however, the subhuman Christ-creature crawling pathetically on the ground like some wild beast is a devolution and descent toward something much more pathetic and disreputable: the type of human capable of loading millions of people into gas chambers and thus reifying them as desubjectivized *things* to be transformed into ash heaps.

But the production of technologies for reducing humans to ash heaps on a mass scale was one of the major industries of World War II: for the degree to which technology could be pushed toward recreating eschatology on earth was one of its main projects. The nomenclature of World War II technologies all have a faintly apocalyptic ring to them: *Vergeltungswaffe*, the Final Solution, the atom bomb, etc. These are eschatological technologies produced by human beings attempting to appropriate the powers of the gods, but not to nobler purpose, rather for more and more efficient ways of wiping out larger and larger populations. And these are the kinds of technologies that segue us effortlessly into Foucault's and Agamben's Biopolitical Age,[11] in which the concentration camp becomes what the prison, the hospital, the clinic, the school and the factory had been for the previous Institutional Age.

For the first time, during World War II it became possible to actualize the Last Judgment using technological systems of mass extermination. And hence, the human being, viewed through the lens of such technologies, shrinks precipitously to the level of an insect, precisely in the manner, and from the vantage point in the heavens, from which a God might view him. The ontological status of such a creature is no longer human at all, but rather sub-human.

And so, Beksinski's demorphosized Christ-creature becomes for those of us living at the threshold of the twenty-first century an image of the Last Man at the End of History, the posthuman being of Heidegger's *Letter on Humanism*,[12] whose humanistic tradition of dictating to Being has led to apocalypse and mass atrocity. Humanism, as Heidegger pointed out in that essay, has failed us, leading only to the brink of an abyss from which we might not be able to turn back. Using technology to dictate to Being, instead of listening to its shepherd-like call, has led to the meltdown of our cities and of our properly human status, once celebrated so nobly by Pico della Mirandola in his essay *Oration on the Dignity of Man*.[13]

In that essay, written during the height of the Rennaissance, Pico placed the human on an ontological scale between the angels up above and the beasts down below. But in Beksinski's painting, the posthistoric human now exists somewhere between the insects and the beasts. His is a being that *crawls* upon the ground and who studies it for *signs*. Its axial orientation is horizontal, like that of an animal, and it can only look down (insofar, that is, as it can see anything at all) at the earth, never up. Few characteristics, other than the palpating right hand, remain to differentiate such an entity from the beasts. *The hand now reads the ground, as it once read the stars.* The image icon appropriate to such an age (and the very icon that appears on the cross of a 1978 Beksinski crucifixion, where it has displaced the signifier of the human Christ with that of a spider-like insect[14]) is rather that of Kafka's Gregor Samsa lying in his bed on his back, unable to right himself while squirming his many insectile legs. Kafka's image, take note, is essentially that of a horizontal crucifixion in which the signifier of Christ has slid away from its signified anchor as "man-God" and been replaced by the signifier of a giant man-bug.

Thus, Beksinski's image of the crawling, devolved man-creature has traded the heaven archetype out for the earth archetype, for in almost precise proportion to the degree to which, with ever mightier and more astonishing technologies man has raised himself to the status of the ancient gods, technologizing their powers, he has lowered himself ontologically to the status of a posthuman creature of a Biopolitical Age in which, as Agamben has pointed out, the concentration camp is the emblematic institution.

Indeed, Beksinski's creature has been, like Agamben's *homo sacer*, desubjectivized: that is to say, unplugged from the signifying and post-signifying sign regimes (in which, as D&G pointed out, he was configured as a passional subject) and stripped clean of all individuality. (In the post-signifying regime initiated by the Hebrews, who did away with human sacrifice at the precise time in which they punctuated, in Lacan's sense, the creation of the human being as a Subject, Moses becomes the first Subject; later, with Descartes, who inherits and combines the post-signifying regime with the paranoid signifying regime, the point of subjectification becomes the *cogito*).

Hence, the significance of the bandages that defacialize and effectively wipe the slate of the face clean, for whereas the bandages of Grunewald's Christ serve to highlight his humiliation and underscore his humanity as a suffering subject, the completely covered face of Beksinski's Christ-creature has been defacialized, its human visage effaced and removed so that no trace of its subjectivity remains. It is a *thing*, in other words, not a three-dimensional human individual. And the defacialization, which Beksinski, from his earliest work in photography had been concerned with all along, serves to reduce the visage to a posthuman prosthesis and blank slate awaiting the inscription upon its surface of new codes and new signifiers. The defacialized man, with which twentieth century art has been so preoccupied, is essentially *inhuman*, a visage created not by the process of what Peter Sloterdijk calls "protraction,"[15] in which the human visage has been, through interfacial relationships between humans over the millennia, extracted from its animal origins as a snout with fangs, but rather "detraction," in which the *portrait* becomes a *detrait*, and the face dismantled. This is not the face of the metaphysical age in which, as in Lacan's mirror stage, the image staring back at the infant essentially humanized it and created the fiction of its ego in response, but rather, the face staring into computer monitors, security cameras and other electronic apparatuses that rob and disinvest the facial visage, conferring on it an apathetic and indifferent countenance. The posthuman face, in other words, created not by looking and interacting with other human beings, but by interacting with dehumanizing machines.

The posthistoric human is *a*-signifying: numbers, as at Auschwitz, are more appropriate designations for him than names derived from humanist and mythical narratives. This is a type of being who has been stripped of all protections of the juridical macrosphere that once guaranteed and gave him his rights and reduced to the status of a *homo sacer* who can be killed with impunity precisely because he *has* no rights.

But these posthistoric humans of Agamben's Biopolitical Age are precisely what Beksinski is foreseeing here: his creature crawling along the ground, from which all protective civilizational macrospheres have been stripped away, is precisely Agamben's *homo sacer* who presently inhabits all the refugee camps of the world in places like Darfur, Rwanda, Serbia, etc. He is the biopolitical human, stripped clean of subjectivity, faceless, nameless and without rights. Such negentropic places in the world, where displaced populations are rounded up into camps, are becoming more and more common and may indeed, constitute the Wasted Life of the human being in the coming future, a future of mass exoduses and population displacements due to environmental catastrophes, water and food shortages, and so on.

Beksinski, as all great artists do, clearly foresaw what lay ahead for the posthistoric human being, now polarized into Fukuyama's Last Man at the End of History and Hobbes's First Man of prehistory. The Last Man is the human being as ubiquitous consumer, capable of participating in global free trade agreements and the endless circulation and proliferation of free floating signs and signifiers; and Hobbes's First Man, whose life is nasty, brutish and short, that is to say, the life of the Third World human being who is slowly proliferating around the planet and may even, as Hurricane Katrina showed us, slowly begin to irrupt into the civilizational fabric of our megalopolitan world cities everywhere.

As theoretician Heiner Muhlmann pointed out, the Roman gladiatorial arenas were essentially zones of exception, of maximal stress, that is, that were demarcated on the *inside* of zones of cooperation (i.e. cities), so that the brute struggle of zoological existence walled onto the outside of cities as eternal zones of stress and conflict could be carefully caged and staged on the *inside* of city life as zoological exhibits.[16] But nowadays, such zones of exception, of stress and conflict, are constituted not by gladiatorial arenas but by refugee camps that are slowly emerging within zones of cooperation and juridical order everywhere, as posthuman fabrications of purely zoological human beings who have no rights because they have no cities.

Beksinki's art, therefore, is an art that captures the revised ontological status of the posthumanist being of the biopolitical age. It is a being for whom all systems of signification have disintegrated and who sits atop the middenheap of the metaphysical age, picking through the discarded signs and wondering what they must once have been used for.

Odd Nerdrum

Miniature Cosmos
Cosmologies, when they become obsolete, do not just disappear. Rather, they are miniaturized by the poets, artists and painters of subsequent generations who thereby preserve them in diminished form. The Arabian cosmological image of the world as a gigantic cavern, for instance (realized in their mosques) – an image which once held together an entire civilization – returns in science fictional narratives of the domed city in films like *Logan's Run* or *The Truman Show*, or in popular novels like Stephen King's *Under the Dome*. The Paleolithic cosmology of the Hunt for the great Beast, likewise returns, scaled down for mass consumption, in the lowbrow kitsch of a movie like Steven Spielberg's *Jaws*.[1]

In art history, though, it was the Flemish painters of the 15th century who were the West's first great miniaturists of a vanishing cosmology, in this case, the disintegrating Christian macrosphere which, with the gradual development of perspectival space during that very century, was then on the verge of extinction. Flemish painters, correspondingly, like Robert Campin or Dirk Bouts, created the bourgeois interior precisely by scaling down and miniaturizing the Christian cosmos, carefully fitting it *inside* the interior living spaces of Flemish houses. As a result, in paintings like Campin's *Annunciation*, the great Christian cosmological Event looks like it is taking place inside of a doll house. Thus, in miniaturizing the vanishing Christian macrosphere, the Flemish painters created the bourgeois interior, the very same interior that will later, in the 17th century, be blown up to life size in the interiors of the great Dutch painters like Vermeer and Rembrandt, *minus the Christian iconotypes,* which had by then largely disappeared from Northern European art.

The Norwegian painter Odd Nerdrum, as it turns out, is also a kind of miniaturist, not so much of the Medieval macrosphere in terms of its content, but rather of its *structure*. What had been, in other words, an entire cosmology holding civilization together by means of a series of iconotypes becomes, in the case of Nerdrum, the private microsphere of a single man. The signifiers are, of course, no longer the same. If I am a Flemish artist living in the fifteenth century, I have a large, but very limited number of thematic iconotypes available to me to paint, such as the Annunciation, or the Last Supper, or the Nativity, or Mary's Death, or the Resurrection, etc., but it is a decidedly narrow and very limited range of iconotypes.

Nerdrum's microsphere is also held together by a series of iconotypes, although they are mysterious iconotypes for which the corresponding signifieds are missing. Nerdrum, that is to say, paints the images for stories and iconotypes *as though we knew what myths and stories these images referred to.* He constructs a thoroughly consistent cosmology of iconotypes such as the bathing *Hermaphrodite*,[2] a painting which is faintly evocative of Rembrandt's *Susannah and the Elders*; or *The Ultimate Sight*, an image for a non-existent mythic Event;[3] or he paints *The Man with Catfish*[4] as though we knew the parable which this image referred to; or the Cain and Abel-like image of *Woman Killing Man*,[5] and so forth. A whole galaxy of images and signifiers referring to vanished, or else non-existent, signifieds.

The Christian iconotypes were, of course, signifiers that referred to and were firmly anchored in established and very stable transcendental signifieds. They were signifieds which, during the epoch of the Medieval macrosphere, controlled and held together the entirety of Western European civilization. But, as Derrida pointed out in his essay "Structure, Sign and Play in the Discourse of the Human Sciences," there is nowadays an absent ontological center at the heart of our contemporary understanding of Being.[6] The transcendental signifieds like God, or the Subject, or Kant's Ideas of the Reason, have now vanished, leaving the signifiers free to play and skid and slide across the ontological canvas of the Western mind. This surplus of signifiers, together with the increased play of meaning, now supplements the absence of the transcendental signifieds.

And, as we saw with Mark Rothko's multiforms of about 1946 or so, the disintegration of the iconotypes -- or else call them, as

Derrida did, transcendental signifieds if you prefer -- of the Modernist macrosphere was made very clear in the evolution of both his and Pollock's canvases. The Modernist iconotypes melted away with the collapse of the Integral macrosphere during World War II, leaving behind precisely the absent ontological center which Derrida found there in his 1966 paper.

Odd Nerdrum's miniaturization of the iconotypical *structure* of the Medieval Biblical macrosphere is an attempt to *fill in* this absent ontological center, this void at the heart of the Western clearing (*die Lichtung*) with a new self-enclosed and self-contained cosmology, a cosmology structured, like the Christian one, by mythic forms. But the Biblical iconotypes have, in Nerdrum's art, been reterritorialized into the language of a science fictional utopia. They are signifiers without signifieds, or images of non-existent myths, myths which it is left up to the viewer himself to supply. Nerdrum's cosmos is a highly participational one in which the viewer of the canvases is invited to supply the missing myths which the images illustrate. It is, therefore, a cosmology with its own absent center, and this is why Nerdrum belongs, despite all protestations by both him and his critics, firmly to the epoch of contemporary art.

Missing Maximal Stress Event
The Medieval macrosphere, though, together with its Christian iconotypes, was brought into being for a very specific set of reasons, reasons which are *absent* in the case of Nerdrum's microsphere. The iconotypes of Medieval art, that is to say, constitute a kind of *stepping down* of the acute stress of an original founding event, what the German theoretician Heiner Muhlmann has called a "Maximal Stress Cooperation (MSC)" event. These are cultural events, such as wars, battles or the murders of religious founders, that involve a single population's cooperation in staving off a mortality that threatens the group as a whole. The Trojan War was an event of this kind, or the Persian Wars of the Greeks, the Maccabean Revolt, the American Civil War, etc.[7]

The MSC event, according to Muhlmann, has two phases: a stress phase, during which the population is united together to avert disaster, and a relaxation phase which can only set in if the preceding stress phase has been positively assessed (in other words, registered as a victory of some sort).[8] The maximal stress event is an event of major stress that activates strong emotions and those intense emotions become memoactive, that is to say, they engrain the event on the collective bio-memory of a people. This is a type of acute stress that is then stepped down, as though by a transformer, into latent stress in the form of cultural media that record the event. The writing down of the Gospels, for instance, translate the acute stimuli of the founding event of the Crucifixion into latent stimuli; but these latent stimuli can then always be reactivated into the original acute stimuli by a culture through liturgical and ritual acts that retrieve the original emotions associated with the stress of the founding event.[9]

Thus, the Christian iconotypes of the Medieval macrosphere refer *back* to the maximal stress, the acute stimuli, that is, of the founding event of the Crucifixion. They are translations into image form of the Gospels, which are themselves a downloading of the original acute stimuli into latent stimuli. A culture, according to Muhlmann, passes the MSC model along through the generations vertically by handing it down through media, but if there is a break in the tradition, and an event continues to exist *only* in the form of words and images and *without* the emotional liturgies and rituals to reactivate the original stress, then cultural disintegration sets in, almost as a kind of Alzheimer's, that gradually causes a culture to "forget" the original sense of the stress events. The culture, at that point, ceases to exist.

`This entire cultural dynamic, however, is precisely what is *missing* in the case of Nerdrum's miniaturized Medieval microsphere. He proceeds to paint like an artist who is embedded in an already existing World, in which such events have long since taken place, and in which it is therefore assumed that everyone knows and recognizes what events he is talking about. His cosmology is therefore a *simulacrum* of the Medieval macrosphere, for his iconotypes do not refer to an original maximal stress founding event that brought them into being as a means of culturally storing the event; they are, rather, images for which the texts and Gospels that would explain and make sense out of their existence, are *missing*. They are, in other words, latent stimuli with no original acute stimuli or founding events that preceded them. They are a micro-cosmology in search of a history.

Which explains both the strangeness of the images, and also why they can never be taken up the way Nerdrum would like them to be, as iconotypes for the society as a whole. His microsphere is an attempt to fill in the missing ontological center that has resulted from the collapse of both the Perspectival and the Modernist macrospheres, gone since World War II, but it can never perform this function because it is operating under the conditions of an ahistorical cultural moment. History does not exist any longer: we are living in a historyless age, and a historyless age is one in which cultural founding events no longer occur. So Nerdrum's microsphere can never be provided with the historical stress events that would give it the necessary emotional stress which would cause it to be relevant for, and thus taken up by, the civilization as a whole. It is, instead, an abortive cosmology.

But this does not mean that it is irrelevant: if we take a closer look now at the specific images and iconotypes which compose its internal structure, we will be able to see how Nerdrum's microsphere functions as a counter-environment (in McLuhan's sense) or counter cosmology – instead of a World (in the Heideggerian sense) -- which makes visible certain otherwise hidden structures of our present environment.

Parallel Universe
From the early 1960s until about 1983 or so, Odd Nerdrum was largely a painter of social realism whose main theme tended to focus on the troubled relationship of the isolated individual to his society. But in 1983, he painted a canvas entitled *Iron Law*,[10] which takes this theme and uses it as a bridge from consensus reality into the parallel micro-world that he creates. Like Joseph Wright's depiction in his 1771 painting *The Alchemist in Search of the Philosopher's Stone* of an alchemist who is creating his own micro-world inside of the alembic that now harbors a nascent chemical cosmology that radiates its own

inner phosphorescence from inside the beaker, so Nerdrum, too, becomes the demiurgic creator of his own mini-world from this point on. Though the world that he makes appears to represent a post-apocalyptic society of some future sort along the lines of the *Mad Max* movies, Nerdrum has denied this, insisting instead that what we are looking at in these canvases is a world that parallels our own as a sort of alternate universe. And the painting *Iron Law* represents the bifurcation point at which this parallel world begins to break off into its own separate and self-contained universe.

The image shows a man submitting to the punishment of being beaten by another man with an iron staff while in the distance beyond this foreground violence, a third man can be seen wandering off into the landscape which, from henceforth, becomes characteristic of Nerdrum's parallel world: a waste land of rocks and earth barren of trees, vegetation or indeed even civilization of any kind. Nerdrum's self-contained world island, that is to say, eliminates *both* Nature and Civilization from existence, leaving behind only the residue of human culture locked into a tribal mode. Thus, it is not Civilization which interests Nerdrum, for he, just like Oswald Spengler, Martin Heidegger and Rudolf Steiner before him, regards contemporary civilization with skepticism, as something corrupt and not to be trusted, since it is based upon the realization of a worship of machines which are hostile to human values. Western industrial technology has triumphed over humanity, scaling him down to the size of an ant. But Nerdrum, in his canvases, eliminates this technical civilization so that the properly human world can scale itself back up into our view as the thing in all this which *matters*.

But in doing so, he has also eliminated Nature from his parallel world, for unlike Joseph Beuys, who eliminated the human element from his compositions in favor of an interest in vast, impersonal spiritual – macrocosmic processes, Nerdrum retains his uchronic society at the human scale, and builds it *around* the human being, never losing sight of him. By eliminating Nature (i.e. in clearing away the trees and forests and greenery from his canvases), Nerdrum ensures that no larger, more sublime macrocosmic elements may arise to impede the view of his little alchemical homunculi.

Also, in centering his concerns on the human body in a way that is not too dissimilar from that of the Greeks, (especially those of the Hellenistic Age with which Nerdrum aligns himself and his kitsch aesthetic), he has felt it necessary to retain the perspectival space of the Old Masters since, for him, it is essential that the motif of the human body be recognizable.[11] The human body, for Odd Nerdrum, is the axial center around which his entire cosmology revolves. And since his imaginary society is post-literate and has reverted back to an oral-tribal mode, the body itself is retrieved, as it is in primitive territorial regimes (as D&G point out in *Anti-Oedipus*), as the main surface of inscription.[12] Scarring, tattooing, deforming, defacing, incising, cutting, slicing: these are the forms of mediatic incision in an oral society, and this is why in Nerdrum's art, we see the body so often deformed, cut, mangled, amputated, etc. It is the only surface of inscription that his post-literate society has available to them, and they use it precisely to construct their cultural memory out of the mnemo-technics of pain.

Which brings us back to *Iron Law*, in which the nearly naked human being is submitting to a ritual of being beaten and thus, of offering his body as a surface of inscription with which to encode and engrain cultural memory as a mnemo-technique of pain. The painting is actually illustrating the way in which mediatization now takes place in Nerdrum's parallel universe: the staff becomes the substitute for the pen which now writes in blood upon the surface of the body in a code which is permanently stored in the memory, and will thus never be forgotten. Pain, as Nietzsche put it, is the most effective mnemonic device there is.

The other important aspect of *Iron Law* is that, as Jan Ake Pettersson has pointed out, it visually evokes Masaccio's 1426 painting of the *Expulsion from Paradise*, in which Adam and Eve, with postures very similar to the beaten man in Nerdrum's painting, are being chased out of Eden by an Angel behind them with sword raised in a gesture that evokes the raised staff of the punisher in *Iron Law*.[13] This marks Nerdrum's painting as an exospheric image, for the expulsion of Adam and Eve from the Garden is tantamount, a la Peter Sloterdijk, to a spherological collapse and its ensuing crisis of transition from one sphere to another. In Nerdrum's case, the image of exile in *Iron Law* suggests the bifurcation point at which his world breaks off from the mainstream world of social reality into its own spherological exile in the creation of a private universe, a universe that is closed and contained, completely broken off, from our own consensus reality.

In the painting entitled *The Transfiguration*,[14] which shows a man waking up, surrounded by sleeping companions, and arising into a sphinx-like posture with the dawn breaking over a desolate landscape all around him, we see Nerdrum's avatar, as it were, awakening into this new reality that he is painting. He, the artist, is now awakening into a world that he is dreaming forth while we, the viewers of the canvas, are merely the sleepers stuck into the mode of banal reality.

In *The Ultimate Sight*, painted in 1984,[15] we see a group of three men looking out over the world from an elevated viewpoint at the top of a cliff edge, a point that is much higher than the clouds. They appear transfixed as though by the awe of a religious revelation, and what it is that they are beholding we cannot see, but one has the sense in this painting that we are at the edge of Nerdrum's cosmos looking off into the abyss where, in *his* world, the ancient cosmological myth of The Edge of the World is retrieved and made active. This painting captures the mythical Edge of Nerdrum's cosmos, a theme that he will return to in the Limbo paintings of the late 2000s.

And in the 1984 painting of *The Mother*,[16] Nerdrum returns to the sleeping theme and shows us a mother wrapped up in an animal hide together with her two infants in a sort of sleeping bag in a completely desolate landscape. The key thing about the painting, though, is the curvature of the horizon, a motif that has existed in three of these first paintings of Nerdrum's alternate cosmos: in *Iron Law* and *The Mother*, especially, but it is also dimly perceived in *The Ultimate Sight*. The horizon in Nerdrum's cosmos is *always* curved, but it is a degree of curvature that can only be glimpsed from being very high up in the air.

Nerdrum's microcosm, then – and this is an important point -- is taking place as a drama that is unfolding upon the surface of a cosmic ball, a ball that is perhaps too small for it.

Expanding Bubble

In the 1985 paintings, *Revier*[17] and *The Night Guard*,[18] the curvature of this horizon is more and more pronounced as the earth itself appears to be rising higher up into the field of view, slowly pushing the sky out of the frame. This is even more evident in the 1986 paintings, *Sleeping Courier*[19] and *The Black Cloud*,[20] in which the part of the canvases exhibiting the sky is gradually diminishing. (Indeed, the character who gestures to the small black cloud does so almost as a means of coming to grips with a heavenly world that the expanding earth is pushing him into).

Something strange, then, happens to Nerdrum's microworld as he goes along: it is expanding. The brown sphere of earth upon which he paints his dramas is itself actually *growing*, pushing against the frames of the canvases, slowly getting larger as though Nerdrum's spherical cosmos were a ball that were being inflated like the glowing bubble in Joseph Wright's 1773 painting *Two Boys Blowing a Bladder by Candlelight*.

There is an old geological theory (put forth by Roberto Montovani in 1889) that the earth itself, *our* earth, is actually growing larger and that this increase in its size is the real explanation for why the tectonic plates appear to be drifting away from each other, for the planet is actually, somehow, *expanding*.[21] The theory, in our world, was rendered obsolete by Wegener's plate tectonics, but in Nerdrum's parallel universe, that is precisely what is happening. His enclosed spherical cosm is like a bubble that is gradually inflating with time, growing ever larger and larger as it expands into the absent ontological center of the Limbo left behind by the collapse of Gebser's Modernist macrosphere. That black void – the empty space later painted in Nerdrum's Limbo paintings – is the space into which his cosmos is expanding and trying to fill the semiotic vacancy with a new macrosphere.

The process becomes visible when one considers the evolution of the following canvases: in the 1987 painting, *Sleeping Twins*,[22] the sky is completely gone, for we are hovering over a pair of twins, looking directly down at an earth that seems to be alive and pulsing with its own internal energies; in the 1990 *Wanderer Imitates a Cloud*,[23] the curvature of the horizon is the most blatant yet, and indeed, the earth is rising so far up into the sky, that its cloud forms are beginning to be imitated by Nerdrum's protagonists on the ground below; the man with the downward pointed knife in the 1990 *Contra Natura*,[24] attempts to stop the process by actually threatening the earth itself, but his attempt is a failure, as shown by the 1990 painting *One Story Singer*,[25] in which a man with magical singing powers actually brings a cloud down to the earth, which lands upon a distant mountain peak and begins to take on the corporeal form of some as yet undefined shape, as though an avatar were arriving; in the famous painting from the same year, *Dawn*,[26] in which four men sitting on the ground are singing, a line of jagged mountains (in direct opposition to the downward pointing knife in *Contra Natura*) pushes *up* against the diminishing strip of sky above them (as though the magic power of their voices were actually *causing* the rocks and mountains to grow and push up towards the sky); in the 1993 *Dying Couple*,[27] a pair of lovers is expiring in agony on an earth that has all but completely covered the canvas, for the sky is now a thin, barely visible strip at the top of the canvas; and in the 1995 *Baby in a Deserted Landscape*,[28] the earth is so severely curved that it is actually tilted, threatening to let the baby slide off the ground and out the other side of the canvas. In this painting in particular, one can feel the vitality of Nerdrum's pulsing, inwardly throbbing earth: its geomorphic powers are visible in the steam vents beyond the baby, as well as in many of the volcanoes so often depicted in his other paintings. The 2005 sequel to this painting is *Study for Five Singing Women*,[29] in which we see a group of five women and one boy on a ground that curves tumescently and powerfully up at us, pushing everything else out of view.

The end result of all this?

In the 2005 painting, *Man in Boat*,[30] Nerdrum's avatar, lying prone in a small boat, floats up off the ground altogether and when next we see him it is in *Self-Portrait in Void*,[31] where the avatar has floated off into the Limbo of the black empty void that Nerdrum's microsphere is expanding into. His recent paintings, which show groups of discarnate human souls floating in a black void, or else a single man with a burning head drifting in darkness,[32] are images of the void that surround Nerdrum's cosmos and into which it is expanding and attempting to fill up with a new World. It is precisely the void that Western man, during the metaphysical age, had immunized himself against by erecting philosophical thought systems, but with the collapse of those systems, this void of semiotic vacancy and meaninglessness now threatens to overcome contemporary man with depression, anxiety and ennui.

Nerdrum in these later canvases has moved from an exploration of the earth to the outer astral shell surrounding it. These are also snapshots, as it were, of the souls who inhabit Nerdrum's cosmos, for this is the world that they reincarnate *from*, descending into their physical bodies down on the expanding earth below from this floating void of astral presences. It is an image of materiality surrounded and encapsulated by spiritual substance, but it is also an image that replicates our current technological surrounding of the earth in a sheath of electromagnetic pulse signals in which discarnate human entities float in the form of coded signals that travel at the speed of light around it.[33] We have recreated a technological version of the ancient astral spheres that were once imagined as surrounding the earth, and Nerdrum's late paintings perfectly capture this.

And the significance of Nerdrum's expanding earth?

Nerdrum terms his type of art "kitsch," meaning thereby not the usual connotation of the term as vulgar reproductions of art, or else simply lowbrow art for the living room of the mass consumer, but rather a traditional type of art that is concerned, in opposition to Modernism, with the values of craftsmanship, i.e. painting skillfully, and rendering traditional human themes. It is an art of emotions that does not appeal, like Modernism does, to the coldly analytical intellect and its merely disinterested concerns with abstract formal properties, but with the warm, glowing, living world of human life. And so, Nerdrum also terms his "kitsch" art "geocentric," in opposition to what he describes as the "egocentric" art of the academy.[34] Nerdrum's earth is expanding because it is insisting upon its importance, that is to say, insisting upon the importance of its humanistic values in opposition to the nihilism and irony of much of contemporary art. Contemporary art, that is to say, has lost contact with the earth, and like the myth of the Greek giant Antaeus, in losing contact with the real world, suffers from an increasing loss of power in the form of irrelevance and elitism that appeals to ever smaller and smaller audiences.

But Nerdrum's art is also geocentric in another sense, for it is as though he were retrieving the geocentric Ptolemaic cosmology of the ancients, in which, because the earth was at the center of the universe, so too was the human world and all of its concerns. As Rudolf Steiner has remarked, the Copernican shift may have decentered the earth from the cosmos *physically speaking*, but in a way, it still remains at the center of the human drama *spiritually speaking*, since it is precisely upon the earth that the solar system's spiritual drama is unfolding through and by means of human cultural activities. If Nerdrum is insisting upon the earth as the center of his cosmology, it is only because he believes, like Steiner did, that it is precisely on the earth that the spiritual drama is being played out.

Counter Environment

As a counter-environment, however, I have said that Nerdrum's microcosmology does make certain structures of our present age visible. It is a truism to say that science fiction is never about the future, but is always a form of disguised commentary on the present society and I think the case is no less so in the paintings of Odd Nerdrum. That his world is a waste land that is devoid of trees, animals and vegetation (for the most part) is the simplest and clearest example of this, for it is a way of saying that *our* civilization is a waste land void of spiritual values.

But his imaginary society, as I have remarked, is one which has regressed back to the level of oral-tribal media of communication. It is, in other words, a Dark Age society in which all mediatic structures, whether electronic or Gutenbergian, have collapsed and disappeared. In a way, Nerdrum is therefore saying that *our* society is already living in a post-humanistic world of disintegrating literacy and vanishing (Gutenbergian) media.

Peter Sloterdijk, in his controversial essay "Rules for the Human Park," describes how the book lost the battle against the gladiatorial arenas in ancient Rome, a process which he describes in terms of "constraining" or "inhibiting" media vs. "disinhibiting media." Inhibiting media are the traditional texts and books of humanistic civilization that tame and domesticate the human animal, constraining and inhibiting his bestial impulses with the power of cultivated Reason; disinhibiting media, on the other hand, like today's Hollywood movies and video games or the Roman gladiatorial arenas, do not do this, but rather encourage the human toward his bestial impulses, inviting him to routinely resort to violence as a means of problem solving. And since, in ancient Rome the inhibiting media typified by the book lost out against the battle with the disinhibiting media of the arenas and stadiums, Sloterdijk sees the same process happening today all over again. With the decline and collapse of humanism and its literary activities with the rise of mass (circus) culture, Sloterdijk sees us entering already into a kind of post-humanistic Dark Age in which the archivist comes to replace the humanist. And the archivist merely catalogs and labels his books; he is not so much interested in reading them.[35]

So Nerdrum's Dark Age society, with its post-literate, tribal – oral structures, is a comment on the lineaments of a new Dark Age which Nerdrum sees emerging through the surface structures of our contemporary electronic society. And when literate structures break down, the body does indeed resurface back into view as the new locus of inscription, a tribal locus, as it were, for tattooing, piercing, scarring and inscribing icons and signifiers into the flesh has been on the rise in the tribal cultures of our youth and hooligan societies of the past four or five decades.

But then, perhaps Nerdrum's earth is also *shrinking*? Perhaps the visibility of the curvature of the horizon is actually an effect of an earth that is *too small* for his gigantifying human inhabitants? Perhaps the very reason we can see the curvature is not so much that it is expanding as that it is a ball that is too small to comfortably accommodate its giant human inhabitants whose culture is too large and therefore out of all proportion in relation to it?

As Paul Virilio has remarked, with Google Earth, the planet now reveals itself as too small for human civilization.[36] We have turned it into a toy and a plaything for a civilization that has surrounded and encompassed it to the point where it has actually eliminated Nature – as in Nerdrum's paintings – by placing the earth *inside* the dome of human civilization. If it has become so small that we can now actually *see* the curvature of its horizon, then perhaps we have grown too big for it, like a child that has outgrown its old toys and clothes.

Then perhaps, as Nerdrum's late paintings seem to suggest, there is more room for us in Limbo than upon the earth's surface?

And in that case, perhaps we need a new Eschatology, a new theory of vanishing horizons and world closures. A new understanding of Being, in other words, as Heidegger in his essay on "The Turning" has suggested, of a coming epoch in which the enframing of the earth by human technical systems will gave way to the framing of the human being by the gods themselves.

Maybe Heidegger was right.

Only a god can save us now.

London

Francis Bacon – Damien Hirst – Anish Kapoor

The British artists which I discuss in this next section have an altogether different "feel" about them than either the Germanic artists or the New York group: for one thing, they are not haunted by a catastrophe that has leached the metaphysical certainties out of their work, as was the case for the Germanic grouping; and unlike the New York group, they are not quite so anxious about the Void – and hence, with filling it -- that looms over contemporary post-history. Instead, they have proceeded to construct their own semiospheres almost out of whole cloth, for their work, as different as that of each artist is, nonetheless is involved with kinds of "world-making."

Francis Bacon constructs a world of demons, monsters and shadow-forms that are entirely unplugged from narrative traditions of any kind. His tortured humans are not enacting scenes from ancient myths and they do not refer to any known historical events or episodes. Bacon is a kind of alchemist who constructs a laboratory out of his semiotic cubes, inside which he creates agonized homunculi that he then proceeds to torture. It is an entirely self-contained and enclosed world – a world of suffering beings crossed with geometrical forms -- that does not refer to anything beyond the walls of its own rectangular boundaries.

Damien Hirst, who originally patterned himself after Bacon – Bacon's hermeneutic cubes become Hirst's vitrines, as is well-known – is concerned with analyzing the a priori *structures, indeed the very skeleton, of the global anti-world that we currently find ourselves living in. All the entities of his work – which, unlike Bacon's, have expanded to include a veritable bestiary – are ontologically deworlded entities cut off from the conditions of their lifeworlds and thrust, as modular units of disposability, into circulation on the inside of the capitalist ecumene. His formaldehyde animals, his spots, his jewels and cigarette butts have all been cut from the contexts of their particular worlds and plugged into the capitalist grid of seriality and repetition.*

Anish Kapoor, meanwhile, has been busy creating cultural hybrids between West and East by genetically cross-splicing Hindu religious signifieds that have been cut free from their religious environments and setting them loose into the global metabolism, where they drift, literally, across the planet's countryside as bizarre, wayward objects that have escaped confinement from their own semiotic world containers. Kapoor's anti-objects, like Hirst's entities, are ontologically deworlded signifieds that have been unprooted from their originary ground and set circulating around the planet via the world interior of capitalism, where they take on unspecified and indeterminate "meaning functions."

Thus, these British artists have set about the creation of radically new anti-worlds that are not concerned so much with the anxieties of meaning – as was most emphatically the case with the Germans – but rather with Being; living, that is to say, under the conditions of the new world interior of the global ecumene that cuts the individual off from all his traditions. Bacon ejects the traditions altogether while Kapoor hangs on to some of them, and Hirst simply analyzes a cross-section of Existenz *under the new environmental conditions of the planetary society.*

Francis Bacon

Monsters

Francis Bacon's art is the kind of art that surfaces into view when a World collapses. Like the art of Hieronymus Bosch or Pieter Bruegel, which unleashed a cavalcade of horrors at precisely the time when the Christian macrosphere was undergoing disintegration due to the impacts of new tools and principles of the scientific age then dawning – i.e. the perspectival grid captured in Durer's 1525 woodcut of a *Draughtsman Drawing a Recumbent Woman*; the retrieval of Platonic mathematics by Copernicus – such an art opens up the Gates of Hell, as it were, and unleashes a flood of cosmic monsters which the functioning macrosphere had specifically been erected to defend Civilization *against*. Just as the walls of Medieval cities had kept the siegeing armies of the Vikings and later, the Moors at bay, so too, the Western mind had built ontological walls designed to keep the demons from the world Out There from infiltrating the collective consciousness of European society.

In Bacon's case, it wasn't the Moors armed with their newly acquired technics of gunpowder that brought down the walls, but the Nazis with their V2 rockets and their corporately manufactured Zyklon B nerve gas that ruptured, and then exploded, the West's final metaphysical bubble, that bubble which the Swiss philosopher Jean Gebser termed "the Integral sphere," and which had come into being as a collective endeavor of all the arts and sciences of the nineteenth century, where it had served as an ontological sphere that gave a unity of purpose and metaphysical meaning to the project of Modernity taken as a whole.[1]

It was in the aftermath of the great apocalyptic war that ended history, then, when the ancient monsters which the Christian mythos had captured, bound and thrust down into the underworld – sealing it with a huge cosmic rock – found that the entrance to their world had been blown open and that they were free, once again, to crawl about the surface of the earth. Such monsters, like the cosmic beings out of a Lovecraft tale, are invisible and not readily apparent to the senses, but it is precisely the task of the artist – of *any* age – to make the invisible visible.

And so the canvases of Francis Bacon came into being as an attempt to render these demons perceptible to our faculties of vision and sense in an age in which the structuring scaffolds of grand metanarratives no longer existed to defend us moderns against them.

Embryogenesis

The first such group of monsters to concern us are, of course, the three creatures of Bacon's inceptual great work, *Three Studies for Figures at the Base of a Crucifixion* (1944), a work which he himself always regarded as marking the birth of his oeuvre.[2] He had already been painting since 1929 or so, but he regarded these early works as gauche and awkward attempts to find a style, a style which crystallized all at once in the 1944 triptych, his first real achievement as an artist.

It is important to note that, as the title indicates, this is *a* crucifixion, not *the* Crucifixion, for Bacon's work is concerned with the formation of singularities, not the repetition of archetypes, which had been one of the main concerns of Modernism. For Bacon, it is true, does borrow the three figures at the foot of Grunewald's great Isenheim *Crucifixion* – Mary Magdalene (left panel), Christ (center panel, indicated by the blindfolded Christ he has taken from Grunewald's *Mocking of Christ*) and the lamb (right panel), but he transforms them beyond all recognition into monsters, and in doing so, articulates (albeit in the picture language of images) a complex theory of the morphogenesis of monsters. For Bacon's work, despite all his hand waving at any attempts to find meaning in his canvases, is about the formation of singularities, and this early triptych represents the inception of that project.

Bacon's theory here – even if only unconscious on his part – is that monsters are created through a complex process of morphological folding and stretching of organisms such that they are torqued and twisted until they no longer conform to any preexistent animal patterns. As Deleuze and Guattari point out in *A Thousand Plateaus*, it was the eighteenth century biologist Geoffrey St. Hilaire who proposed, in opposition to Cuvier, that all animals in nature are really only *one* animal, a primordial Ur-animal that has been elongated, stretched and twisted during the processes of embryogenesis in order to specify all the earth's animal forms.[3] You get a cephalopod, he said, by folding a vertebrate in half from head down to tail: voila, a squid! Or a giraffe by stretching the neck of a vertebrate while simultaneously shortening its torso. Or a snake by removing the legs of a lizard and stretching it out lengthwise. And so on.

Deformities, St. Hilaire held, were created when a human being was born before the morphogenetic process was completed: a heteradelph, for instance, is really an individual arrested at a very early stage of embryogenesis before the organism has been fully differentiated.[4] And indeed, when one glances at a page of nineteenth century drawings of embryogenetic processes throughout the animal world – such as those famously drawn by Ernst Haeckel[5] – with all their pre-formed, half-formed and yet-to-be-formed embryos, and then back again at the creatures of Bacon's triptych, one does begin to see that monsters are indeed created when the morphological folding of the organism during embryogenesis is arrested.

Certain things can happen to an embryo which would destroy the skeleton of a fully formed vertebrate: it can be folded in half, twisted asunder and shifted around as though it were a Creature Without Organs.[6] But it is only the finished creature which corresponds to a pre-existent animal pattern and which is therefore *not* a singularity, but rather conforms to a Type that is already in existence. If the embryo, however, is born *before* the topological foldings are complete, then you have a monster: that is to say, a creature that does not conform to a pre-existent and therefore recognizable pattern.

Bacon's project, then, which he announces in this first great triptych, is to create *new* forms, whether human or animal, by appropriating the folding and stretching processes of embryogenesis, forms which are, therefore, completely novel and which correspond to no known patterns or archetypes: singularities, in other words. This is why his project is so radically different from Modernism – despite its superficial similarities of figuration, etc. – because it is based on an ontological theory not of *matching*, but of *making*. Modernism, and indeed, the entire history of Western art, was based on – or at least, consistent with – the old *adequatio* theory of truth in which there exists a correspondence between things and pre-established truths. A thing is true because it can be said to correspond to a pattern, usually Platonic, that pre-exists, and makes possible, the truth itself.

But in an ontology of singularities, such as that which, for example, Deleuze articulates in his *Difference and Repetition*, truth is not about the correspondence of knowledge with its objects. For Deleuze, the philosopher *creates* concepts by extracting singularities from the flow of clichés, banalities and convention. Truth is not, for Deleuze, an old-fashioned matter of Platonic matching of the thing with the archetype that makes it possible in the first place, but rather the creation of really novel, and therefore *fresh* ideas, or in the case of Bacon, new forms.[7]

Modernism, on the other hand, despite its ethic of "make it new," was nonetheless Platonic in essence, since it was all about the rediscovery of mythic – and mathematical – archetypes, precisely the Jungian archetypes of the collective unconscious, which it made visible through the works of Picasso, Klee, Beckman, Chagall, etc. etc. who were all concerned, to one degree or another, with myth-making.

This is not the case, though, with contemporary art, which actually *creates* its own truths as it goes along. It does not match them to Platonic Forms, Ideas or otherwise already known categories, and it is therefore based on an ontology of *making*, not *matching*. This is why it is so hard for most people to grasp: because it does not *refer* outside of itself to some other, already known metaphysical world of Forms, and the mind therefore has difficulty getting a grip on it.

And this is precisely why Bacon belongs as one of the founding fathers of contemporary art and *not,* as he is commonly seen, as one of the last belated stragglers of Modernism. Everything in his work is new: nothing corresponds to or refers to other worlds or archetypes, mythic or otherwise, beyond the work of art itself. Bacon *creates* his own world as he goes along, constructing a semiotic of meaning that is entirely his own and which has significance *only* within the world of unique forms that he creates. It is, therefore, a hermetically sealed, self-enclosed -- and also self-referential -- world whose semiotics derive only from signifiers that refer to his own made-up signifieds.[8]

It is an art that takes place *outside* the metaphysical age, and all of its structures and metanarratives, which ended with Modernism and also, incidentally, History itself during World War II.[9]

And so, lacking a pre-existent metaphysical universe within which to make sense out of his images, it seemed to Bacon (mistakenly) that what he was doing had no meaning and meant nothing at all. On the contrary: Bacon was like an alchemist constructing a tiny world of his own inside of a glass beaker; hence the significance of the famous perspectival cubes that he often used as staging for the exhibition of his images. They are hermetically sealed vessels inside which he invents tiny homunculi that he then proceeds to torture with his experiments. But what takes place inside these glass terrariums has no reference to any other world existing outside them. Such meaning as they have refer *only* to Bacon's microverse and not to any other metaphysical cosmos inside which his art takes place.

Bacon, that is to say, does not create *in* a world; his images *are* worlds unto themselves and therefore cannot be understood on the lines of any sort of Platonic theory of matching that tends to burden much art criticism, which usually proceeds by examining the relation of this or that painting or work of art to earlier pre-existent works of art by way of which they are measured. There is *some* dialogue with the past, it is true, in Bacon: his fascination with Velazquez and Van Gogh come to mind. But of course his semiotic is not a pure one: it is still mixed with striations of Modernist agendas in which dialogues with the Old Masters were *de rigeur*. But such dialogues do not compose the *fabric* of Bacon's microverse. They are merely atavistic organs left over from previous epochs of art evolution which are in no way essential to understanding how the new organism functions in the contemporary milieu in which it finds itself situated.

Bacon Descends Into Hell
The first such archetypal atavism, then, that we encounter as we proceed through Bacon's oeuvre is his descent into the underworld,

which begins with his shocking *Painting 1946*. This painting of a hanging side of beef split down the middle, and a man with the top of his head sheared away standing beneath an umbrella, functions in a way that is directly analogous to the ancient entrances to temples and cathedrals that were usually adorned with frightening threshold guardians. Think of the Kirtimukkhas of the Far East or the apocalyptic Christs on the west portals of European cathedrals.

Indeed, for the next decade or so, Bacon will spend his time sojourning in a murky, cavernous World Below populated by self-luminous figures that radiate their phosphorescence out of a dim and uncertain all-surrounding darkness: a collection of Popes and mysterious, anonymous businessmen that remind one of Homer's twittering shades. This is the period of Bacon's dialogue with Velazquez's portrait of Pope Innocent X, which appears to grow out of the series of heads that he paints beginning with *Head I* of 1948, especially since *Head IV* is actually the first of the Pope paintings. It is in *Head I*, furthermore, that Bacon first begins to construct his hermetic cube, a corner of which can be glimpsed surfacing into view above the screaming head in the top right corner.[10] By the time of the first of the Velazquez Popes with *Head IV*, the construction of the cube has been completed, and the screaming Pope sits securely within it, a prisoner of its semiotic overcoding.

This geometrical cube is a sort of apparatus of semiotic capture that Bacon constructs as a miniature coordinate system within which his laboratory experiments can take place. In the Age of the World Picture, as Heidegger described it,[11] back in the 17th century, the entirety of Western science and philosophical thinking unfolded inside of a similar cube in the form of the Cartesian x, y and z axes, which were also an apparatus of semiotic capture, since anything that appeared inside them, such as the standard Scientific Object or Philosophical Self, was immediately overcoded by the sign regime of the scientific episteme of Foucault's classical age. Objects were deworlded, becoming pure things in themselves, and the Subject, too, in philosophy from Descartes's *cogito* to Husserl's Transcendental Ego, became a pure subject-in-itself, floating free of all world parameters. That particular cube signified the knowledge apparatus during the metaphysical age, and in the nineteenth century it disintegrated and gave rise to an epistemic sphere: as Gebser points out, Modernist art is painted on the curved spaces of non-Euclidean geometry. By Bacon's day, however, both Cube and Sphere were gone, bombed out of existence by the horrors of World War II, horrors which were so extensive that they reached all the way into the metaphysical plane and wrecked it, too, with the thoroughness of one of those Allied firebombings of German cities. Bacon, therefore, had to construct his own apparatus of semiotic capture in his art since there was no longer an extant one to overcode all of his art inside of a metaphysical and encompassing sphere of significance. Thus, it is precisely while journeying through his underworld that this semiotic cage, essential for all the rest of his art, is constructed.

The other thing that Bacon works out during this sojourn is his particular facial semiotic. It is precisely on the features of his anonymous businessmen that he proceeds to recode the human face by "defacializing" it, to use D&G's term, in which he scrambles facial features in order to undo their signifying codes.[12] Bacon's faces are masks that do not signify on the West's traditional plane of signification, but are, rather, asignifying masks that refer to nothing beyond themselves. In contrast to tribal art – which Picasso's facializations often signify – in which the mask is always a mask *of* some spirit being or other entity that pre-exists the individual wearer and defacializes him by absorbing him back into the ancestral realm of the tribe, Bacon's masks do not point to a signifying plane of recognizable entities or archetypes, for their facial features are completely scrambled and therefore signify, as he always said, nothing. They are, rather, masks that undo the codes connecting the figure to this or that pre-existent system of meaning, masks in which Bacon is unplugging the human figure from *all* such narrative systems whatsoever.

Color Event

Long about 1956-57, an Event transpires in Bacon's art, an Event that indicates his emergence from the underworld. This is the Color Event that begins with his dialogue with Van Gogh in the series of eight paintings that he did in 1957 as reworkings of Van Gogh's

1888 *Painter on His Way to Work*. It is as though Bacon has come up from the dark, lightless underworld that had formed the interior of his world space for a decade, and brought up from that underworld with him the shade of Van Gogh, like Orpheus attempting, but in this case, succeeding, in bringing Eurydice back to the day world with him.

In Van Gogh's painting,[13] furthermore, there is a shadow cast upon the ground by the artist as he strides down the road in the middle of the day, and in reworking this image, the figure of the Shadow enters into Bacon's canvases as a permanent acquisition, a sort of etheric scar of his journey into the underworld, which is composed of nothing *but* shades. In his lightless underworld paintings, there had been no shadows because there was no exterior light source, and a shadow cannot be cast without one. The figures were themselves self-luminous shadows. But once he emerges from the underworld into the day world, with all its primary colors, the shadow can now be cast upon the ground before him as a reminder of the underworld etheric double that trails us as a sort of absent signifier throughout all our life, as Peter Sloterdijk puts it in his *Bubbles*.[14]

From this point on, Bacon will keep largely within the daylight world in his canvases, where objects are not self-luminous but rather illuminated by exterior light sources (Van Gogh was a painter who was at his best in daylight scenes). Indeed, it is almost as though the shade of Van Gogh has been brought forth from the underworld, so that Bacon can sacrifice him and infuse his substance into Bacon's canvases as a new Color Event that signifies the artist's shift from Night to Day.

But the Shadow, from henceforth, never leaves Bacon's canvases, where it remains as a floating signifier waiting to be filled in, as indeed, it was, by the time George Dyer entered his life.

n-Dimensional Images

Dyer entered into Bacon's life in 1964 and became his primary lover until Dyer's death by suicide in 1971. Bacon's first portrait of him, a triptych, appears in 1964[15] at just about the time that Bacon was becoming preoccupied with portrait studies of specific individuals, an obsession that would be characteristic of his canvases for the next decade (in addition, of course, to his interiors). Bacon painted very few portraits of people he did not know, and his immediate circle of friends appear and reappear all throughout his canvases,[16] sometimes as close up head shots, sometimes as figures in his interiors, during this period: Muriel Belcher, Isabel Rawsthorne, Lucian Freud, Henrietta Moraes and Dyer himself all form a kind of tribe for Bacon, whose features he defacializes and then refacializes onto the plane of his own signification.

In doing so, Bacon is, of course, operating within the convention of the portrait study that extends back to Jan van Eyck and Giovanni Bellini, but whereas those portraits took place within the great metaphysical age, Bacon's take place within the *post*-metaphysical age and therefore, do not have the same codes of signification as the great portraits of classical Europe. The great European portraits are facializations of men and women that signify their coding into the Age of the World Picture, in which they are transformed into Pure Subjects beholding a realm of Pure Objects in infinite space. The *cogito* of Descartes and the transcendental subject of Kant are basically the metaphysical scaffolding into which the great European portraits are plugged, and from Descartes to Husserl, the subject of the Portrait is simultaneously the transcendental subject of the metaphysical age.

But with the collapse, as I have said, of Cartesian phase space by the time of Modernism, the portrait study had to be reterritorialized onto the curved sphere of non-Euclidean geometry that formed the cosmology of Modernism, an art of which Picasso was, of course, the great master. By the time of Bacon, this world is gone, and so his portrait studies no longer refer to such planes of signification. The asignifying mask that he had developed during his journey through the underworld in the 1950s of his anonymous businessmen is now transplanted to the specific faces of real, actual individuals, who are thereby refacialized onto the plane of Bacon's own personal realm of signification, which is a realm of singularities and novelties, and not, as I have pointed out, Platonic archetypes.

His 1968 painting, *Two Studies for a Portrait of George Dyer*,[17] is the closest thing to an aesthetic credo that can be found in his art, for it shows the viewer exactly what he is up to: Dyer is depicted sitting cross-legged in a chair beside one of Bacon's own portraits of him, which leans up against a blue wall. The portrait is a work in progress, and only the figure of Dyer, with a head that looks like it has been split in half, has been completed.

Dyer is, of course, Bacon's main subject during this period: he is painted so often as a figure in Bacon's art that one begins to suspect that he functions in the role of Bacon's alter ego (Bacon, in the early 60s, had just begun to execute self-portraits, but when Dyer showed up in 1964, these largely ceased). In this respect, he functions as an equivalent to the electronic avatar which all of us, nowadays routinely, cast forth as a shadow into the electronic landscape, one of Baudrillard's famous simulacra that are currently replacing the Real.

So, in other words, the Shadow that had first appeared in any significant way in Bacon's art beginning with the Van Gogh series in 1957, is a role that is now taken over by Dyer himself, who becomes a sort of three-dimensional personification of it. Dyer was, in other words, Bacon's shadow, and Bacon plugs him into the role of the Shadow in his art.

Thus, in the painting *Two Studies for a Portrait of George Dyer*, Bacon is showing us how Dyer functions as Bacon's Shadow, his substitute avatar, as it were, on his canvases, by representing a half-finished canvas of him as figure minus ground leaning against the wall. The series of nails that Bacon has painted onto Dyer's image on the unfinished painting within the painting tell the viewer that Bacon is nailing his refacialized figures onto the plane of his own semiotic significance (in this painting, represented by the black, unfinished surface of the canvas which functions as a stand-in for the hermetic cube) where, because they do not refer to any pre-existent faces or archetypes, they signify non-specific, that is to say, *n*-dimensional entities. They are like topological complexities in *n*-dimensional space that are very difficult for the mind to get a grip on. But the key thing to understand is that, by not referring back to the plane of Modernist signification, where they would be tribal or mythic figures, they are *not* merely two-dimensional figures, for the figures of myth and tribal facializations are of *fewer* not *more* dimensions than the physical world. Myth flattens out three (or perhaps four) dimensional reality into the two-dimensional world of eternal repetitions and shorthand abbreviations into single images of complex cosmological processes. Myth compresses and flattens; it does not complexify.

Bacon's project in this respect should be starkly contrasted with what Andy Warhol was up to at exactly the same time in New York City. Warhol, as I have discussed in my study of him in *Dead Celebrities, Living Icons*,[18] was *the* great Icon painter of the world of the celebrity. What Warhol captured in his silkscreens was not three-dimensional celebrities themselves but rather their two-dimensional avatars as processed through electric and photographic vision machines. The celebrity's descent into electric circuitry, which really began to take off in the 1950s with James Dean, Elvis Presley and Marilyn Monroe, was a process of generating two-dimensional avatars that took on their own independent life in the mediatized world, often gaining strength in direct proportion to the loss of the real celebrity's own vitality.[19]

But the classic 1950s larger than life celebrity was a forerunner and prophet of the world which we all inhabit today, for with the democratization of the cult of the celebrity via YouTube and other social media, everyone nowadays generates their own electronic avatars as a matter of course. We now live in the Two-Dimensional Society that came into being immediately after the collapse of the Modernist hypersphere at the end of World War II, during which period a landscape of shopping malls, resort hotels, business buildings and theme parks emerged as a world of non-places void of meaning and historical significance, culturally denuded and therefore flat. A world of advertising logos, in other words, that has come to replace the traditional complexities of the Old European metaphysical world of nation states signified by flags and coats of arms.

But the task of the contemporary artist is to resist all this by creating microworlds as little machines that reverse entropy with n-dimensional, not two-dimensional, constructions that no longer refer to traditional planes of signification, such as those of the mythic or Cartesian kind, but which also do not refer to the two-dimensional plane of virtual reality, either. Bacon's facializations of the 1960s, then, counter this flattening of the human being into electric avatars by creating a plane of signification upon which his Figures are n-dimensional complexities that must be understood in their own terms. Bacon's project, then, though it may not have been known to him consciously, was nevertheless to create a realm of singularities and complexities that specifically function as a counter-environment to the prevailing ad logo world that was then in process of closing down around us and has now since captured all of us into its codes.

Disintegration of a World

With Dyer's death by drug overdose, then, in 1971, another major Event transpired in Bacon's art, the last, and perhaps the most transformative of all. In committing suicide by drug overdose, Dyer played the role that is normally played by the disoriented celebrity whose avatar has the paradoxical effect of shrinking him down into a realm of dissolution and disintegration into drugs and alcohol. But it is Bacon who is the star of the show, not Dyer, who merely played the role of the shadow, but a shadow which, by being represented obsessively in Bacon's paintings, was nevertheless made famous. When Dyer died, however, two things happened: first, Bacon began to represent himself in a series of obsessive self-portraits that extended all throughout the 1970s, as though he were trying to fill in the gap left by the missing signifier of Dyer's sudden absence from his world. And secondly, the impact of Dyer's death resulted in the slow, gradual disintegration of Bacon's interiors along with his hermetic cube.

At first, Bacon wrestles with Dyer's death in a series of triptychs, as for instance in the 1971 triptych called *In Memory of George Dyer*,[20] in which Dyer is represented in the center panel specifically and unmistakably as a shadow reaching up to unlock a door (probably on his way back to Bacon's underworld). And in the famous *Triptych May-June 1973*,[21] where Dyer's death is represented in a sequence of images that show him vomiting into a sink in the right panel and dying on the toilet in the left. But in the center panel Dyer is shown being nearly engulfed by an ominous and mysterious Shadow with a shape that does not resemble Dyer, or any human being at all, but which is unmistakably that of a demon, and specifically the demon that most art scholars identify with the Furies that now come to haunt Bacon's work from henceforth.

Monsters, mostly absent from Bacon's art for nearly a decade, now begin to reappear in his art, heralded by the death of Dyer at precisely the point at which the walls enclosing his interiors in a protective membrane now begin to come down, leaving him vulnerable to their impact. This is immediately evident in the *Triptych May-June 1974*, which depicts, for the first time, one of Bacon's interiors as a sandy island out on a beach with the sea and the sky looming in the background. Dyer, significantly, is represented as a figure in all three of the panels.

With the opening up, then, of what had hitherto functioned as a closed, hermetically sealed box inside which Bacon's experiments could take place, the monsters begin to enter in: the creature that had formed Dyer's shadow in the *Triptych May-June 1973* makes its first appearance in the *Seated Figure 1974*,[22] where it is seen floating into one of Bacon's interiors where a seated figure is turning away from a rectangle that opens up the entire right side of the canvas to a blue void (the sea?) from whence the ominous creature comes floating in. We also see this same creature hovering over the geometric cube in the 1976 *Figure in Movement*,[23] as though it were an avenging angel of death come to destroy Bacon's semiotic machine. The same figure turns up in its most vivid form as the left panel of Bacon's 1981 *Triptych Inspired by the Aeschylus of Oresteia*, which confers on it its identity as an avenging Fury.

But all through the later 1970s, the walls of Bacon's interiors have been melting away into featureless orange or vanilla colored voids; or else huge black rectangles begin to come in like swallowing mouths where they dominate the canvases, as in *Triptych August 1972*.[24] It is at precisely this point that Bacon's landscape paintings begin to appear, just as the walls of his interiors are disintegrating. With this spherological collapse, as Peter Sloterdijk would put it, the outer world of Nature which Bacon had so assiduously excluded from his canvases for so long begins to surface into view, announcing the end of his microworld. In *Landscape 1978*,[25] the semiotic cube becomes transparent to a field of grass upon the curved surface of the earth; then it disappears altogether in *A Piece of Waste Land* in 1982.[26] In the first version of *Jet of Water* in 1979 (reworked in 1988 as one of his final canvases)[27] a gush of water that had first been glimpsed as the sea on the horizon in the earlier triptych now comes in like a drowning flood to begin washing Bacon's interiors away for good. By the time of the 1983 *Sand Dune*,[28] the semiotic cube that had once contained his hermetically sealed interiors is now completely buried beneath a huge hill of sand, like a civilization that has been swallowed up at the end of its cycle by Nature.

It was Dyer's death that had set in motion this chain of disintegration that led to the collapse of Bacon's microsphere and his semiotic cube, and so, with his last painting, the *Study from the Human Body* of 1991,[29] the viewer is confronted with a final, enigmatic image, one of the strangest and most innovative of Bacon's entire career: Dyer is depicted at the edge of one of Bacon's interiors, now shown receding into the background, but he has somehow sunken halfway down into the floor of the interior, while the semiotic cube has retracted and withdrawn to the point where it just frames Dyer's head. Dyer's form hangs near the edge of a precipice, and it is as though we are shown, for the first time, the hidden stage set, constructed out of a series of wood panels, upon which Bacon had been staging all of his art for his entire career. The image is like the final image of Peter Weir's film *The Truman Show*, in which the character of Truman, while guiding his boat, punches a hole into the stage wall of what he had assumed to be a real sky but which turns out only to be a set. In Bacon's final image, the exhibition space is gone, and Dyer is shown as though he were the meteorite that had crashed into it, signifying the beginning of its dissolution into the abyss. Whatever world exists on the canvas to the left of the painting, we cannot see.

But perhaps it is only Death.

Damien Hirst

The Artist as Metaphysician
The thing about Damien Hirst is that he is not, strictly speaking, an artist; he is, rather, a *metaphysician*. The vast majority of his work, as is well known, is delegated to others for their realization, since Hirst cannot paint, draw, sculpt, carve, shape or *make* anything. He simply visualizes the ideas, draws a quick sketch, and then gets busy on the phone. He is not, in short, a *craftsman*, for the artist as skilled craftsman is one who is concerned with the *efficient* and *material* causes of a work of art. Hirst deals only with the *formal* and *final* causes that visualize the works as singularities brought into being through the processes of Difference and Genesis.

It was the 17th century British philosopher Francis Bacon who separated out the formal and final causes of a thing as belonging to metaphysics, whereas the efficient and material causes were the domain exclusively of science, that is to say, of physics proper. The natural scientist was therefore a physician, properly speaking; the philosopher, in Bacon's view, a metaphysician. Hence, Hirst is the artist as a metaphysician, one, that is, who deals only with the Ideas of the work and delegates the realization of those Ideas into specific material substrates by skilled (and largely anonymous) craftsmen. This enables him to work with a vast profusion of media, and to convey the illusion that he is master of them all. This is one of the reasons why he says that at the beginning of his career, he was torn between being an artist and being a curator of exhibitions. Hirst is a master of *arrangements*; hence, his early facility with collages.[1]

Artists, of course, have always delegated tasks to assistants and pupils; this is nothing new. What is new with Hirst is the scale and degree of the delegation, since it is there *from Day One*. Warhol, in his factory, may have had other artists do projects for him, but Warhol began, and always remained, a craftsman: as one who could, if sufficiently motivated, *do things*. This was *never* the case with Hirst.

And so, Hirst represents something new in art, the ontological crisis of the status of the artist *as an artist*. There has been a slippage between the artist and the material construction of his works that, with Hirst, is almost complete, a near total divorce of mind from matter. Of course, this has been the case with the architect since about the year 1800 or so when, with the rise of new kinds of architectural materials like iron and glass and steel-framed skeletons, the engineer came into being as a separate phenomenon from the architect, and upon whose skills the architect has had to rely ever since in order to realize the formal causes of his visions in specific material substrates. For the past two centuries, the architect, too, has been almost exclusively a metaphysician. And as a metaphysician, the architect can get into the deep ontology of a civilization in ways that are difficult for the average artist: indeed, the architect can define the entire ontology for a civilization, in just the way that ours has been defined by the architecture of Nowhere: shopping malls, airports, office parks and other forms of corporate architecture.

And so, Hirst as a metaphysician has likewise been privileged to a deep access to the ontology of our civilization. He is *not* an example of McLuhan's dictum that the artist is a creator of a counter-environment to the prevailing technological environment of a civilization, in the way, say, that the Romantic poet was retrieving ancient agrarian myths to create a counter-world to the Industrial environment. Hirst as an artist-metaphysician, rather, is performing a sort of X-ray analysis for us of the prevailing global world order of our civilization, revealing, as it were, the transcendental (*a priori*) skeleton of that civilization.

Hirst, in other words, is the Immanuel Kant of globalization.

Deworlded Entities

Let's begin with something as banal and apparently trivial as the spot paintings, the first few examples of which in 1986 and 1988 were painted by Hirst himself.[2] These are simply white canvases upon which Hirst or his many assistants paint rows and rows of multi-colored spots arranged into a grid. But in commenting on these paintings, Hirst has this to say: "Imagine a world of spots. Every time I do a painting a square is cut out. They regenerate. They're all connected."[3]

When Hirst says "every time I do a painting, a square is cut out," he might just as well be talking about every work of art he ever does, especially the vitrines, which are, after all, just squares and rectangles cut out of this grid and in which other entities or elements are substituted for the spots. The spots are actually semiotic place-holders, then, for which one can substitute absolutely any entity: rows of cigarette butts, say, or serialized fish all swimming in the same direction. It doesn't matter so much what the particular entity is that is plugged into Hirst's semiotic grid of place-holders, for what matters is the fact that anything plugged into this grid immediately takes on the ontological status of Seriality and Repetition. It is the repetition of the entity, as with Warhol's Coke bottles or Campbell's Soup cans, that is the point.

In plugging various entities into this grid, which acts as a kind of phase space underlying all of Hirst's work as its transcendental schema, the entities themselves, in being reiterated to infinity, have changed their status. They are no longer singularities that belong to specific lifeworld contexts. In Heideggerian terms, they have become ontologically deworlded entities. They are pure Figures minus all Grounds.

In today's global hypercapitalist world order, we are *all* ontologically deworlded entities, pure Figures minus Grounds, pure entities minus the conditions of our originating Worlds. And once the conditions of an originating World are subtracted from an entity, one can do certain things to that entity that could not have been done when the entity was embedded in the context of its lifeworld.

One can, for instance, serialize it. But one can also treat it as an entity unto itself, capable of infinite modulation. The entity can also be cloned. It can be hybridized, modified, cut open, rearranged, altered, spliced, diced and otherwise interfered with. Lacking dependency for its existence upon the conditions of its originating World – the breathability of an atmosphere, say, or the nutrients from the earth taken into the body to heal it from illness

– the entity now becomes dependent instead upon management by large and impersonal scientific institutions, such as hospitals, genetics labs, pharmaceutical industries and the like, which have to provide the circumstances of its life conditions for it. Artificial conditions are provided for the entity, which has now become merely a prosthesis of a scientific establishment that regards it as capable of Infinite Operability and Modification.

And so, it is not just Hirst's formaldehyde animals that have become the new objects of the Gaze of this global deworlding operation, but each and every one of us. We are *all* deworlded entities in the eyes of Big Science, capable of endless modification: the human body, in such a world order, is composed of a series of modules, each of which, and any of which, can be moved around, subtracted, replaced, substituted and altered, for whatever reason any of these institutions sees fit, whether they are hospitals, pharmaceutical laboratories or genetic engineering firms.

Hirst's art, then, is an art for capturing the age of the ontologically deworlded entity.

Medicine Cabinets

Hirst's first two medicine cabinets, entitled *Sinner* and *Enemy*,[4] were actually built by himself in 1988. The first one, *Sinner*, is the prototype – and in many ways, serves as the overture to all the rest of his work – which features his grandmother's medicines, arranged into rows on six shelves. Instead of serialized spots, we now have rows of medicine bottles plugged into the grid and contained in a rectangular box that will later evolve into his rectangular vitrines. In the left corner (uniquely amongst all his medicine cabinets) Hirst has placed a small anatomical model such as might be assembled by a child, as a signifier for the object of all these medicines: the human body, or rather, the *pathologized* human body. Each medicine in each bottle corresponds to one or another organ of the diseased human body which, in the global world order, has components which can be removed and switched out, just like the little plastic pieces of the anatomical body. Everything is modular in this transcendental schema: no piece has its own authenticity or singularity, and each can be simply traded out for another, or else its mechanized equivalent (such as a mechanical heart or a metal-jointed hip).

Hirst's medicine cabinets are like one of those distant stars studied by astrophysicists who infer the existence of the invisible planets orbiting them by studying the gravitational wobbles of the stars: the cabinets, in other words, function as a sign that something is missing, for the very existence of these drugs implies an invisible order of sick human beings orbiting about them. Not only does their existence imply the corresponding reality of a society of the sick and the infirm as a norm, but they also imply that the illnesses managed by the producers of these drugs are seen in a certain way: that is to say, in a one to one correspondence between each symptom and each drug. The symptoms, like the diseased organs that can be swapped out, can also be traded out for each other: each drug will eliminate each symptom, but will cause many more symptoms to appear that guarantee the existence of the other drugs to manage them in turn. The symptoms themselves are infinitely operable and can be switched out like the components of an anatomical model.

But the drugs arranged in the rows on the shelves can also be regarded as elements in a set, as in the case of mathematical set theory, in which brackets are drawn around a finite (or perhaps infinite) number of elements that are then *set off* in order to be mathematized. This analogy becomes more clear in the vitrines, to which Hirst, in 1990, then turned. (The grid of spots is still in operation; in the vitrines, the grid has simply become three-dimensionalized, and its elements reduced).

In his first great vitrine, *A Thousand Years*,[5] Hirst isolates just a few elements from the infinity of possible elements that form the continuum of the real world: in the first, smaller scale version, *A Hundred Years*,[6] this consisted simply of two glass cubes connected together (like mathematical brackets) isolating the set of elements composed of an Insectocutor, flies, a smaller white box which hatched the larvae, and some dishes of sugar cubes. The flies are the entity taken from the physical world that now stand in for the spots (in an interview Hirst called them simply "black dots"),[7] and it is the function of their life cycle, of their birth in the white cube and their death by the Insectocutor, that is now isolated in the brackets formed by the vitrine. The smaller virtine of *A Hundred Years* even becomes a subset of the larger vitrine *A Thousand Years*, since the latter contains all the elements of the former, with the addition of one more element: the severed cow's head which the flies can feed upon or lay their eggs in.

The vitrine thus functions as a mathematical bracket, or a slice of the spot grid that has been three-dimensionalized, inside which entities, *any* entities, can be removed from the conditions of their lifeworld and studied, isolated and analyzed. It is like the artistic equivalent of a scientific experiment. The larger implication, of course, is that we are *all* flies bracketed and studied, isolated into the grid of the scientific world order that has subtracted us from the conditions of our locality in a specific place and a specific time.

Formaldehyde Bestiary

In 1991, Hirst had a kind of creative explosion, in which vitrines now began routinely swimming forth from his imagination. The most famous of these is, of course, the formaldehyde shark, which Hirst entitled *The Physical Impossibility of Death in the Mind of Someone Living*.[8] Whereas with the flies, he had extracted an entity from its lifeworld in order to study the conditions of its life cycle while alive, now Hirst proceeds to extract an animal, a very dangerous one, from the conditions of its lifeworld in order to freeze and arrest it into a state of permanent suspension, as though one had simply pressed the "pause" button on one of these creatures just as it was about to take a bite out of someone. By capturing the animal and suspending its processes of decomposition with formaldehyde, Hirst is essentially demonstrating the ability of science to arrest the laws of nature as they would normally operate. It is, indeed, the physical impossibility of the death of the animal, since the formaldehyde suspends its natural decomposition process.

In ancient Egypt, the organs of the body were removed and placed into canopic jars with various kinds of salts and other chemicals to dry them out so that they would cease to decay. In mummifying the body, the Egyptians were trying to arrest the natural processes of decomposition for religious reasons, namely to extract the body from "nature" and to displace it into a "supernatural" order of eternality. By contrast, the animal that is captured and preserved in formaldehyde by science is chemically mummified, but not for religious reasons; it is, rather, to demonstrate the power of science over nature, of its ability to seize and capture all natural flows of any, and every, kind. Suspending the animal's decay rate with chemicals is a way of placing it *inside* the phase space of the scientific anti-world, which removes all entities from the circumstances of their local environments, in which they are embedded in, and governed by, temporal metabolisms. It is the triumph of science over the organism, over Nature, and over environmental circumstances of all kinds. The animal, in other words, is an animal no longer: it is, rather, a *thing*, transcendental object x, whose properties can be studied and mapped objectively. It is not the animal painted by the Paleolithic artist on the walls of his cave, which is captured into a magical order of timeless Platonic essences, but the animal as scientific object, flayed, splayed and transformed into a timeless *function* in a bracketed set of equations. And whereas the Paleolithic Animal Form could, through proper use of the rites of regeneration, become the template from which endless physical copies could be made, so too, the scientifically deworlded animal can become the template from which, through the processes of cloning and genetic engineering, an endless procession of serialized forms can be made.

And indeed, Hirst proceeds to serialize his shark by miniaturizing it, scaling it down and multiplying it into a grid of small fish for his two vitrines entitled *Isolated Elements Swimming in the Same Direction for the Purpose of Understanding*[9]. These two vitrines, one oriented to the right and one to the left, are composed of six rows of fish all aligned like spots on one of his grids (or bottles in the medicine cabinets). They, too, are deworlded entities, cloned, replicated and plugged into a bivalent ontology of pure Platonic Left and pure Platonic Right. Like Kant's problem of the identity of indiscernibles, in which the left hand cannot be mapped onto the right hand no matter which way you turn them, entities in a bivalent ontology must be oriented along symmetrical axes that govern, in *a priori* fashion, their manifestation in time and space.

Human and Animal

In the 1994 vitrines, *Still*,[10] *Naked*[11] and *Doubt*,[12] which are composed of glass encased cabinets with glittering arrays of stainless steel surgical instruments, all laid out into rows, we are treated to a vision of the fate of the body in the scientific world order. These vitrines, of course, are an outgrowth of the medicine cabinets, but whereas those imagine the body as composed out of an infinite assemblage of chemical compounds (capable of endless deconstruction and reconstruction, like Lego blocks) the surgical vitrines present the body as a mechanical assemblage of moveable parts: if an organ is diseased, you simply cut open the body and remove it. If a limb is wrong, you hack it off. If a tumor is present, you cut it out. The body is a machine composed of parts which can be switched out at will. It is capable of infinite analysis and breakdown by the scientific gaze.

Likewise, with the apotheosis of his formaldehyde vitrines, *Some Comfort Gained from the Acceptance of the Inherent Lies in Everything.*[13] Here, a cow and a bull have been sliced into a series of pieces, and each vitrine contains one slice, interfiled with the others. The animal here, too, is modular: it can be carved up and analyzed; pulled apart and catalogued, inventoried and assembled. In other words, in the global scientific world order, *there is no ontological difference whatsoever between the human and the animal*. Forget Heidegger's insistence on the "abyss of difference" between them: in this world order, the human being is just as much composed of a modular array of parts, like moving units in a Japanese house, as an animal, and both are susceptible of modifying, packaging and assembling like parts in a factory. The human being, in this flattening world order which crushes all hierarchies down onto a single plane of horizontal homogeneity, is just a displaced animal. He, too, can be captured like the formaldehyde shark, and placed into an eternal phase space where he is transformed from an ontological singularity into a mathematical function.

Hence, with the other apotheosis of his formaldehyde animals, the series of 12 vitrines, each of which contains a sheep's skull floating in formaldehyde and entitled *XII Disciples*,[14] each one given the name of one of the Apostles, it follows that, since there is no difference ontologically speaking in this global world order between humans and animals, the Apostles may just as well be represented *as* animals. This "scientific" civilization, in other words, has reversed thousands of years of careful religious evolution, in which the human was gradually extracted ontologically from his animal substrate. With the Sphinx of Giza, a human head sits on an animal body, but with the Greek centaur, half the body is a horse and the other half a human. By the time of the Apostles of Christ's days, the animal-headed Egyptian gods were regarded as a religious atavism, a holdover from the days of the pagans, all of which imagery was anathematized in the fourth century AD by Theodosius the Great.

But with the collapse of this difference in the evolution of science from its "humanist" Renaissance backdrop, the Apostles in the art of Damien Hirst can just as well be pictured as sheep, since there is no longer any difference between them ontologically speaking. Their only differences nowadays are biological and anatomical, but not metaphysical. Both are simply kinds of entities that can be plugged into the grid, where all entities are the same and equally capable of infinite iterability.

Hirst Phase II

Long about 1997-98, Hirst's career as an artist began to falter. He bought a restaurant, which he called *Pharmacy* (named after his 1992 installation), and tried to run it for a time, while his art began to flicker and slowly, to fade out. By then he was very nearly the most famous artist alive, and interviews conducted with Gordon Burn at this time show him wrestling with the problems of fame and what to do with himself as an artist. He wasn't sure.[15]

So this period neatly divides Hirst's career (like one of his vitrines) in half: there is the Hirst of Phase I and the Hirst of Phase II, and they are actually very different artists. They continue, however, with the same project of excavating the ontological structures of globalization, but they do so from different angles and begin to bring in new media (such as painting).

The key work that marks the rebirth of Hirst's art, and inaugurates Hirst Phase II, is a 1999 vitrine entitled *Adam and Eve (Banished from the Garden)*.[16] This is actually composed of two connected vitrines, inside each of which a corpse covered by a sheet (one male and one female, apparently) rests upon a mortuary gurney. They are arranged end to end, rather than side by side.

By splicing together the visual signifiers of these two corpses with the linguistic signifiers "Adam" and "Eve," Hirst in a certain sense revisits the Life and Death thematic of his very first vitrine *A Thousand Years*. Adam and Eve are the first two seeds, as it were, of the human species; they are the seeds which, when planted, result in the germination of the swarms of human beings that follow them throughout the millennia. They are like the fly larvae planted in the cow's head: in Zoroastrian mythology, the first man, Gayomart is killed at the same time as the first bull, the Cosmic Ox. From the bull's semen come all the world's animals; from its spinal marrow, all the plants, while from the bones of the dead man come all the world's metals and minerals. According to the same mythology, at the end of Time, Gayomart will be the first man resurrected, and the fact that, in Hirst's vitrine, we are also confronted by a pair of corpses obliquely suggests the resurrection of the dead at the end of history during the Last Judgment, in which Adam and Eve would be the first to crawl forth from their graves (like flies from the cow's skull) to begin the process of Apocalypse.

Thus, by cross-splicing religious signifiers now into his vitrines, Hirst's work begins to open up a new hyperdimensional phase space around his earlier flattened ontology of a grid of semiotic place holders. That ontology had been the ontology of the scientific world order in which entities could be removed from the conditions of their lifeworld contexts and simply treated as Derridean units of iterability. This was a flat, horizontal and two-dimensional world view, and it was a world view, moreover, directed entirely and exclusively at the physical body. The subtle, or metaphysical body, and the dimensions of the spirit world, were left out of account.

But now, Hirst, in his second phase as an artist, and increasingly more and more often, begins to genetically modify his works by cross-splicing them with religious signifiers that begin to open a new "vertical" dimension of meaning that "crosses" in an almost perpendicular manner the horizontal plane of his grid of deworlded entities.

The religious signifiers, at first, begin to crowd in only through the titles, as in the case of *Adam and Eve (Banished from the Garden)*, or two other important works from this period, *Hymn* (1999)[17] and *Trinity: Pharmacology, Physiology, Pathology* (2000).[18] *Hymn* is simply a twenty foot tall bronze monumentalization of the anatomical model from his first medicine cabinet, *Sinner*, although both its title (which suggests a religious hymnbook) and its scale (which suggests something like Michelangelo's *David*) have religious connotations. And *Trinity*, which is a series of three vitrines jammed full of plastic anatomical models of various bodily organs and parts, provides us with the missing half of the medicine cabinets, for Hirst is here displaying *all* the organs that each of the pills in the medicine bottles on the shelves of those earlier vitrines were designed to treat as remedies. So, in a way, Hirst rebegins his art by returning on the spiral in a classic Hegelian *Aufhebung*, back to his first works and recoding them: scaling them up, multiplying them, miniaturizing them, providing their missing halves, etc. The process, however, is not just one of repeating himself, as many of his critics have accused him; rather, the second half of his work consists in *recoding* the earlier works by genetically modifying them with religious signifiers in an effort to create entirely new signifieds.

Hymn, for example, becomes the template for a number of religiously themed works of this period. His *Virgin Mother* of 2005 is essentially Degas's sculpture of a fourteen year old dancer combined with the anatomical cut away of *Hymn* and cross-spliced with the motif of the Virgin who is about to give birth to a god. The same thing applies to his 2008 sculpture, *Anatomy of an Angel*,[19] half of whose body is an anatomical cut away, and to his recent 2010 and 2011 sculptures, *Myth* and *Legend*, which are visions of a unicorn and a Pegasus horse with half of their bodies anatomically cut away.

But soon, the religious linguistic signifiers begin to give way to religious images which infect the actual works themselves which, by 2005, have been almost completely overcoded by religious themes.

The Inescapable Truth, for example, is a vitrine containing a dove hovering above the top of a human skull, in an oblique reference to the baptism of Christ. In *The Sacred Heart of Jesus*, Hirst gives us a bull's heart inside a vitrine that has been lacerated with pins and needles like a displaced image of Saint Sebastian, while *In the Name of the Father* gives us a sheep in place of the crucified Christ. In 2007, he even creates a series of statues of Saint Bartholomew complete with flayed skin and scissors and knife.

In her essay on Hirst's work, Marina Warner dismisses these images as "obvious" and not worth a second glance, but they *are* worth a second thought, especially by comparison with the works he was doing in the first half of his career.[20] In cross-splicing religious signifiers (in both linguistic and imagistic form) into his works, Hirst is not only creating a second, vertical order (of religion) to cross (over) the horizontal plane of his earlier flattened ontology of science, but the religious signifiers themselves, it is important to note, have been deworlded just like the entities of the first vitrines and spot paintings. The religious signifiers, that is to say, like the formaldehyde animals, have been ontologically removed from the circumstances of their lifeworlds, although not the lifeworlds in the physical environmental sense, but their *religious* lifeworlds. Hirst's religious signifiers have been extracted from the Catholic tradition that he grew up in and placed into the ontological phase space of his grid, just like the animals, the flies, the spots and all the other entities of the earlier vitrines. Once inside this phase space, where they have been cut free from the *Abgrund* of their lifeworld tradition, they can now be genetically cross-spliced with the other signifiers. The signifier of the Virgin Mother, let's say, can now be hybridized with an anatomical model; or the signifiers of the arrows that killed Saint Sebastian can be spliced together with a bull's heart; or the dove of the Annunciation removed from the life conditions of its traditional painting where it is shown descending toward Christ's head, and placed on the inside of a scientific vitrine that mathematically brackets it and cuts it off from all traditional systems of meaning whatsoever.

These signifiers, in other words, decontextualized from the grounds of all their traditional religious worlds, *no longer mean what they did in those traditions*. They have become floating signifiers in the capitalist phase space, where they point to the meta-processes of the conditions that make that very phase space possible in the first place: splicing, hybridizing, modifying and creating the equivalent of religious GMOs. These genetically modified images have altogether different meanings on the inside of this global phase space than what they had before. These meanings, furthermore, are not specified or predetermined in advance, but left up to the art viewer to decide for himself. Hirst, in these religious GMOs, provides the viewer with the signifiers, but it is the viewer who must now assemble them to create new signifieds.

For instance, the descent of the dove toward the skull in the vitrine called *The Inescapable Truth* no longer signifies the descent of the Holy Spirit into Christ at the moment of his baptism by John. Christ, for one thing, was never signified by a mere skull (that signifier usually referred to Adam). So what does the dove's descent refer to?

Who knows? That's up to the art viewer to decide for himself. The artist doesn't know, either, for in the age of contemporary art, it is now up to the viewer to create his own Truth Event.

The needles piercing the bull's heart in *The Sacred Heart of Jesus* no longer refer to Saint Sebastian, who didn't have a bull's heart. What, then, do they refer to? The signified is missing, and has to be constructed by the viewer.

So, Hirst's religious works, I think, *do* deserve a second, more thoughtful glance, since they are essentially syncopated images left incomplete in order to invite the viewer to fill in the missing dimensions of meaning. (In this sense, they are equivalent to Lacan's variable sessions, in which he would terminate the session when the patient was mid-sentence, or when a silence had fallen, in order to invite the "fill in" on the part of the patient's unconscious.)

In the global capitalist phase space, all the signifiers have come uprooted from the earth and are floating in the air, along with all the other entities, in strange new configurations that might, or might not, amount to anything meaningful. They cannot simply be dismissed, however, and taking an attitude of superiority toward such works of art will only succeed in underestimating their imagination-stimulating properties.

In the Middle Ages (and even in the Renaissance), we were force fed meaning. The meanings of the images were prefabricated and they left no room for the viewer's imagination to interact with them. An image of the Baptism of Christ or the Last Supper was simply that: the Baptism of Christ and the Last Supper, whose meanings had already been fixed and worked out in the various Christian councils over the centuries.

Even in Modernist Art, the meanings of the images – though considerably more fluid than in Medieval or Renaissance art – were still largely fixed by the processes of what Modernist Art, taken as a whole, was doing: creating hyperdimensional objects in a multi-perspectival phase space, for instance, or updating Jungian mythic archetypes.

This is no longer the case in contemporary art, in which the meanings are as fresh as whatever the viewer brings to the art works. There is no fixed meaning associated with them: only hermeneutical constructions that incarnate each specific work as a Truth Event (a descent of the dove, perhaps?) that is recreated for each viewer in that viewer's intimate interaction with the work.

Such is the fate of meaning in the age of post-historic civilization.

Anish Kapoor

Ruptured Worlds
In the post-metaphysical age, civilization is no longer protected by spheres or membranes of any kind. All the boundaries, walls, mandalas and macrospheres which, in the mythical and metaphysical eras, once contained and organized civilizations, have been shattered and now lie in pieces all about us. And when something ceases to function or breaks down, that is precisely the moment when it surfaces into visibility by crossing the threshold of our subconscious awareness into conscious perception. Environmental backgrounds, as McLuhan always liked to point out, are unconscious precisely because of their all-immersive ubiquity. Heidegger's proverbial hammer is invisible to circumspective concern so long as it is working and embedded in that mode of being which he terms *Zuhandenheit*. It is only once the hammer ceases to function properly, however, that it becomes visible and shifts from its *Zuhanden* mode to the mode of *Vorhandenheit*, where it now stands out as a theoretical problem to be solved.

In the history of civilizations, likewise, once cosmologies break down or cease functioning, they do not just disappear without a trace, but are retrieved from the ancient middenheap by the artist who catches them, miniaturizes them, and transforms them into works of art in the new environments constructed by new technologies and other modes of Being. Thus, the Renaissance artist retrieves the *Laocoon* from the middenheap of antiquity and it becomes the inspiration for a *Moses*, which becomes the constitutive work of art of the new Renaissance world city under Pope Julius II or Leo X.

Thus, in the art of Anish Kapoor, all the ancient containers – mandalas, macrospheres and various uteromorphic cosmologies – which once served during the mythical age as world bounding horizons have reappeared on the *inside* of the global capitalist anti-world as art objects scaled down and miniaturized for mass consumption. The global ecumene of late capitalism is absolutely hostile to all such world-spheric containers, for it has engulfed all of them, thus neutralizing their ontological efficacy and melting them down into the metaphysical slag heap of ancient cosmologies and lost civilizations that now fill the exhibits of our natural history museums.

All metaphysical walls, membranes and boundaries have nowadays ceased to function – hence, the present anxieties that fuel the building of walls and fences along nation state borders everywhere – and the signifying contents which they once held in place, furthermore, have been disgorged across the planet via contemporary art. The ancient religious signifiers which these huge global containers once used to hold in place have escaped capture from their various worlds and come loose, and now they are presently tracing lines of flight through the capitalist ecumene as uncoded flows anarchically rupturing meaning systems everywhere.

The art of Anish Kapoor is a massive reterritorialization of some of these ancient signifiers onto the global body, or socius, of the late capitalist hypersphere.

1000 Names

Kapoor's first great work, *1000 Names,* is a good example of this phenomenon.[1] First exhibited in the Paris studio of Patrice Alexandre in 1980, *1000 Names* (which refers in Indian religion to all the names of the god Vishnu) is a display of signifiers torn from the Hindu tradition and littered across the floor of the studio in glowing red, yellow, white and black pigments. The forms are all geometric: circles, squares, domes, obelisks, crescent shapes, etc. and they have been represented in such a way as to suggest their self-emergence from below out of the very floor of the studio itself.[2] The forms are evocative of Hindu signifiers: the obelisks recall transformed Shiva lingams; the white domes suggest miniaturized stupas; the squares and crescents are ancient symbols for the elements of earth and water. One of the forms is a red cone up which a serpentine shape spirals,[3] exactly like the kundalini serpent in the Tantrika tradition that is traditionally depicted as being wrapped around a lingam. The colors, furthermore, are those associated with Indian thought systems: red, white and black are the colors of the three *gunas*, or qualities, that matter possesses: *rajas, sattva* and *tamas* in the Sankhya philosophical tradition.

According to Sankyha cosmology, the world of matter created itself, for it is a system of cosmic autopoiesis that does not feature the gods as the creators of the world. Rather, the world is thought to have emerged as the result of the interaction of the twin forces of matter or *prakriti*, and mind or *purusa*. The three *gunas* which characterize matter – *rajas* for fiery passionate activity, *tamas* for heavy, slow torpor, and *sattva* for luminous clarity -- were set into agitated activity by the presence of thousands of these *purusas* which acted upon it in a manner similar to the way magnets cause iron filings to line up. Consciousness, or *buddhi,* is created first, and then, along a stream of parallel evolution the subtle elements – which are self-luminous, or *sukshma* forms – known as the *tanmatras* are created. The first atoms, also subtle, and known as *paramanus*, are created, and eventually give rise to subtle forms of the first elements. The entire cosmos up to this point is self-luminous and autopoietic: that is to say, it creates itself from out of its own substance.

The subtle elements soon give way to what are known as the concrete or gross elements, the *sthula bhutani*. *Akasha*, or ether, which is the first of these elements to emerge, is actually space itself as a humming morphogenetic field that creates forms simply by making a sound. It is associated with the geometrical figure of the sphere. Air comes next, which is associated with the circle, while fire is associated with the triangle, water with the crescent moon and earth with the shape of a square. Thus, the creation of matter according to Sankhya cosmology.[4]

Kapoor's glowing forms, likewise, might be regarded as self-luminous *sukshma* forms arising from a kind of *akashic* field. However: they are deterritorialized forms which have been torn from their original apparatuses of semiotic capture. Such apparatuses are the various mandalas and yantras which the Hindu tradition imagines as the structuring fields within which these signifiers take on their meanings. Such forms would traditionally find their place within a geometric apparatus of semiotic capture such as a Tibetan mandala, where cosmic mountains are, for instance, placed in the center, with gates opening up into the four directions, while the five elements are each nailed down to their proper place within the apparatus, just as is the case, likewise, for an Aztec sun calendar.

But Kapoor's self-luminous and autopoietic forms have escaped capture by these ancient cosmic apparatuses, for they have been torn loose from the world-bounding horizons of their tradition and set free into the global capitalist ecumene, where they can trace new lines of flight into meaning systems that are totally "other" than what they were originally designed for. Kapoor's exhibition space is the very opposite of a Tibetan mandala, for in it, the forms have all broken loose from their original world-structuring contexts. It no longer matters much – semiotically speaking – whether this or that crescent shape used to symbolize water, or this or that red square once symbolized earth, for in Kapoor's art all that matters now is that they are self-luminous apparitions that appear to be emerging from some other dimension below the studio floor. They are "thus come" as the Buddhists would say: self revelations of their own mysterious luminosity. They are therefore, to a large degree, semiotically undetermined.

Once the forms have been deterritorialized from the contexts of their original world-bounding horizons and set free into the capitalist anti-world of contemporary art, they are now free of all traditional meanings and can be recoded to perform new functions. The forms can now mutate, change and transform in surprising ways.

Megaliths

In the late 80s, Kapoor's medium undergoes a shift from forms made out of colored pigment to a fascination with megaliths and megalithic cosmologies. Indeed, just as the cosmology of Sankhya envisions the world shifting from self-luminous and subtle forms into a cosmology of *sthula bhutani*, or the solid forms of concrete matter *inside which* the earlier cosmology of light has fallen and become entrapped, so too, it is as though Kapoor's earlier self-luminous works disappear into the heavy, concrete forms of his megaliths. We can actually see the process happening in the work which he created in 1988 that is entitled

Wound,[5] which shows a bloody vertical rift in the wall with two long stones and one short one set on the ground in front of it in such a way as to suggest that the blood is running out of the wall and pooling into little basins on the stones. In a manner of speaking, the blood running from the wall stands as part for the whole of Kapoor's earlier cosmology of self-luminous forms now leaking out and draining off into the stone, where it is captured and imprisoned, as it were, just like the subtle forms of Sankhya cosmology trapped inside of heavy matter.

In the 1989 work known as *Void Field*,[6] the floor of the museum space is filled with large square-shaped blocks as though the ruins of a collapsed temple had been gathered together and arranged neatly for inspection. Each of the stone blocks, however, features a hole in the center, like the *bindu* at the center of the Shri Yantra in the Hindu tradition, which is regarded as the cosmic origin point from out of which matter, both subtle and heavy, emerges, only in this case, Kapoor has reterritorialized the *bindu* as a sort of cosmic drain, down into which his entire earlier cosmology has disappeared.[7]

In a number of works dating from the early 1990s, Kapoor is fascinated by drilling holes into huge stones, and with representing monoliths, such as in the 1990 work *It is Man*,[8] with large black rectangles in their centers. This is a period of Kapoor's work in which he is concerned with Depths, rather than Surfaces: his monoliths, such as the *Adam* of 1989,[9] represent upright stone blocks as though they were fragments taken from some larger whole, and featuring a black rectangle like the monolith from *2001: A Space Odyssey* on the surface. This is, perhaps, a way of giving depth to the image: the stone block, he would appear to be saying, is not just a stone block – anymore than the human being is just made out of physical matter – but has a depth interior to it, a realm of hidden consciousness that is on the *inside* of the block.

In the ancient megalith cults of the mythical age which Kapoor's work seems to be referring to, it was commonly thought that the worshipped stones and lithic forms had fallen from the heavens to the earth, and were therefore revered, like the Ka'ba of Islam, as revelations of the descent of heavenly powers to the earth. In the work entitled *Angel*, of 1990,[10] Kapoor represents one of these monoliths with a black rectangle in the center as presiding over a museum floor littered with chunks of blue-painted sandstone. Blue, of course, is the traditional symbol of the sky (especially in the Western tradition), and in Kapoor's work it is as though pieces of the heavens had broken off from the sky and fallen to earth. Kapoor's installation, then, shows us the collapse of the blue sky that once formed the ontological canvas of the Western tradition, discovered in the paintings of Giotto in the 14th century, who was the first artist to substitute a blue sky for the gold background of Byzantine icons. Thus blue became one of the central and most important colors of the metaphysics of Northern Europe down to Goethe's day and beyond (he regards blue, in his *Theory of Colors*, as the signifier of the infinite[11]) symbolizing space itself until, during the falling bombs and V2 rockets of the Second World War the Western understanding of Being collapsed and the sky fell to earth along with it in a rain of bombs, fragments and missiles. The West has suffered ontologically from the lack of a protective and immunizing macrosphere ever since, and has substituted a pulsating grid of electronic signals in its place.

And so Kapoor's work during this period is characterized by a fascination with the depths of things, which is perfectly exemplified by his architectural work of 1992 entitled *Building for a Void*,[12] in which he has designed a round tower with a spiral walkway like the mosque at Samarra such that, when one walks inside of it, there is a black hole in the center of the floor leading to a three-meter wide chasm below, while an oculus at the top of the ceiling is open to admit the light of the heavens into the dim interior. The work thus captures and reterritorializes the ancient three tier cosmologies of the mythical age, in which the earth was imagined as enclosed by a cosmic dome situated above an abyssal underworld and open to the spiritual energies of the heavens located in the realm beyond the dome above.

All through the 1990s Kapoor is concerned with burrowing holes into rocks, monoliths and floor surfaces, as though he were excavating stone in search of his lost cosmology of light. But beginning with *Turning the World Upside Down* in 1995,[13] and *Turning the World Inside Out* from the same year,[14] Kapoor gives birth to a new cosmology of self-luminous surfaces, for the former work is a convex, gold-colored mirror on a wall, while the latter work is a large silvery sphere with an indentation on the top. These works now begin to radiate light, rather than to absorb it, and they reflect an ever-increasing preoccupation of Kapoor throughout the rest of his career with mirrors and reflective surfaces.

Depths

So, Kapoor's work is structured largely in terms of a central bipolarity of Depths vs. Surfaces. His holes in the floors of museums and in monolithic rocks continue, but with the work of 1999 known as *Taratantara*,[15] they begin to be detached from floors and walls and to expand to monumental size: this is a work composed of 50 meters of red PVC forming a tunnel between two voids at either end of an old Baltic flour mill in Gateshead, England. Thus, Kapoor's basins of attraction have here been scaled up to an all-encompassing environment that tyrannizes over, and swallows up the human being. This is even more true of his 2002 work *Marsyas*,[16] also composed out of red PVC, and filling the museum space of the Tate Modern with 155 meters of it stretched across a frame with two funnels at either end. Another monumental work called *Dismemberment, Site I* in New Zealand, from 2003,[17] also constructed out of PVC held together, in this case, with steel cables, and resembling nothing so much as a huge vaginal orifice, simply rests incongruously in the middle of the New Zealand countryside.

The 2008 work known as *Memory*,[18] furthermore, is a sort of giant egg made out of rust-colored Corten steel and set into a hallway of the Guggenheim where an entrance from another corridor gives access to the structure's single, square-shaped opening. But the culmination of all of these Depth-works comes with the gigantic 2011 piece called *Leviathan*,[19] which Kapoor had constructed in the shape of a three-chambered, spherical cross in the middle of the Grand Palais in Paris: when the viewer steps inside this work, he is confronted with a mysterious red-colored wombsphere that surrounds, encloses and contains him. It is the "nobjective space" of the embryo in its mother's womb, as described by Peter Sloterdijk, in which the pre-subjective embryo but dimly perceives various "non-objects" such as the placental blood, the placenta itself, or the soft walls of the uterus.[20]

Thus, the thread of Kapoor's work that develops into these ever-gigantifying uteromorphic structures points to ancient signifiers of the mythical understanding of being-in-the-world as a being-in-the-Great-Mother: they are attempts to capture, scale down and miniaturize the ancient cosmos of the mythical age, in which the earth was depicted as a central island surrounded by an amniotic sea with an enclosed ceiling of cosmic spheres surrounding it like a womb.[21]

Kapoor's structures are evocations of the body of the Great Mother – which became *the* central religious figure of Hinduism – cut into pieces as a series of partial objects that have been deontologized and set into circulation in the capitalist world space of the global anti-world. These uteromorphic cosmologies once held together entire civilizations and formed their bounding world horizons that protected and immunized the human being, locking him in place inside of a reassuringly enclosed, womb-like cosmos. Now that these cosmologies have disappeared as valid forms for structuring civilizations, they become visible in the capitalist ecumene as works of art, scaled down for mass consumption. The body of the Great Mother, in Kapoor's art, has been cut into pieces, deworlded, and scattered across the earth's landscapes as a series of vaginal and womb-shaped structures that evoke the old experience of the world-as-cavern which formed civilization's basic cosmology until Giotto pierced it by discovering the blue sky of infinite space that lay beyond it.

Surfaces

But Kapoor's ontology of mirrors is also scaled up in his work at this time, not only to the monumental proportions of a work like *Cloud Gate* (2004),[22] which he had built for a public monument in Chicago, but as an obsessively recurring theme all throughout his work of the 2000s. His various Sky Mirrors, scattered across the earth's countrysides and civic spaces, are circular disks which capture and reflect bits of the sky, as though to suggest that it has fallen to earth.

Indeed, all the old bivalent ontologies supporting a heaven / earth dichotomy have, in the post-metaphysical age, been dismantled and deconstructed: the horizon line which once separated them has now gone, for this horizon line wasn't just a line, but functioned as an actual membrane that separated the realm of the heavens and the gods up above from the realm of mortal humans and animals here on the ground below. Kapoor's various sky mirrors, including *Cloud Gate*, are indeed pieces of the sky that have fallen to earth, precisely because the horizon-as-bounding-membrane that once separated sky from earth has been ruptured and has ceased to function (along with all the other world-bounding membranes). The laws of the heavens nowadays form a seamless continuum with those of the earth, for it is all one giant cosmosphere ruled by the four fundamental forces of physics. There are no gods up above, and humans have already demonstrated their prodigious technical-problem solving abilities in sending men into outer space as though to prove that they could exist there just as well as down on the planet below.

The sky, furthermore, was, in point of fact, the first mirror: all ancient cosmologies were reflected onto the heavens as cosmograms. The heavens were giant mirrors that reflected back at us humans our projections in the form of gods, deities, souls and constellations. The sky, then, was once *the* great mirror whose contents reflected the interior of the human psyche and its deep, unconscious contents.

But Kapoor's mirrors are part of his ontology of pure Becomings, for he uses them to strip the skin from the surface of the world, as it were, and set it into a parallel dimension of pure events, to borrow from the language of Deleuze in his book *The Logic of Sense*. In that book, Deleuze points out how the Stoics separated the realm of effects from causes by Platonizing them: events for them were pure Becomings without causes that existed in a kind of flat surface world that they separated from the concrete world of causes and states of affairs between bodies. The Stoics, in other words, decorporealized effects-as-events from their material substrate, and put them into a realm of pure Becomings.[23]

Kapoor, with his mirrors, it seems to me, is doing something similar: in stripping the skin of the surfaces of things from the world and setting it into a parallel reality inside of his various mirrors, he is decorporealizing events as effects from things as states of affairs, for his mirrors always transform and distort what they represent into a realm of two-dimensional reflected surfaces without causes, for the causes of the distorted images do not lie within the mirrors themselves, but outside them. His mirrors create a realm of pure effects without causes, a realm of pure surfaces without depths. Just as Deleuze points out that Lewis Carroll, in his Alice novels moves from concern with depths (Alice, for instance, falling down the rabbit hole) into a realm of pure surfaces (i.e. mirrors, playing cards, chessboards),[24] so too, Kapoor's art moves from an excavation of the world's ontological depths into the construction of an ontology of mirrors as pure surface effects. In doing so, he is paralleling the way in which our electronic video screens and monitors act as mirrors which reflect back at us a two-dimensional surface world of effects without causes, a world of phantoms, ghosts and avatars that is no more substantial than a fleeting dream made out of subtle matter. We, too, like Kapoor with his mirrors, are engaged in the creation of an ontology of pure surface effects without causes.

Red Wax

Now, with Kapoor's red wax works of the 2000s, he is attempting to create a three-dimensional parallel to his mirror-world of surface effects. Beginning in 2003, with *My Red Homeland*,[25] in which Kapoor creates a sculpture out of 25 tons of red wax swept in a circular motion by a pestle revolving once per hour, he creates a self-making work that illustrates the pure process of Becoming. Like one of D&G's plateaus, it is a work without a goal or a telos that never develops *into* something, but simply illustrates autopoiesis as a pure process of self-making that is indifferent to the nature of the actual *thing* made.

His work *Svayambh* of 2007[26] is perhaps the most exemplary illustration of this, for it is a slab of dark red wax set on rails which is moved slowly through the doorways of the gallery such that the wax takes on the shapes of the doorways as it is pushed through them. The thing that is made here, which is simply a huge indeterminate hunk of red wax, is not the point so much as the process of *self-making*, since *Svayambh*, according to Kapoor, is a Sanskrit word that means "self-making." But of course, as we have seen, the narrative of cosmogenesis in the Sankhya system was a narrative precisely of the self-making of the cosmos by the twin principles of matter and consciousness, and so Kapoor's work bears the vestigial ghost of the Sankyha cosmology along with it. However, the thing that is actually made by this process – in contrast to the Indian philosophical system -- is not a specific, determinate thing, for Kapoor has deliberately left it semiotically undetermined. The work is a pure Deleuzian event of the making of a thing that makes itself as the three-dimensional illustration of the process of autopoiesis: *what* is made is not the point as much as the actual *process* of self-making that is being illustrated.

The object as it travels along its track through the galleries and doorways does evoke associations, though: birth, for instance. The object, in passing through the museum, transforms its various entrances and doorways into vaginas that are imagined as giving birth to something parthenogenically, which means without insemination by a male. This was precisely the nature of the old self-making models of cosmogenesis of Indian and some early Greek traditions (in Hesiod's *Theogony,* for instance, in which Gaia gives birth to the cosmos spontaneously, from out of her own substance). The entire Hindu cosmology is an autopoietic one, and it is also one in which the myth of the goddess is the strongest and most prominent of all the world's existing religious traditions today. Kapoor's work signals a shift in contemporary art from an ontology of poiesis (or making, as in the case of Yahweh on the first page of the Book of Genesis) to autopoiesis (in which the cosmos – together with the entities inside of it -- grows like a plant from out of its own soils).

Svayambh, then, is a three-dimensional work that illustrates Kapoor's event ontology, for it is an event that has been decorporealized by being removed from the conditions of the physical world's specificity, or states of affairs of concrete things. It is semiotically indeterminate, and therefore invites the viewer to complete it by territorializing it with his own signifieds, for it is a work which *has* no signifieds other than what the viewer ascribes to it.

Indeed, all of Kapoor's red wax works of the 2000s, such as *Up Down Shadow* of 2005[27] or *Push-Pull II* of 2008,[28] are depicted as objects making themselves by emerging from another world into this one. The objects of these works are like spinning wheels that emerge spontaneously through the floor or else slice through the museum walls as though they were irruptions of self-luminous forms from another world like those of his early great work *1000 Names*.

In carrying all this out, Kapoor is creating a kind of rhizome between the ancient Indian thought systems and the modern hypersphere of capitalism, for just like the viruses that create rhizomes between humans and animals by shuttling genes back and forth between them, so Kapoor, as a transnational artist, is creating cultural hybrids by shuttling the cultural genes of two worlds back and forth to create interesting and novel forms. Rhizomes, as Deleuze and Guattari point out in *A Thousand Plateaus*, are lateral connections between multiplicities that create new and surprising assemblages between them.[29] Thus, the value of such a deontologizing age as the one we're living in today is that connections are now open as never before between the various world civilizations for creating unprecedented cultural formations. Homi K. Bhaba is therefore dead wrong when he says, in his essay on Kapoor's work,[30] that such cultural backgrounds are disposable in considering the work of a transnational artist like Kapoor. Indeed, they are precisely the whole point and essence of what he is up to as an artist in a cosmopolitan age. Other transnational artists – such as Cai Guo-Qiang or Zaha Hadid – are doing something similar: that is to say that their work in contemporary art cannot be fully understood without knowing something about the cultural backgrounds that they carry with them from their own respective traditions.

Worldless Objects

Kapoor's artworks, then, are deterritorialized signifiers that have been cut free from the bounding horizons of world specificity and let loose into the capitalist anti-world, which has melted down all the traditional bivalent ontologies of heaven / earth, up / down, nature / spirit, light / dark etc. in the very process of creating itself as a scientific superstructure. With the impacts of science on the one hand, and Deconstruction on the other, such ontologies no longer have the world-shaping functions which they once conferred on their local horizons.

Set free from those horizons, Kapoor's works are like mysterious objects that have thrust through into this world from some *other* dimension where they might have had specified meanings in their original contexts but which now have come unmoored from their traditions and are encountered as worldless objects unto themselves. It is as though Kapoor transforms us into astronauts in outer space floating in a world without horizons who encounter these strange objects as artifacts from an alien world. They confront us as enigmas to be solved, purely worldless objects in the problematic mode of *Vorhandenheit* that require completion by the viewer. They have lost all touch with Being (which is always world specific), and so, contrary to Gadamer's aesthetics in *Truth and Method*, in which he says that the work of art is an emanation or avatar of Being that takes the viewer up into it and increases the Being of the object in the process,[31] these works have lost all connection to their originary Being-worlds, and so they have to be considered as miniature worlds unto themselves. They are not avatars of Being, but create and generate their own Being-thereness from out of their own presence.

Each of Kapoor's objects is a self-making entity from another dimension that requires the viewer to actively reterritorialize it. They are deliberately semiotically indeterminate, for in the capitalist anti-world which they inhabit, meaning is provincial and specific to place and therefore, unwelcome. The capitalist world space is full of meaningless objects a la Baudrillard, signs that proliferate like viruses without aim or purpose. Specific meaning – as opposed to the diffuse quantum wave-like meaning function of Kapoor's works -- is world-specific, however, and so it does not fit well within the world order of late capitalism, which deontologizes everything it encounters. Meanings must be left open and semiotically indeterminate in order for the various worlds encountering each other in such an age to translate the various works of contemporary art across cultural boundaries. When meanings are as specific and pre-determined as they were in the mythical and metaphysical ages, they leave no room for dialogue and become authoritarian, generating only friction, tension and, in worst case, scenarios, war. ("My metaphysics are greater than yours, which I will now proceed to demonstrate by decimating your population," etc. etc.)

So, for a global anti-world, an art full of worldless – although not necessarily meaningless -- objects becomes the *only* art that counts.

Rome and Paris

Jannis Kounellis – Christian Boltanski

The work of the displaced Greek artist Jannis Kounellis (who moved, early in his career, to Rome, where he became part of the Arte Povera *movement) and the French artist Christian Boltanski, despite their differences, do have something in common as contemporary artists: they are both concerned with what is* missing *from the world of consumer hypermodernity. In contrast with the British artists, such as Damien Hirst or Anish Kapoor, whose worlds are full of the plenitude of the being-thereness of the planetary society, Kounellis and Boltanski are artists engaged in the construction of a counter-environment to the prevailing world situation.*

Kounellis's art is full of an anxiety regarding the changed ontological status of place *under the conditions of globalization. His works are attempts to reconstruct a very specific world horizon, that namely of the Mediterranean with all its ships and docks, stone houses and amphorae, horses and olive trees, etc. He is worried that the world of his Greek origins – as Heidegger warned in his late writings of the fate of place generally in this new distanceless world of planetization – might be forgotten or obscured, or might lose its actual being-thereness in a world in which the near is made far and the far made near and no place, consequently, has any essential difference from anywhere else. Kounellis is obsessed with history, place and space: exactly the opposite to the concerns of Damien Hirst, in whose work it is precisely these structures which no longer matter, just as they no longer matter much in the age of Free Trade Agreements and Planet Hollywoods.*

And though the French were late on the scene with contemporary art, a movement which even Boltanski admits they did not generally understand, in the work of Christian Boltanski, they have produced one of contemporary art's finest artists. Boltanski, too, like Kounellis, is concerned with what hypermodernity is overlooking: namely, an axial relationship to the cult of the dead and the ancient Underworld. If Kounellis is involved with constructing the mesocosm of Greek civilization, Boltanski's work recaptures the Homeric journey to the realm of Hades, the world beneath *the Greek mesocosm that fell into a darkening beginning with Homer's twittering shades and Plato's cavern of insubstantial shadows. Boltanksi's work insists that the dead, especially those who died in the apocalyptic conflagration of the Second World War, should not be forgotten, but remembered through the construction of altars, monuments, plaques and memorials. And it is not the famous dead that he is anxious about, but the anonymous dead, those who died in the bombing raids and gas chambers and who left nothing behind them to signify their ever having existed but piles of their clothes.*

Thus, the work of Jannis Kounellis and Christian Boltanski is making visible for us what has disappeared in the construction of globalization: history, place and space; the cult of the revered dead, and the memory of, and respect for, the ancestors. It is precisely the Past that is now disappearing, as civilization enters into an amnesic phase that insists upon the relevance of an ever-present Present that has no regard for, or interest in, the past.

Jannis Kounellis

Horses

In Paleolithic art, the magic of the paint which touched the surface of the rock walls of the cave had the effect of symbolically *dissolving* the walls so that they could become transparent to the presence of another world, composed of grazing animal herds, which could be seen as actually *coming through* the liquefied rock like a portal to another dimension. Thus, the walls of one world were eroded in order to make the reality of *another* world present.[1]

In like manner, Jannis Kounellis's famous 1969 *Untitled*,[2] in which he placed twelve live horses *inside* the space of a gallery in Rome, had the effect of dissolving the boundaries of one world in order to make tangible the presence of another. Kounellis's horses were materializations into the museum space from another world -- not, in his case, from a parallel reality -- but a world from the past: the equestrian world of stables and horses, meadows and fields, barns and ranches. A world, in other words, of specific *places* with connotations for human *Existenz* of meaning and significance conferred on life lived in those agrarian places.

But in the world configured by technological globalization, it is precisely the significance of such places that ceases to matter, for in the global ecumene, as Heidegger pointed out, one place is ontologically no different from any other, since the far is made near and the near made far. The result is distanceless nihilism.[3] Specific places – this or that bridge, barn or hilltop – with their historically acquired meanings and significances, are effaced and erased as they are overcoded by the value-neutral grid of electronic pulse signals and GPS maps which have the effect of rendering one place just the same as all other places. This or that hilltop where a god, perhaps, once made its presence known, or where a historical battle was fought, is rendered meaningless.

Kounellis's horses, then, are part of a *worlding* process that is here taking place inside the the space of the museum, as also happened, once upon a time, in the Paleolithic. In dissolving the walls of the museum as a space set aside for art objects and recoding it as a place for the materialization of entire worlds, Kounellis is, of course, also dissolving the partition that separates the traditional art museum from the natural history museum, which is also a space set aside for the construction of worlds. Both types of museum, created as separate entities in the nineteenth century, are now colliding together, losing and effacing their own significances as separate spaces.

But Kounellis's horses are only *fragments* of another world: they are living entities torn from their agrarian world horizon which, like the figures in a Chinese landscape painting, have had all the syntactical connections removed, requiring "fill in" on the part of the viewer, who must now supply the missing world-ground to the figures. With his horses, the gallery space is transformed before the viewer's eyes into a portal to another world in which the viewer must supply the missing trees and barn, the meadows and hills. One is, thus, not just looking *at* twelve live horses, but looking *into* another space and another time. Another space and another time, that is, which has *lost* its significance in the distanceless world of late capitalism.

Gigantic Humans

In his 1975 work, *Civil Tragedy*,[4] Kounellis highlights this loss of significance even further. In this work, a single, lonely coat rack with a hat and coat upon it stands morosely before a wall that is entirely covered in gold leaf. An illuminated oil lamp burns on the adjacent wall, casting a dim and viscous light upon the scene.

The obvious point to make, of course, is that the gold leaf is an allusion to the Byzantine icon paintings of the Middle Ages, when gold backgrounds prevailed as the cosmic frame surrounding the images of the saints and heroes of the Christian cosmos. But notice that, once again, the viewer must supply the missing world – in this case, the *figures*, since the *ground* has already been provided -- to the fragment from a larger universe that Kounellis gives him here, for it is precisely the *absence* of saints and heroes which matters in Kounellis's image. In the age of Byzantine icon painting which lasted from the sixth century until about the time of Giotto (who substituted the blue sky for the traditional gold background), the human being was a figure of cosmic importance, scaled up and gigantified to the level of a Christ with piercing eyes that followed the viewer wherever he went. This was an age of giant humans magnified onto the walls of churches at places like Ravenna and Thessaloniki, where figures like Christ Pantocrator or St. George or the Emperor Constantine stared down upon the viewer from out of the faintly gleaming gold walls of the murky cavernous recesses of these buildings. In other words, the human being in those days *mattered*, for the cosmos was an artifact constructed by anthropogenic gods using anthropotechnic means.

The other thing about these old icons is that they were essentially two-dimensional: not only were they perspectivally flat, but they were ontologically flattened, as well, since an icon is a hieroglyphic version of a human being simplified to the level of a cosmic stencil.

But with the presence of the coat rack, with its single hat and coat standing in for the traces of an absent human, we have a signifier from the present day world, for Kounellis specifically modeled the coat rack on those found in Viennese coffee houses.[5] The hat and coat are of a kind that might have been worn by a Kafka character (one of Kounellis's favorite authors) and so it is, perhaps, an oblique reference to the labyrinthine landscapes of Kafka's fiction, in which the human being is a cosmic entity no longer, but has been shrunken down to the level of a mouse running a maze.

As in the contrast between the Mycenaean heroes and the Greeks of the sixth century BC who regarded themselves as but diminished shadows of those mighty warriors – Herodotus writes of the Spartans finding the bones of Orestes, which were those of a ten foot tall skeleton[6] – so too, in our modern civilization there has been a loss and a diminishment of the status of the human being, ontologically speaking. The Byzantine icons have shrunk, while the gold background of a universe animated by magical powers has disappeared, and the cosmos itself has enlarged to incredibly vast proportions which have all but dissolved the human entity into a mere speck of dust.

The contemporary human being may be a three-dimensional subjectivity by comparison with the hollow icons of the Byzantines, but he has suffered a corresponding diminution in his ability to inscribe a mark – in Derrida's sense -- on the cosmos. (In Derrida's cosmology, he can only inscribe marks on texts since, for Derrida, there *is* no cosmos, ontologically speaking, structured by transcendental signifieds any longer). The various projects and projecting(s) of the sciences has sundered him from any kind of integration into a cosmic whole, and he now stands on his own – like the coat rack -- as a fragment torn from a once mighty but now murky and obscured world picture. He is like Rudolf Steiner's historical human being, who has differentiated himself as a subject, but has lost all contact with spiritual powers in the process.

As in the essays of Heidegger, the human being in Kounellis is at home in the universe no longer, but finds himself rather in an *un-homed* situation.[7]

Two Worlds

Another work which performs a similar contrast between worlds is Kounellis's *Untitled* of 1991[8] in which, in a museum in Naples, he exhibited a collection of traditional Mediterranean peasant amphorae, all compressed tightly together in a rectangular shape on the museum floor, and in which all the vases but one contained seawater, while the remaining one contained blood. Aligned at eye level along the wall was a series of steel plates (Kounellis's preferred "canvas") upon each of which had been mounted, in pairs, a sack of coal with a bent metal rod protruding from it.

For Kounellis, coal always signifies the industrial capitalist imaginary: the coal that was used to power the steam engines, for instance, of the various railroads that constructed the early phases of industrial capitalism as a world ecumene. The phase of commercial capitalism which preceded industrial capitalism was, of course, largely a Mediterranean invention of sea-faring merchant ships crisscrossing the world's various oceans from Venice and Genoa to ports in India and China. As Fernand Braudel has described it in his three volume opus, *Civilization and Capitalism*, this was an affair not of the manufacture of new goods, but rather of the trading of already extant ones such as spices, metals, tobacco and textiles, coffee and liquors, etc.[9]

The world configured by the various amphorae gathered onto the museum floor, however, is a much, much older world than that of the capitalist imaginary in either one of its early phases, for the amphorae signify the ancient world of the Greeks and the Romans, of a much earlier commerce of exporting olive oils and wine from the Greek islands all over the Mediterranean. Kounellis's amphorae are not of the painted type, but rather traditional vases of the kind used by the Greek peasant in the countryside for hauling wine and water and grains. They stand metonymically as part for the whole of a *very* ancient way of Greek and Roman village life.

But the fact that the vases are full of seawater, while one of them is filled with blood, suggests the contrast of something living vs. something dead, and the implied notion of death thus evokes the ancient Greek cult of the dead, which also centered on amphorae. The Greeks burned their dead, and they placed the ashes of the dead body inside amphorae which they then set into graves such as at the Kerameikos cemetery at Athens which, as the name suggests, revolved around this whole custom. Nearly the entirety of Greek art, furthermore, came out of this funerary cult: the custom of Geometric vase painting and the early, sixth century BC cult of the Kouros statue which functioned as the prototype for the later statuary of the fifth century BC, for instance. In placing these vases inside the museum in Naples, Kounellis, as with his horses, is once again placing an entire world on the inside of a museum, although it is only a fragment of that world, which must be completed by the viewer.

And it is a world that is now in fragments precisely because it has been enframed and encircled by the capitalist imaginary of industrialization which surrounds and engulfs it like the sacks of coal along the wall of Kounellis's installation. The industrial world was a coal powered one, a world of steam ships and locomotives, of factories and soot-blackening mill towns that saturated the atmosphere with a brown patina of CO_2, which now today is creating the heat dome over the planet that is causing its sea levels to rise, a sea level rise that will, one fine day, swallow up many of the Greek islands.

As though they had never even existed.

Falling Bodies

As Stephen Bann rightly points out in his monograph on Kounellis, there is a certain *weight* and *gravitas* about Kounellis's work.[10] All the vectors of his art point decidedly *downwards*, for it is the earth archetype itself that is the dominant structuring feature of his works. It is almost as though Kounellis, as an Italian artist, had rediscovered Galileo's Law of Falling Bodies all over again, for whether we are thinking of the various rocks and stones that he has hung suspended from the ceilings of various buildings,[11] or the rows of furniture hanging by cords along the inside gallery of a piazza in Naples;[12] or the wall composed entirely out of chiseled stones at a gallery in Naples;[13] or the various scales weighed down by coffee grounds that he has hung at several locations;[14] it is all very weighty and heavy, very solid and *very* material.

Galileo's discovery of the Law of Falling Bodies supplied Western science with its visionary frame of a material world governed by material forces that could be enslaved and manipulated by trapping them into heat engines and various combustion machines. From Leonardo to Galileo and Torricelli, it is a world that was first unveiled by the Mediterranean imagination, in which the most important motif of the Christian imaginary is that of the Deposition of Christ, where the accent is placed upon the weight and heaviness of Christ's body as it is taken down from the cross in the various imaginings of this event from Fra Angelico in 1432 to Rembrandt's *Descent from the Cross* in 1633 (precisely the time in which the inertial laws of physics are being worked out from Leonardo to Newton). It is the depleted *body* of Christ which becomes the iconographic prototype of Western science and medicine, as depicted, for example, in Arnold Bocklin's 1868 *Mary Magdalene Lamenting the Body of Christ*, an object that has become bereft of life and as a result, can be dismembered and taken apart by the processual analysis of the scientific scalpels of reason.

The dead body of Christ has been carved and cut into pieces – like the Egyptian Osiris – and has disappeared into the various works of Kounellis torn and scattered into the stones and rocks and walls of his constructions. It is this body of the dead Christ, not the descent of the Living Spirit, that forms the (implicit) subject matter of Kounellis's material cosmos, with all its ancient gravitas. This becomes momentarily explicit in his *Untitled* of 1972,[15] which features only the bottom part of the cross with the structure known as the *suppedaneum* upon which Christ's feet rest, signified in the image by a golden pair of child's shoes. The emphasis of this rather unique image of the Crucifixion (characteristically, only a fragment that must be filled in by the viewer for completion) is upon the feet resting on the ledge that supports them. But the Deposition is also indicated more directly in works like the one in the Teatro Margherita in Bari, 2010,[16] in which a symbolic cross is configured by two intersecting girders tilting towards, as well as touching, the ground.

Kounellis's semiotics are, in this sense, diametrically opposed to those of Damien Hirst, whose world is a capturing of the transcendentalist imagery of late hyper-global capitalism, with all its ontologically deworlded entities that have no relationship to being-in-a-world of any kind. Hirst's luminous butterfly windows, for instance, form a decided contrast to Kounellis's rock walls that are frequently placed inside of window frames to block out, rather than facilitate, the flow of light.[17] And Kounellis's entities, like his museum horses, are never deworlded, but are always embedded in a specific world from a specific earthly place, although it is a world that must be supplied by the viewer in order to complete the (syncopated) image.

Fire

But there *is* a principle of luminosity in Kounellis's work: that of fire, although it is not the fire of the tongues of flame of Pentecost that signifies the ability to communicate and disperse the power of the Word through media that eventually become electronic and self-luminous; it is rather fire understood in the sense of the old alchemical use of fire to melt down and transform matter in order to use it to shape new materials, which process later became the basis for the production of new materials through chemistry and industrial design.

In the *Untitled* of 1985, for instance, in which the walls of a gallery space in Milan are lined with a horizontal row of steel plates across which propane gas torches are arranged like arrows moving from left to right, a series of these arrows is aimed directly at the fragmented Crucifix which Kounellis had used in the earlier 1972 Crucifix with child's shoes.[18] These are the fires of Western industrial transformation that melted the cross down as a signifier and traded out the Christian imaginary for the industrial capitalist imaginary. But this meltdown of Christian signifiers left a series of semiotic vacancies in the fabric of the Western cosmos, and it is precisely these vacancies which Kounellis depicts in works like his *Untitled* of 1984 in which 32 steel shelves are arranged in rows along the gallery wall, each with traces of burn marks where previously oil lanterns had been lit.[19] The lanterns have been removed, and Kounellis's emphasis here is on what remains: the scars of semiotic vacancies which once used to be filled with meaning. It is a portrait of a cosmos of depleted signifiers where the flames of transformation have all long since disappeared. It is not a universe that communicates to us any longer, but only a realm of shadows where forms once used to reside.

Art as a Singularity

Kounellis's later works have a tendency to monumentalize and apotheosize his earlier works. A good example of this is the exhibition held in 2010 at Ambika p3 at the University of Westminster: the centerpiece of this exhibition is a series of eleven steel bins raised on benches elevated slightly above the floor, with coal deposits at the top of each bin. The bins form the shape of the letter "K," and many of the sides of these bins feature rows of empty glass bottles, as though to allude to Warhol's rows of Coke bottles.[20]

Seriality and repetition of the bottles suggests capitalist mass production, which is also signified by the coal; but most of the cases feature a black or a white muslin cloth that has been tied across the center of the composition in such a way as to suggest the crossing out or effacing of this principle of mass production which Kounellis sees as inimical to the work of art. For him, mass production of the glass bottle or the beer can, as he has elsewhere stated the matter,[21] is part of the capitalist consumer imaginary which is completely opposed to the work of art that functions as a singularity designed to rupture and neutralize this commodification process. Hence, the black muslin cloths are Kounellis's way of crossing out the effects of capitalist consumerism with the singularity of the unique, and never to be repeated, phenomenon of the work of art as a whole.

In an adjacent corner of this exhibition space, Kounellis has created a little alcove which features workers' jackets hanging at intervals along the wall. Cases of serialized bottles are arranged on the wall above them, together with their black muslin cloths which have been wrapped around them.

The coal bins which have been arranged into the "K" shape not only refer to Kounellis's last name, but also to "Kafka," one of Kounellis's favorites. The labyrinthine design of the exhibition refers us to the labyrinthine corridors of the topologies of Kafka's novels, in which various office clerks are swallowed up into the bureaucratic machinery. The character of Joseph K. in *The Trial* is engulfed by the machinery of the judicial system which swallows him alive, never to be heard from again.

Thus, Kounellis's world here – the same space also features the hat and coat rack of *Civil Tragedy* – is a return to that 1975 work on a higher turn of the spiral: for now the hat and coat signify not the Viennese coffee houses that were earlier contrasted with Byzantine civilization, but the industrial factory world of capitalist mass production and its transformation of the human individual into a mere servant of the hive. The shrinkage in stature of the human being across the centuries reaches here its final phase: from the gigantified human of the Byzantine icons to the Medieval grail quester, and then down to the silly antics of Don Quixote and onward to Kafka's Gregor Samsa, in which the human being becomes ontologically no more significant than a bug on the floor, the gradual dismantling of human autonomy as the result of the diminishment of the human presence in the cosmos has resulted in the waste land of fragmented meanings from broken cosmologies that now surrounds the human being today.

The human world that was once a *humanistic* world has now become a world of factories and automation in which the human presence is negligible at best, and serves only to keep the machines running.

Kounellis's overall vision, then, is one of fragmentation and loss: throughout the entirety of his works, he has striven to piece together from the collapsed middenheap of European civilization the once mighty age of what Fernand Braudel has called "Memory and the Mediterranean":[22] a world of ships and ports, of the transportation of coffee beans and lentils; of Homeric voyages and discoveries; of buildings made out of stone and wood, and quiet little peasant villages and towns tied to specific places and spots of the earth that once conferred meaning and significance upon those places. Places in which, as Heidegger put it, things *thinged* and worlds *worlded* precisely because they integrated concrete objects – buildings, bridges, jugs – into the ordered cosmic fourfold of earth and sky, mortals and divinities. The global capitalist world order, on the other hand, is what ruptures such connections by effacing place and rendering locality obsolete.

It is as though Kounellis's Mediterranean cosmos were a lost world that he, like an archaeologist, were trying to reassemble bit by bit: some scraps in a museum here; some horses in a gallery there; broken stones negentropically arranged into various meaningful patterns in various places. A world that is today shattered and lies in ruins, but from which, Kounellis insists, meaning can still be found through the patient processes of reconstruction.

Thus, the resurfacing of a submerged civilization that has been paved over by the freeways and shopping malls of hypercapitalist consumerism has been the main thrust of Kounellis's project as a contemporary artist of place and space, memory and meaning.

It is *not* a world that is indifferent to place, or in which distance is meaningless: but rather a world of specific spaces and places that requires journeys and travels in order to get to them.

In the process, the museum and the gallery are reterritorialized by Kounellis for becoming portals of entry, at various access points, to this one single (largely hidden) world that he is busy unearthing. Each exhibition and each installation opens up a different window onto this lost cosmos: an age of boats and ships powered by wind, water and wood and later, railroads and factories powered by steam and coal.

It is art as Earth used to build up a World and to set it forth in classic Heideggerian fashion.

Christian Boltanski

Hand of God
In the *Monumenta* Exhibition of 2010, Christian Boltanski constructed a work on the inside of the huge interior space of the Grand Palais in Paris entitled *Persons*, in which he reworked the imagery of the Last Judgment: the entire space of the floor was ordered into rows of rectangular-shaped piles of clothing which the visitor could walk between, like Turkish rugs. At one end of the installation, there was a huge pyramidal-shaped mountain of clothes which a red metal crane periodically lowered from the ceiling dipped into with its claws, grabbing piles of indiscriminate heaps of these clothes which were then raised up and dropped back onto the mound, over and over again. At the opposite end of the exhibition space, there was a wall of rusty metal bins: one of Boltanski's famous archives, each monogrammed with a different number.[1]

The red metal crane was, of course – as Boltanski has explained – the hand of God, seen depicted, for instance, on the tympanum of the Last Judgment at Autun cathedral as a pair of hands looking very much like the clawed grip of a crane, reaching down and grabbing the dead in order to sort them into not one, but rather, *two* piles: the blessed over here (to the right) and the damned (over there, to the left). (A similar sorting process, we note, went on at the camps during the Holocaust: the healthy to the right, the sick to the left, etc.). But the fact that there is only *one* pile in Boltanski's reworking of this imagery implies that no such distinction exists any longer for us moderns: we are, today, *all* damned.

The piles of clothing – as has been endlessly pointed out – do suggest the processing of the possessions of the Jews during the Holocaust into separate, neat little mounds: a mound of suitcases, a mound of teeth, a mound of jewelry, etc. etc. Thus, for Boltanski the

Last Judgment at the end of the world becomes recoded as World War II, the apocalyptic war that ended history.

But of course, the piles of clothes need not *necessarily* refer to the Holocaust, for they imply a larger structure of that war of which the Holocaust was only a specific instance: namely, the biopolitical processing of entire populations at genocidal scale which that war turned into a mass industry. The six million Jews exterminated in the camps were done so in linear, so to say, *alphabetic* fashion: bit by bit, person by person, on linear rails standing in lines in accordance with *lists*. All very Gutenbergian: first one thing, then another.

But the other great extermination event of that war which Boltanski's piles of empty clothing suggest is that of Hiroshima, a *non-linear* extermination event in which the entire population of a booming metropolis is blinked out of existence all at once, with electronic instantaneity. One hundred thousand people suddenly deleted – as it were – from existence in their tracks, their clothes falling to the ground out of the blue sky like the scraps of clothing in Spielberg's *War of the Worlds* that drift to the earth from the people scooped up by the alien tripod machines.

In either case, though, the ontological consequences are the same, for Boltanski's famous piles of clothing refer to the management of entire populations during the Biopolitical Age which Foucault was the first to name, and which, with the various genocidal Events from Cambodia to Darfur that have since followed, we find ourselves still living in to the present day.[2]

Thus the hand of God in the Medieval imagery of the Last Judgment is mechanized in Boltanski's artwork, in which it becomes an eschatological technology for eliminating entire populations in mass human extinction events.

Catacombs

But Boltanski's work is not primarily about the Holocaust, or even the End of History. It is, rather, an attempt to reestablish a relationship with the ancestral dead. It is the dead that he is always searching for, and it is the Underworld of ancient Western tradition going back to Homer that he is attempting to unearth and unconceal back into the light of the Heideggerian Clearing.

Consider his first important work in this respect, the 1985-86 *Children of Dijon*,[3] in which he illuminated the interior space of a cathedral with black and white photographs of dead children, each one surrounded with a halo of electric light bulbs. The walls of the cathedral are thus brought into life as a cloud of dead human souls gathered like gnats in the late afternoon sun across walls that, once upon a time, featured iconic saints. Under the hand of Boltanski, however, the saints have been replaced by the anonymous dead of a group of children, for in the Biopolitical Age, it is not the exemplary individual that counts, but rather the absorption of the featureless human entity into the mass grouping.

An additional effect of the dark squares of the photographs – especially as seen from afar -- is to convey the illusion of little niches and crevices opening up within the walls, like a honeycomb, inside each cell of which rests the soul of a dead child. Boltanski thus reterritorializes the cathedral as a Christian catacomb, for the dark squares remind one of the rectangular -- and sometimes, crescent-shaped -- cells recessed into the walls of the catacombs, in each of which lay a carefully preserved corpse.

It is always the Underworld, in one way or another, that Boltanski has in mind in his art, which is perhaps why he prefers to place his installations in the unused basements and cellars of museums and galleries, as well as in churches, for they are all spaces that are evocative of the *world below*, where the souls of the dead glow with self-luminous incandescence.[4]

Pendulation

Ever since Homer, our Western dead have had less being than the living, for Homer is the first to relegate them to the status of mere "twittering shades."[5] When Odysseus encounters the dead shade of the ghost of Achilles, he no longer possesses any power and claims that he would rather be a paid servant in the house of the living than a prince among shades in Tartarus. Achilles, that is, has less *being*, ontologically speaking, than Odysseus, who is *more real* than he (of Agamemnon's ghost, Homer says that "he had no strength nor substance anymore"). This is why the *Odyssey* should be read *after* the *Iliad*, for the great deeds of the short life of Achilles in the latter epic is a stark, and rather sobering contrast to the paltry and impoverished phantom that confronts Odysseus in the *Odyssey*.

According to Franz Borkenau, in his book *End and Beginning*, the history of Western civilization has been marked by a back and forth pendulation in which the ontological status of the Underworld has variously taken on more being, or less being, depending on the civilization in question.[6] For the archaic societies of Egypt and Mesopotamia, Borkenau ascribes to them the appellation of "death transcending" cultures, for these were societies that did not accept death as something final but rather to be transcended in the imagery of an afterlife that was brilliantly illuminated and in which the cult of the ancestral dead took center stage in these societies. But beginning with Moses and Homer (and foreshadowed by the pharaoh Akhenaten's war against the gods and funerary deities of the astral plane), the Underworld was devalued and grew dark, and the role of the dead diminished to the status that we find it in *The Odyssey*. Thus, the societies of the Jews and the Greeks were what Borkenau termed "death accepting." But then, with the rise of Christianity, a "death transcending" attitude was revived, in which the soul's salvation became of primary importance and the Biblical apocrypha, accordingly, are filled with luminous descriptions of the journeys of saints like Paul or Enoch, Baruch or Elijah, to the realm of the dead, which is described in these texts not as dark at all, but as radiant with the silvery effulgence of the starry heavens.

But then, according to Borkenau, by the time of the Renaissance, the Greek attitude of "death acceptance" once more came to prevail, where it has remained ever since, and the cult of the ancestral dead has correspondingly diminished in Western civilization to a virtual non-existence. Indeed, the dead are *so* unimportant to us moderns that Borkenau suggests a new, and hitherto, unprecedented attitude of "death denial" that has gained the field of our society, in which death, for the first time, is regarded as the complete cessation of consciousness and the existence of the soul or the Afterlife denied altogether.

However, what falls off the radar of a particular society – or, using Heideggerian terminology, what withdraws into concealment – is picked up by the artist, whose job is precisely to make invisible, or otherwise hidden (because subliminal) environments visible. Thus, in the work of Christian Boltanski, the dead begin to resurface into the Clearing once more, for Boltanski is like the girl with the candle in Picasso's etching (*Minotauromachia*, 1935) who has climbed the ladder down into the Underworld, where she holds up the light to reveal the various monsters of the abyss that she finds down below.

Boltanski's descent into the Underworld has revealed to us moderns that the dead have become, as it were, the scar tissue of Being: like DayGlo colors in a fun house, they radiate their own internal luminescence as scars on the black walls of Being.

In his 1996 work, *The Concessions*,[7] for example, we see them glowing on linen sheets attached by curtain hooks to portable frames: each sheet has a face projected upon it in an eerie blue glow, while a series of images of deformed bodies, each one covered up with a black cloth, has been hung on the walls of the museum space surrounding them. The covering up of the images on the walls reminds one of the old custom of covering up mirrors in houses when their occupants died, so that one would not encounter their images by accident.

In a work of 1996 entitled *Passion*,[8] the walls are covered with actual mirrors while bare light bulbs dangle from the ceilings. Lined in frames along the floor, the faces of the dead glow back at us from behind weirdly illuminated fabrics, like modern incarnations of the veil of Veronica upon which the image of Christ had miraculously appeared.

Thus, the dead are everywhere in Boltanski's work, for his art is tantamount to a reconstruction of the Underworld, hitherto left in ruins, after the traumatic population extinction events of World War II.

Halo

Each one of us, according to Boltanski, is surrounded by a halo of dead ancestors. Physiognomically, we are jigsaw puzzles composed out of traits of the dead: this nose, those eyes, these cheekbones, all taken from the dead, who live in us and through us as a kind of genealogical swarm.[9]

Consider his 1990 work *Reliquary*,[10] in which five vertical stacks of metal tins have been arranged with black and white photographs of the dead, in blurry focus, each lit with a single lamp that tilts down over the visage and illuminates it. The blurred faces make it appear that we are looking at a single, multiplied individual, as though to imply that the dead are entities which have lost their individualizing characteristics and devolved back into the level of a transindividual species type. Thus, Boltanski's dead have melted back into a collective species pool: to a certain extent they have *lost* ontological being, but nonetheless they glow back at us from out of the murky darknesses into which they have receded with their own self-luminosity.

Boltanski's various *Shadow Theaters* (of 1986 or 87), which sometimes use candles and sometimes electric light to project spooky shadows of skeletons, angels of death, specters and other revenants upon the walls of churches and cathedrals, are essentially images of the dead as shadows, and as such they point to the myth of Plato's cave as the beginnings of the ontological derealization of the dead into a mere bundle of squirming shades.[11] Plato's shadows, it is true, are meant to be the forms of the sensory world mistaken for substance, but the fact that he has chosen the cave as their setting suggests that he is miniaturizing the ancient Underworld inside his myth, for caves have *always* been the abode of the dead. Indeed, the earliest origins for human burial anywhere comes to us from a cave in Atapuerca, Spain dating from the absurdly early period of 400,000 BC, in which the species of proto-Neanderthals known as *Homo heidelbergensis* simply tossed their dead into a pit at the bottom of one of their caves.[12] Later Neanderthals of the time of Shanidar, circa 60,000 BC, continued to bury their dead in caves in just about the same region of Palestine that Abraham would later purchase a cave from the Hittites for his own burial plot.[13]

But the Underworld is not necessarily the realm of those who have been simply cast aside and forgotten, for all during the long, long thousands of years of the ancient Neolithic, the dead were everywhere, their skulls lined along lintels and doorways, lovingly reconstructed at Jericho and set into niches in walls, and even buried under the sleeping quarters in places like Catalhoyuk. Indeed, the entirety of the Neolithic seems to have been situated down *inside* the Underworld, where the human domus existed amidst a swarm of dead ancestors. Technological change, accordingly, was slow to come about in those days, for the weight of the dead lay so heavy upon the decisions of the living that new ideas were rarely welcomed, or even entertained. It was not until the Minoans of ancient Crete stopped burying their dead under the floors of their living spaces and started putting them out into separate cemeteries that the "death accepting" civilization of the West got fully underway, and the Underworld, accordingly, darkened and dimmed to the ontological status of Plato's cavern of illusions and Homer's twittering shades.

Now, in the work of a contemporary artist like Christian Boltanski, the Underworld is lighting up once more, and the faces of the dead are staring out at us, demanding recognition after the traumas of the mass extinction events of the Second World War. Art after Auschwitz, to answer Adorno's question, is an art that takes its lead from recognition given to the dead, for in Boltanski's work, the dead are not forgotten, since his installations constitute one long process of "unforgetting."

Thus, the work of Christian Boltanski is an attempt to reconstruct, brick by brick, the shattered vault and crypt of the Western Underworld, an underworld that caved in somewhere between Nietzsche's annunciation of the death of God and the bombing runs on cities during World War II. Boltanski's Underworld is one in which the dead have resurfaced as a kind of *physis* of self-showing, in which their faces loom up at us out of the dark like some Heideggerian entity unconcealing itself, where they shine forth and then withdraw from us like phantoms. It is an Underworld characterized, though, by ephemerality rather than permanence, for Boltanski's entire ontology is one of vanishing and disappearance. He is concerned with the traces and scars that are left behind as marks on the walls of Being, for even if the dead have left behind only a name or an anonymous photograph, they are still marks capable of Derridean iterability in Boltanski's art, where they are charted, mapped, catalogued and collected as so many signs of the Vanished and the Disappeared.

Archives

Hence, the nature of a work like *The Missing House* of 1991,[14] in which Boltanski places placards of the names of all those who had died in a house that sat in between two houses and was destroyed by a bomb, together with all its occupants, during the war. The house has vanished, but through the work of Boltanski, it has left behind the traces of its occupants as one-dimensional names inscribed on placards mounted on the walls of the exteriors of the two surviving houses. Boltanski cannot bear to let the former occupants be forgotten.

Hence, too, the ambiguous nature of all his various archives: in the 1991 work, *Reserve: the Dead Swiss*,[15] Boltanski arranges stacks of vertical tins adorned with the faces of dead Swiss on the face of each tin. In the 1994 work, *The Lost Workers: the Work People of Halifax 1877-1982*,[16] he arranges rows and rows of cardboard and metal boxes with the names of all the workers inside them. And we have already seen the collection of archives in his reworking of the Last Judgment at the Grand Palais in 2010.

Boltanski's archives are part of a technique for treating entire populations as his primary sculptural material: if Michelangelo used marble to create his masterpieces, Bolstanski on the other hand uses *entire populations* as the *prima materia* for his works. And it is most especially the populations of the *disappeared* which interest him: those who are no longer with us, and who, during the statistical treatments of the methods of the Biopolitical Age have, for one reason or another, simply been deleted from existence.

Thus, it is not the individual as such that interests Boltanski – that would be the case for Foucault's anatomo-politics of the disciplinary age – but rather the molar aggregation of large groups of the disappeared and the deleted, the forgotten or the unknown. Boltanski's art is a biopolitical art for an age of biopolitical methods.

And let us not forget the ancient association of the archive with the realm of the dead, for in the earliest texts that come down to us from Mesopotamia, we know that when the dead person went down into the Underworld (then known as *Irkalla* or *Arallu*) to stand before the throne of Ereshkigal (the Mistress of the Dead) for his sentence, his name was recorded by the goddess Geshtinanna on a clay tablet to be stored in the archives of the dead.[17] In ancient Egypt, Thoth was the scribe who recorded the names of the dead, and in Chinese mythology, Yen-lo-hwang was the god of the Underworld who kept huge archives in which all the birthdates and death dates for the dead were recorded.

Thus, the archive was not biopolitical in origin, but rather thanatological.

Hence, the significance of the huge archive in the *Persons* exhibit at the Grand Palais of 2010, for it is, in essence, the record of all the names of the dead at the apocalypse.

Indeed, even Boltanski's ongoing project of gathering up all the world's phone books in order to store the names of every living person on the planet in an installation entitled *The Subscribers* (of the year 2000) has something faintly apocalyptic about it.[18]

All the names – to use Jose Saramago's phrase -- will be accounted for, the work implies, once Gabriel's horn resounds.

A Final Word

Art used to be a function of the city. Once upon a time, its task was to adjust and orient the gaze of the inhabitants of Paris or Rome or London to the outer world that lay beyond the city, using the optical structures of the city like a lens through which to view that outer world. At first, as we have seen, it was the City of God as a vast ecumene identified with the earth itself, variously inflected at Ravenna or Siena, Florence or Autun. But then, with the collapse of the City of God, all that was left was the City of Man, an optical creation on a three-dimensional x,y,z coordinate system. Eventually, it was only the city of Paris, which demolished those optical structures of the Baroque into a spatially flattened yet four-dimensional hypersphere.

But today, the city of man is everywhere: the earth now exists on the inside of a huge, global megalopolis. There is no place where city is *not*, for as McLuhan once remarked, even a truck stop café out on the Interstate highway, with a television and a newspaper, is as cosmopolitan as Paris or New York. Paradoxically, however, the artist is no longer essential to the realization of the City's vision which, somewhere during the time of Modernism, was slowly taken over by Adorno's Culture Industry, whose task, from henceforth, became what had once been that of the artist: to adjust and orient the city inhabitant – now a swarming, formless mass – to the technological devastations wrought upon its sensibilities decade by decade. New technologies mean new environments, and their ever-increasing frequency demanded a popular art that could keep up with its transformations in a way that the slow-moving, patient metabolism of High Art could never do. Hence, bestsellers, movies, radio plays, television shows and now digital media such as YouTube, which are constantly providing narratives whose task it has been to counterbalance the disturbed sense ratios of the masses with visions, dreams and nightmares concerned with technological possibilities. Science fiction, whether in literature, comic books or movies, has perhaps been the genre that is best adapted to take on this function.

But the artist, once he had become ontologically superfluous to the task of civilization, found himself on the *outside* of the city and began to be targeted by the city itself as suspect: hence, the ontological status of a street artist like Bansky, who must get in under the radar, as it were, in order to paint his caricatures on the walls of a city that has immunologically targeted him as a criminal.

The artist has become an entropic waste by-product of the City, and so contemporary art, in contrast to the arts of the past, has more and more come to be composed of city exiles. Whereas Modernist art had been inhabited by ex-patriates, contemporary art is an art of artists who have come unplugged from the City: hence, Pollock at Fireplace Road; or Anselm Kiefer inhabiting the ruins of La Ribaute; Bruce Nauman on his ranch at Galisteo, New Mexico or Susan Rothenberg at Santa Fe; or Andy Goldsworthy, whose miniaturization of Land Art transforms the entire earth itself into his canvas, a canvas which produces self-luminous forms that hum and crackle with their own internal radiance. Or James Turrell, meanwhile, who has been in process of transforming Roden Crater near Flagstaff, Arizona into one of the world's hugest works of art, a sort of retrieval of the Hohokam Native American Big House at Casa Grande – which was used for astronomical studies – whereby Turrell sculpts both light and the heavens as though they were clay. The French contemporary artist Christo has even decided to wrap cities up like presents, a feat which is only ontologically possible when one is already on the *outside* of the city, and therefore capable of seeing it as a whole.

One is, then, forced to pose the inevitable question: is such an art necessary? Or, in other words, can civilization survive without it? And the answer, of course, is that, yes, it can. It does not need this art any longer. Art is now on the *outside* of the city, just exactly where Jean-Michel Basquiat was always already finding himself.

Such an art, like the Hellenistic art of the ancients which it so closely resembles, is a worldless art that has come unplugged from all world-structuring cosmologies. It is an art performed by the exiled artist-as-monk, who must survive on his own out in the hinterlands, like the Egyptian anchorites of the third and fourth centuries AD. The art, therefore, functions like a sort of private mystery cult for the initiated. The aesthetically-inclined individual can travel from one artist's private microsphere to the next, exactly as he could be initiated in the ancient world into each one of the mystery cults in turn. Each mystery cult – the Eleusinian mysteries, those of Osiris and Isis, or Mithras – functioned as a scaling down and miniaturizing of the civilizational detritus, the *ontological* detritus, of antiquity's dying societies. To participate in each cult was therefore tantamount to a participation in a series of different ethnoscapes.

And so today, with contemporary art, there is no single world that is being articulated. Each artist is busy constructing his own plane of signification on the inside of his or her own semiosphere, and the interested individual can either show up to view the experiment, or else completely ignore it. He is under no obligation to such an art, for the society does not need, or require, *any* of it.

However: we *are* living in an age when all the previous structuring Forms of civilization – Derrida's transcendental signifieds, Castoriadis's imaginary significations, Heidegger's various turnings of Being – are in complete disintegration and disarray. And in such an age of breakdown, the contemporary artist *is* necessary as a sort of fisherman of Forms: he is busy extracting from this middenheap temporary singularities that may serve, at some point or other, to construct a new cosmology for a new epoch. The artists of contemporary art are experimenters with new forms: most will fall by the wayside, but then, as with the mystery cults of the ancient Mediterranean that eventually produced the single world-sphere of the City of God, it is possible that one or two of them might stumble upon a new set of Forms that will become constitutive of the next, and possibly, the last, phase of Western civilization. And it is *only* the artist, as ontological fisherman, who can do this for us.

Which is why I always keep my eye on the developments of contemporary art, since one never knows what imaginary significations it will produce that may, one day, be taken up to become the structuring forms of a new phase of civilization, or else, an entirely new world sphere altogether.

Contemporary art may be a superfluous art for now, but one day, I imagine it giving birth to some cosmological monstrosity that may engulf us all.

Bibliography

Agamben, Giorgio. *Homo Sacer*. Stanford: Stanford University Press, 1998.

Anfam, David. *Mark Rothko: The Works on Canvas*. Yale University Press, 1998.

Babha, Homi K. *Anish Kapoor*. Paris: Flammarion, 2011.

Badiou, Alain. *Ethics: An Essay on the Understanding of Evil*. New York: Verso, 2002.

Banach, Wieslaw. *Beksinski I*. Lesko, Poland: Bosz Art, 2008.

Bann, Stephen. *Jannis Kounellis*. London: Reaktion Books, 2003.

Bauman, Zygmunt. *Liquid Modernity*. UK: Polity Books, 2000.

Baume, Nicholas. ed. *Anish Kapoor: Past, Present, Future*. Cambridge: MIT Press, 2008.

Belting, Hans. *Likeness and Presence: A History of the Image Before the Era of Art*. Chicago: University of Chicago Press, 1994.

Benjamin, Walter. *The Arcades Project*. Cambridge: Harvard University Press, 2002.

Black, Jeremy and Anthony Green. *Gods, Demons and Symbols of Ancient Mesopotamia: An Illustrated Dictionary*. Austin: University of Austin Press, 1997.

Boltanski, Christiand and Catherine Grenier. *The Possible Life of Christian Boltanski*. Boston: MFA Publications, 2009.

Borer, Alain. *The Essential Joseph Beuys*. Cambridge: MIT Press, 1987.

Borkenau, Franz. *End and Beginning: On the Generations of Cultures and the Origins of the West*. New York: Columbia University Press, 1981.

Braudel, Fernand. *Civilization & Capitalism, Volume I: The Structures of Everyday Life*. New York: Harper Perennial, 1985.

___. *Memory and the Mediterranean*. New York: Alfred A. Knopf, 2001.

Breslin, James E.B. *Mark Rothko: A Biography*. Chicago: University of Chicago Press, 1993.

Brown, Peter. *The World of Late Antiquity*. New York: W.W. Norton & Co., 1989.

Campbell, Joseph and Charles Muses, eds. *In All Her Names: Explorations of the Feminine in Divinity*. Harper San Francisco, 1991.

Celant, Germano. *Anish Kapoor*. Milan: Edizioni Charta, 1998.

Chiappini, Rudy, ed. *Bacon*. Milan, Italy: Skira, 2008.

Clark, Kenneth. *Civilisation*. New York: Harper & Row, 1969.

Cora, Bruno. *Jannis Kounellis*. Milan: Silvana Editoriale, 2010.

Cowan, James R. *The Fantastic Art of Beksinski*. Los Angeles: Morpheus International, 1998.

Crone, Rainer and Alexandra Von Stosch. *Anish Kapoor: Svayambh*. New York: Prestel, 2008.

Dalley, Stephanie. *Myths from Mesopotamia: Creation, The Flood, Gilgamesh and Others*. New York: Oxford University Press, 1989.

Danto, Arthur. *After the Death of Art: Contemporary Art and the Pale of History*. Princeton: Princeton University Press, 1997.

Deleuze, Gilles. *Difference and Repetition*. New York: Columbia University Press, 1994.

___. *The Logic of Sense*. New York: Columbia University Press, 1990.

___. and Felix Guattari. *Anti-Oedipus: Capitalism and Schizophrenia*. New York: Penguin Books, 2009.

___. and ___. *A Thousand Plateaus*. Minneapolis: University of Minnesota Press, 1987.

Derrida, Jacques. *Margins of Philosophy*. Great Britain: The Harvester Press, 1982.

___. *Of Grammatology*. Baltimore and London: Johns Hopkins University Press, 1997.

___. *Writing and Difference*. Chicago: University of Chicago Press, 1978.

Ebert, John David. *Celluloid Heroes & Mechanical Dragons: Film as the Mythology of Electronic Society*. Christchurch: Cybereditions, 2005.

___. *Dead Celebrities, Living Icons: Tragedy and Fame in the Age of the Multimedia Superstar*. New York: Praeger / Greenwood, 2010.

___. *The New Media Invasion: Digital Technologies and the World They Unmake*. Jefferson, North Carolina: McFarland Books, 2011.

Elger, Dietmar. *Gerhard Richter: A Life in Painting*. Chicago: University of Chicago Press, 2002.

Eliade, Mircea. *A History of Religious Ideas Volume 3: From Muhammad to the Age of Reforms*. Chicago: University of Chicago Press, 1985.

Figal, Gunter, ed. *The Heidegger Reader*. Indiana: Indiana University Press, 2009.

Flusser, Vilem. *Into the Universe of Technical Images*. Minneapolis: University of Minnesota Press, 2011.

___. *Post-History*. Minneapolis: Univocal Publishing, 2013.

___. *Towards a Philosophy of Photography*. Great Britain: Reaktion Books, 2000.

___. *Writings*. Minneapolis: University of Minnesota Press, 2002.

Foucault, Michel. *The History of Sexuality, Volume 1: An Introduction*. New York: Vintage Books, 1990.

Frankfort, Henri. *Kingship and the Gods: A Study of Ancient Near Eastern Religion as the Integration of Society and Nature*. Chicago: University of Chicago Press, 1978.

Gadamer, Hans-Georg. *Truth and Method*. London and New York: Continuum, 2006.

Gallagher, Ann. *Damien Hirst*. London: Tate Publishing, 2012.

Gebser, Jean. *The Ever-Present Origin*. Ohio: Ohio University Press, 1986.

Godfrey, Mark and Nicholas Serota, eds. *Gerhard Richter: Panorama*. New York: Distributed Art Publishers, 2011.

Gore, Rick. "The Dawn of Humans: Neanderthals." *National Geographic Magazine*, Jan. 1996.

Grenier, Catherine. *Christian Boltanski*. Paris and New York: Flammarion, 2010.

Harlan, Volker. *What is Art? Conversation with Joseph Beuys*. London: Clairview, 2007.

Hansen, Jan-Erik Ebbestad. *Odd Nerdrum: Paintings*. Oslo: Aschehoug, 1994.

Hauser, Arnold. *The Social History of Art, Volume 2: Renaissance, Mannerism, Baroque*. New York: Vintage Books, 1961.

Heidegger, Martin. *Basic Writings*. New York: Harper Perennial, 2008.

___. *Being and Time*. trans. John Macquarrie and Edward Robinson. New York: Harper Perennial, 2008.

___. *Introduction to Metaphysics*. Yale University Press, 2000.

___. *Pathmarks*. Cambridge: Cambridge University Press, 1998.

___. *Poetry, Language, Thought*. New York: Harper Perennial, 2001.

Herodotus. *The Persian Wars*. New York: Modern Library, 1942.

Hirst, Damien. *The Complete Medicine Cabinets*. New York: Other Criteria, L& M Arts, 2010.

___. *I Want to Spend the Rest of My Life Everywhere, With Everyone, One to One, Always, Forever, Now*. United Kingdom: Booth-Clibborn, 1997.

___. and Gordon Burn. *On the Way to Work*. New York: Universe Publishing, 2002.

Hoban, Phoebe. *Basquiat: A Quick Killing in Art*. New York: Penguin Books, 1998.

Jacob, Mary Jane. *Jannis Kounellis*. Chicago: Museum of Contemporary Art, 1986.

Kounellis, Jannis, Mario Codognato and Mirta D'Argenzio. *Jannis Kounellis: Echoes in the Darkness, Writings and Interviews 1966-2001*. Great Britain, Trolley Books, 2002.

Lacan, Jacques. *The Psychoses, The Seminar of Jacques Lacan, Book III: 1955-56*. London: Routledge, 1993.

Landau, Ellen G. *Jackson Pollock*. New York: Abrams, 1989.

Lewis-Williams, David. *The Mind in the Cave: Consciousness and the Origins of Art*. United Kingdom: Thames & Hudson, 2004.

Lommel, Andreas. *Prehistoric and Primitive Art*. New York: Paul Hamlyn, 1966.

Lotringer, Sylvere. *Schizo-Culture*. Los Angeles: Semiotexte, 2013.

Markman, Roberta H. and Peter T. Markman. *The Flayed God: the Mythology of Mesoamerica*. New York: Harper Collins, 1992.

Marshall, Richard. *Jean-Michel Basquiat*. New York: Whitney Museum of American Art, 2001.

McEvilley, Thomas. "Mute Prophecies" in Mary Jane Jacob, *Jannis Kounellis*. Chicago: Museum of Contemporary Art, 1986.

McLuhan, Marshall and Harley Parker. *Through the Vanishing Point: Space in Poetry and Painting*. New York: Harper Colophon, 1969.

___. and Wilfred Watson. *From Cliché to Archetype*. Corte Madera: Gingko Press, 2011.

Mirandola, Giovanni Pico della. *Oration on the Dignity of Man*. Washington, D.C.: Regnery, 1982.

Mookerjee, Ajit and Madhu Khanna. *The Tantric Way: Art, Science, Ritual*. Boston: New York Graphic Society, 1977.

Moure, Gloria. *Christian Boltanski: Advent and Other Times*. Barcelona: Ediciones Poligrafa, 1996.

___. *Jannis Kounellis: Works, Writings 1958-2000*. Barcelona: Ediciones Poligrafa, 2002.

Muhlmann, Heiner. *MSC, Maximal Stress Cooperation: The Driving Force of Cultures*. New York: Springer Wien, 2005.

Naifeh, Steven and Gregory Smith. *Jackson Pollock: An American Saga*. New York: Clarkson Potter, 1989.

Nerdrum, Odd. *Kitsch: More Than Art*. Oslo: Schibsted Forlag, 2011.

___. *On Kitsch*. Oslo: Kagge Forlag, 2001.

___. *Odd Nerdrum: Themes*. Oslo: Press Publishing, 2007.

Panofsky, Erwin. Perspective as Symbolic Form. New York: Zone Books, 1991.

Peppiatt, Michael. *Francis Bacon: Anatomy of an Enigma*. New York: Skyhorse Publishing, 2009.

Pettersson, Jan Ake. *Odd Nerdrum: Storyteller and Self-Revealer*. Oslo: Aschehoug, 1998.

Rappenglueck, Michael A. *Eine Himmelskarte aus der Eiszeit?* Frankfurt: Peter Lang, 1999.

Richter, Gerhard. *Atlas*. Helmut Friedel, ed. New York: Distributed Art Publishers, 2006.

Rhode, Erwin. Psyche: *The Cult of Souls & Belief in Immortality Among the Greeks, Volume 1*. New York: Harper Torchbooks, 1966.

Rosenthal, Mark. *Joseph Beuys: Actions, Vitrines, Environments*. Houston: The Menil Collection, 2004.

Schele, Linda and David Friedel. *A Forest of Kings: The Untold Story of the Ancient Maya*. New York: Quill, William Morrow, 1990.

Schmied, Wieland. *Francis Bacon: Commitment and Conflict*. Munich: Prestel, 1996.

Semin, Didier. *Christian Boltanski*. London: Phaidon Press, 1997.

Serres, Michel. *Hermes: Literature, Science, Philosophy*. Baltimore & London: Johns Hopkins University Press, 1982.

___. *The Parasite*. Baltimore and London: Johns Hopkins University Press, 1982.

Sloterdijk, Peter. *Neither Sun nor Death*. Los Angeles: Semiotexte, 2013.

___. "Rules for the Human Zoo: A Response to the *Letter on Humanism*." Environment and

Planning D: Society and Space, v. 27, 15, 2009.

___. *Spheres I: Bubbles, Microspherology*. Los Angeles: Semiotexte, 2011.

___. *You Must Change Your Life*. Great Britain: Polity Press, 2013.

Storr, Robert. *Gerhard Richter: Forty Years of Painting*. New York: Distributed Art Publishers, 2002.

Tisdall, Caroline. *Joseph Beuys*. London: Thames & Hudson, 1979.

Troisi, Sergio. *Boltanski: Montedipieta*. Milano: Charta, 2002.

Vattimo, Gianni. *Art's Claim to Truth*. New York: Columbia University Press, 2008.

Vine, Richard. *Odd Nerdrum: Paintings, Sketches and Drawings*. Oslo: Gyldendal Fakta, 2001.

Virilio, Paul. *Art as Far as the Eye Can See*. Oxford and New York: Berg Books, 2007.

___. *Negative Horizon: An Essay in Dromoscopy*. New York and London: Continuum, 2007.

___. *The Vision Machine*. Indiana: Indiana University Press, 1994.

___. and Raymond Depardon. *Native Land: Stop Eject*. Paris: Fondation Cartier, 2009.

Warner, Marina. "Once a Catholic..." *London Review of Books*, July 5, 2012.

Wolfflin, Heinrich. *Principles of Art History*. New York: Dover Publications.

Zimmer, Heinrich. *Philosophies of India*. Joseph Campbell, ed. Princeton: Princeton University Press, 1969.

Zweite, Armin. *Joseph Beuys: Natur, Materie, Form*. Munchen: Schirmer / Mosel, 1991.

Chapter Notes

On the Four Ages of European Art

[1] See "The End of Philosophy and the Task of Thinking" in Martin Heidegger, *Basic Writings* (New York: Harper Perennial, 2008).

[2] Peter Sloterdijk, *Neither Sun nor Death* (Los Angeles: Semiotexte, 2011), 167.

[3] Ibid., 167.

[4] Jacques Derrida, *Writing and Difference* (University of Chicago Press, 1978), 280.

[5] See "The Age of the World Picture" in Gunter Figal, ed., *The Heidegger Reader* (Indiana University Press, 2009), 207.

[6] Jean Gebser, *The Ever-Present Origin* (Ohio University Press, 1986).

[7] Vilem Flusser, *Post-History* (Minneapolis, MN: Univocal Publishing, 2013).

[8] Hans Belting, *Likeness and Presence: A History of the Image Before the Era of Art* (University of Chicago Press, 1994), fig. 100, 176.

[9] Peter Brown, *The World of Late Antiquity* (New York: W.W. Norton & Co., 1989), figs. 95 and 96, 142.

[10] Hans Belting, ibid., 78.

[11] Mircea Eliade, *A History of Religious Ideas Volume 3: From Muhammad to the Age of Reforms* (University of Chicago Press, 1985), 59-61.

[12] Michael A. Rappenglueck, *Eine Himmelskarte aus der Eiszeit?* (Frankfurt: Peter Lang 1999).

[13] Hans Belting, ibid., fig. 27, 81.

[14] Heinrich Wolfflin, *Principles of Art History* (New York, Dover Publications), 210.

[15] Erwin Panofsky, *Perspective as Symbolic Form* (New York: Zone Books, 1991).

[16] Arnold Hauser, *The Social History of Art, Volume 2: Renaissance, Mannerism, Baroque* (New York: Vintage Books, 1961), 218.

[17] See the essay, "Turner Translates Carnot" in Michel Serres, *Hermes: Literature, Science, Philosophy* (Baltimore & London: Johns Hopkins University Press, 1982), 54.

[18] See "The Origin of the Work of Art" in Martin Heidegger, *Basic Writings*, ibid., 139.

[19] Hans-Georg Gadamer, *Truth and Method* (London and New York: Continuum, 2006), 135-36.

[20] Marshall McLuhan and Harley Parker, *Through the Vanishing Point: Space in Poetry and Painting* (New York: Harper Colophon, 1969), 25.

[21] Michel Serres, *The Parasite* (Baltimore and London: Johns Hopkins University Press, 1982), 44.

[22] Arthur Danto, *After the Death of Art: Contemporary Art and the Pale of History* (Princeton, N.J.: Princeton University Press, 1997).

²³ Kenneth Clark, *Civilisation* (New York: Harper & Row, 1969), 345-46.

²⁴ Gianni Vattimo, *Art's Claim to Truth* (New York: Columbia University Press, 2008).

²⁵ Sylvere Lotringer, *Schizo-Culture* (Los Angeles: Semiotexte, 2013), 17-18.

Jackson Pollock

¹ Peter Sloterdijk, *Spheres I: Bubbles, Microspherology* (Los Angeles, Semiotexte: 2011), 49-51.

² See "Paris, the Capital of the Nineteenth Century (1935)" in Walter Benjamin, *The Arcades Project* (Cambridge, MA: Harvard University Press, 2002), 3.

³ See, for example, his essay "The Thing," in Martin Heidegger, *Poetry, Language, Thought* (New York: Harper Perennial, 2001).

⁴ Paul Virilio, *Art as Far as the Eye Can See* (Oxford and New York: Berg Books, 2007).

⁵ Alain Badiou, *Ethics: An Essay on the Understanding of Evil* (New York, Verso: 2002).

⁶ Ellen G. Landau, *Jackson Pollock* (New York: Abrams, 1989).

⁷ For an image of this lion man, see the following website: lotu2.blogspot.com/2008/01/lion-man-of-hohlenstein-stadel.html

⁸ See "1730: Becoming-Intense, Becoming-Animal, Becoming-Imperceptible..." in Gilles Deleuze and Felix Guattari, *A Thousand Plateaus* (Minneapolis, MN: University of Minnesota Press, 1987), 232.

⁹ See "The Epic of Creation" in Stephanie Dalley, *Myths from Mesopotamia: Creation, The Flood, Gilgamesh and Others* (New York: Oxford University Press, 1989), 228.

¹⁰ Roberta H. Markman and Peter T. Markman, *The Flayed God: The Mythology of Mesoamerica* (New York: Harper Collins, 1992), 213.

¹¹ Linda Schele and David Friedel, *A Forest of Kings: The Untold Story of the Ancient Maya* (New York: Quill, William Morrow, 1990), 89.

¹² Gilles Deleuze, *Difference and Repetition* (New York: Columbia University Press, 1994).

¹³ Steven Naifeh and Gregory Smith, *Jackson Pollock: An American Saga* (New York: Clarkson Potter, 1989), 656.

¹⁴ See John David Ebert, *Dead Celebrities, Living Icons* (New York: Praeger / Greenwood, 2010) for a discussion of the phenomenology of the electronic celebrity.

Mark Rothko

¹ Martin Heidegger, *Introduction to Metaphysics*, (Yale University, 2000), 107.

² Ibid. 133-34.

³ Gunter Figal, ed. *The Heidegger Reader* (Indiana University Press, 2009), 216-17.

⁴ Martin Heidegger, *Basic Writings* (Harper Perennial, 2008), 307-41.

⁵ Jean Gebser, *The Ever-Present Origin* (Ohio University Press, 1986).

⁶ Peter Sloterdijk, *Spheres I: Bubbles* (Los Angeles: Semiotexte, 2011), 25.

[7] On Rothko's multiforms, see James E. B. Breslin, *Mark Rothko: A Biography* (University of Chicago Press, 1993), 243.

[8] Zygmunt Bauman, *Liquid Modernity* (UK: Polity Books, 2000).

[9] Arthur Danto, for instance, in his book *After the End of Art: Contemporary Art and the Pale of History* (Princeton University Press, 1998).

[10] David Anfam, *Mark Rothko: The Works on Canvas* (Yale University Press, 1998), fig. 399, 305.

[11] Ibid., fig. 428, 326.

[12] Ibid., fig. 444, 337.

[13] Ibid., fig. 518, 399.

[14] Ibid., fig 438, 332.

[15] Ibid., fig 439, 332.

[16] Ibid., fig. 424, 324.

[17] Ibid., fig. 567, 435.

[18] Vilem Flusser, *Writings* (Minneapolis: University of Minnesota Press, 2002), 21-34.

[19] David Anfam, ibid., fig. 592, 457.

[20] Ibid., fig. 596, 461.

[21] Ibid., fig. 600, 465.

[22] Ibid., fig. 601, 466.

²³ Ibid., fig. 658, 520.

²⁴ Ibid., fig. 657, 519.

²⁵ Ibid., fig. 669, 529.

²⁶ Ibid., fig. 738, 589.

²⁷ Ibid., fig. 740, 590-91.

²⁸ Heidegger, *Introduction to Metaphysics*, ibid., 30.

Jean-Michel Basqiat

¹ See Jacques Derrida, *Writing and Difference* (University of Chicago Press, 1978), 280.

² For the idea of "disinhibiting media," see Peter Sloterdijk, "Rules for the Human Zoo: a Response to the *Letter on Humanism*" in *Environment and Planning D: Society and Space*, 2009, v.27, 15.

³ Jacques Derrida, *Writing and Difference*, ibid., 278-79.

⁴ Richard Marshall, *Jean-Michel Basquiat* (New York: Whitney Museum of American Art, 2001), 73.

⁵ Ibid., 74.

⁶ Ibid., 79.

⁷ Ibid., 81.

⁸ Ibid., 82.

⁹ Andreas Lommel, *Prehistoric and Primitive Art* (New York: Paul Hamlyn, 1966), 23.

10 Richard Marshall, *Jean-Michel Basquiat*, ibid., 92.

11 Ibid., 95.

12 Ibid., 86.

13 See Henri Frankfort, *Kingship and the Gods: A Study of Ancient Near Eastern Religion as the Integration of Society & Nature* (University of Chicago Press, 1978), 7-8.

14 Richard Marshall, *Jean-Michel Basquiat*, ibid., 96.

15 Ibid., 98.

16 Ibid., 125.

17 Ibid., 124.

18 Ibid., 133.

19 Ibid., 131.

20 Ibid., 146.

21 Ibid., 147.

22 Ibid., 135.

23 Ibid., 136.

24 Ibid., 137.

25 Ibid., 143.

26 Ibid., 186.

[27] Ibid., 193.

[28] Ibid., 221.

[29] Ibid., 223.

[30] Ibid., 224.

[31] Ibid., 225.

[32] Ibid., 231.

[33] Phoebe Hoban, *Basquiat: A Quick Killing in Art* (New York: Penguin Books, 1998.

Joseph Beuys

[1] Gilles Deleuze and Felix Guattari, *A Thousand Plateaus* (University of Minnesota Press, 1987), 61-62.

[2] Mark Rosenthal, *Joseph Beuys: Actions, Vitrines, Environments* (Houston, TX: The Menil Collection, 2004), plate 83, 80.

[3] I owe this trichotomous distinction of Beuys' art to Alain Borer, *The Essential Joseph Beuys* (Cambridge, MA: MIT Press, 1987).

[4] Armin Zweite, *Joseph Beuys: Natur, Materie, Form* (Munchen: Schirmer / Mosel, 1991), fig. 19.

[5] Ibid., fig. 28.

[6] Ibid., fig. 32.

[7] Ibid., fig. 45.

[8] Ibid., fig. 43.

9 Caroline Tisdall, *Joseph Beuys* (London: Thames & Hudson, 1979), fig. 92, 55.

10 Ibid., fig. 59, 37.

11 Ibid., fig. 61, 38.

12 Zweite, *Joseph Beuys*, ibid., fig. 59.

13 Joseph Campbell and Charles Muses, eds. *In All Her Names: Explorations of the Feminine in Divinity* (Harper San Francisco, 1991), 42.

14 Zweite, *Joseph Beuys*, ibid., fig. 62.

15 Ibid., fig. 66.

16 Ibid., fig. 68.

17 Ibid., fig. 73.

18 Ibid., fig. 71.

19 Ibid., fig. 126.

20 Ibid., fig. 140.

21 Ibid., fig. 153.

22 Ibid., fig. 175.

23 Ibid., fig. 116.

24 Ibid., fig. 103.

25 Ibid., fig. 128.

[26] See Martin Heidegger, *Basic Writings* (NY: Harper, 2008), "Letter on Humanism," 213-65.

[27] Tisdall, *Joseph Beuys*, ibid., 10.

[28] Ibid., 58.

[29] Ibid., 72.

[30] Ibid., 190-91.

[31] Ibid., 34-35.

[32] Ibid., fig. 90, 54.

[33] Ibid., fig. 82, 50-51.

[34] Ibid., fig. 101, 66-67.

[35] Ibid., fig. 269, 172.

[36] Ibid., 94-95.

[37] Ibid., 101-105.

[38] Ibid, 127-133.

[39] Rosenthal, *Joseph Beuys: Actions, Vitrines, Envrironments*, ibid., plate 22, 38.

[40] Zweite, *Joseph Beuys*, fig. 220.

[41] Ibid., fig. 190.

[42] Rosenthal, *Actions, Vitrines, Environments*, ibid., plate 91, 93.

[43] Tisdall, *Joseph Beuys*, ibid., fig. 198, 134-35.

44 Ibid., fig. 251, 160-161.

45 Ibid., 162-63.

46 Ibid., 166-67.

47 Rosenthal, *Actions, Vitrines*, ibid., plate 77, 79.

48 Tisdall, *Joseph Beuys*, ibid., fig. 433, 248-49.

49 For an excellent example of one of these fat corners, see Volker Harlan, *What is Art? Conversation with Joseph Beuys* (London: Clairview, 2007), fig. 20, 48.

50 Tisdall, *Joseph Beuys*, ibid., 248.

51 See the discussion in Volker Harlan, *What is Art?* ibid, 42-47 and accompanying figs. 17-19.

52 Tisdall, *Joseph Beuys*, ibid. fig. 98, 62-63.

53 Rosenthal, *Actions, Vitrines*, ibid., plate 86, 86-87.

Gerhard Richter

1 See "On the Question of Being" in Martin Heidegger, *Pathmarks* (Cambridge University Press, 1998), 311.

2 Jacques Derrida, *Of Grammatology* (Baltimore and London: Johns Hopkins University Press, 1997), 19-23.

3 Dietmar Elger, *Gerhard Richter: A Life in Painting* (Chicago and London: The University of Chicago Press, 2002), fig. 2.4.

4 Ibid., 48.

[5] See Gerhard Richter, *Atlas*, ed. Helmut Friedel (New York: Distributed Art Publishers, 2006).

[6] Vilem Flusser, *Towards a Philosophy of Photography* (Great Britain: Reaktion Books, 2000), 21-22.

[7] Robert Storr, *Gerhard Richter: Forty Years of Painting* (New York: Distributed Art Publishers, 2002), 115.

[8] Paul Virilio, *Negative Horizon: An Essay in Dromoscopy* (New York and London: Continuum, 2007), 107-08.

[9] Mark Godfrey and Nicholas Serota, eds., *Gerhard Richter: Panorama* (New York: Distributed Art Publishers, 2011), 61.

[10] Storr, *Gerhard Richter:Forty Years of Painting*, ibid., 144-45.

[11] Elger, *Gerhard Richter: A Life in Painting*, ibid., 156.

[12] Godfrey and Serota, *Gerhard Richter: Panorama*, ibid., 91.

[13] Storr, *Gehard Richter: Forty Years of Painting*, ibid., 148.

[14] Godfrey and Serota, *Gerhard Richter: Panorama*, ibid., 92.

[15] Ibid., 100.

[16] Ibid., 98.

[17] Ibid., 98.

[18] Ibid., 99.

[19] Elger, *Gerhard Richter: A Life in Painting*, ibid., fig. 5.20B.

[20] Ibid., fig. 5.20D.

[21] See Gilles Deleuze and Felix Guattari, *A Thousand Plateaus* (Minneapolis: University of Minnesota Press, 1987), 506-08.

[22] Elger, *Gerhard Richter: A Life in Painting*, ibid., fig. 6.1.

[23] Storr, *Gerhard Richter: Forty Years of Painting*, ibid., 152.

[24] Elger, *Gerhard Richter: A Life in Painting*, ibid., 6.2.

[25] Godfrey and Serota, *Gerhard Richter: Panorama*, ibid., 102.

[26] Ibid., 103.

[27] Ibid., 104-05.

[28] See the discussion by Mark Godfrey on "Damaged Landscapes" in Godfrey and Serota, ibid., 78-80.

[29] Godfrey and Serota, *Gerhard Richter: Panorama*, ibid., 108-09.

[30] Ibid., 107.

[31] Elger, *Gerhard Richter: A Life in Painting*, ibid., fig. 7.2.

[32] Godfrey and Serota, *Gerhard Richter: Panorama*, 144-45.

[33] Ibid., 149.

[34] Ibid., 148.

[35] Storr, *Gerhard Richter: Forty Years of Painting*, ibid., 190-91.

[36] Ibid., 196.

[37] Ibid., 197.

[38] Godfrey and Serota, *Gerhard Richter: Panorama*, ibid., fig. 30, 127.

[39] Ibid., 157.

[40] Ibid., 161.

[41] Ibid., 177-93.

[42] Ibid., 189.

[43] Ibid., 189.

[44] Ibid., 184.

[45] Ibid., 185.

[46] Ibid., 222-23.

[47] Ibid., 231.

[48] Ibid., 232.

[49] Ibid., 256.

[50] Ibid., 258.

[51] Elger, *Gerhard Richter: A Life in Painting*, ibid., fig. 12.1.

[52] Storr, *Gerhard Richter: Forty Years of Painting*, ibid., 256.

[53] Ibid., 284-85.

[54] See Martin Heidegger, *Being and Time*, trans. John Macquarrie and Edward Robinson (New York: Harper Perennial, 2008), 262-69.

[55] Godfrey and Serota, *Gerhard Richter: Panorama*, ibid., 244.

Anselm Kiefer

[1] Marshall McLuhan and Wilfred Watson, *From Cliché to Archetype* (Corte Madera, CA: Gingko Press, 2011), 94-107.

[2] See the essay "Differance" in Jacques Derrida, *Margins of Philosophy* (Great Britian: The Harvester Press, 1982), 1-27.

[3] Hans-Georg Gadamer, *Truth and Method* (London: Continuum, 2006), 296-98.

Zdzislaw Beksinski

[1] James R. Cowan, *The Fantastic Art of Beksinski* (Los Angeles, CA: Morpheus International, 1998), 58.

[2] Wieslaw Banach, *Beksinski I* (Lesko, Poland: Bosz Art, 2008), 34.

[3] See the image on the website at http://beksinski.dmochowskigallery.net/galeria_karta.php?artist=52&picture=3359

[4] Jacques Lacan, *The Psychoses, The Seminar of Jacques Lacan, Book III: 1955-56* (London: Routledge, 1993), 258-70.

[5] Vilem Flusser, *Post-History* (Minneapolis, MN: Univocal Publishing, 2013).

[6] Vilem Flusser, *Writings* (Minneapolis: University of Minnesota Press, 2002), 42-50.

[7] Gilles Deleuze and Felix Guattari, *A Thousand Plateaus* (Minneapolis: University of Minnesota Press, 1987), 111-48.

[8] Paul Virilio, *The Vision Machine* (Indiana: Indiana University Press, 1994).

[9] Cowan, ibid., 58.

[10] Cowan, ibid., 23.

[11] Giorgio Agamben, *Homo Sacer* (Stanford: Stanford University Press, 1998).

[12] Martin Heidegger, *Basic Writings* (NY: Harper Perennial, 2008), 213-65.

[13] Giovanni Pico della Mirandola, *Oration on the Dignity of Man* (Washington, D.C.: Regnery, 1982).

[14] Cowan, ibid., 18.

[15] Peter Sloterdijk, *Spheres I: Bubbles* (Los Angeles: Semiotexte, 2011), 164.

[16] Heiner Muhlmann, *MSC, Maximal Stress Cooperation: The Driving Force of Cultures* (NY: Springer Wien, 2005), 64-68.

Odd Nerdrum

[1] I have written in more detail about this process in my earlier book. See John David Ebert, *Celluloid Heroes & Mechanical Dragons: Film as the Mythology of Electronic Society* (Christchurch, New Zealand: Cybereditions, 2005), 194-225.

[2] Richard Vine, *Odd Nerdrum: Paintings, Sketches and Drawings* (Oslo, Norway: Gyldendal Fakta, 2001), 199.

[3] Jan-Erik Ebbestad Hansen, *Odd Nerdrum: Paintings* (Oslo, Norway: Aschehoug, 1994), 175.

[4] Jan Ake Pettersson, *Odd Nerdrum: Storyteller and Self-Revealer* (Oslo, Norway: Aschehoug, 1998), fig. 69.

[5] Ibid., fig. 74.

[6] Jacques Derrida, *Writing and Difference* (University of Chicago Press, 1978), 278-280.

[7] Heiner Muhlmann, *MSC, Maximal Stress Cooperation: The Driving Force of Cultures* (Wien: Springer, 2005).

[8] Ibid., 24.

[9] Ibid., 29-30.

[10] Ebbestad-Hansen, *Odd Nerdrum*, ibid., 168.

[11] Odd Nerdrum, *On Kitsch* (Oslo: Kagge Forlag, 2001), 38.

[12] Gilles Deleuze and Felix Guattari, *Anti-Oedipus: Capitalism and Schizophrenia* (New York: Penguin Books, 2009), 144.

[13] Pettersson, *Odd Nerdrum*, ibid., 62.

[14] Ebbestad-Hansen, *Odd Nerdrum*, ibid., 164.

[15] Ibid., 174.

[16] Ibid., 176.

[17] Ibid., 186.

[18] Ibid., 188.

[19] Ibid., 202.

[20] Ibid., 204.

[21] See the following Wikipedia article, "Expanding Earth" at en.wikipedia.org/wiki/Expanding_Earth

[22] Ebbestad-Hansen, *Odd Nerdrum*, ibid., 216.

[23] Ibid., 240.

[24] Ibid., 256.

[25] Ibid., 258.

[26] Ibid., 266.

[27] Ibid., 314.

[28] Pettersson, *Odd Nerdrum*, ibid., fig. 91.

[29] Odd Nerdrum, *Odd Nerdrum: Themes* (Oslo: Press Publishing, 2007), 455.

[30] Ibid., 226.

[31] Ibid., 521.

[32] Ibid., 544-45.

[33] I have also discussed Nerdrum's painting in my recent book. See John David Ebert, *The New Media Invasion* (Jefferson, North Carolina: McFarland Books, 2011), 185.

[34] See especially Odd Nerdrum, *Kitsch: More Than Art* (Oslo: Schibsted Forlag, 2011), 213.

[35] Peter Sloterdijk, "Rules for the Human Zoo," in *Environment and Planning D: Society and Space*, volume 27, 2009, 12-28.

[36] Paul Virilio, Raymond Depardon, *Native Land: Stop Eject* (Paris: Fondation Cartier, 2009),26.

Francis Bacon

[1] Jean Gebser, *The Ever-Present Origin* (Ohio University Press, 1986).

[2] Wieland Schmied, *Francis Bacon: Commitment and Conflict* (Munich: Prestel, 1996), fig. 2.

[3] Gilles Deleuze and Felix Guattari, *A Thousand Plateaus* (University of Minnesota Press, 1987), 46.

[4] Ibid.

[5] See, for example, the image at www.answersingenesis.org/articles/2009/07/13/results-bloodies-religion-ever

[6] Gilles Deleuze, *Difference and Repetition* (New York: Columbia University Press, 1994), 215.

[7] Ibid., 136.

[8] This is one of the characteristics of contemporary art which Peter Sloterdijk faults it for, insisting that its lack of building a world in the Heideggerian sense is what makes it so "selfish." See Peter Sloterdijk, *You Must Change Your Life* (Great Britain: Polity Press, 2013), 434.

[9] Arthur Danto, *After the End of Art* (Princeton, NJ: Princeton University Press, 1997), xiii.

[10] Rudy Chiappini, ed. *Bacon* (Milan, Italy: Skira, 2008), fig. 5, 231.

[11] Gunter Figal, ed. *The Heidegger Reader* (Indiana University Press, 2009), 207.

[12] Deleuze and Guattari, *A Thousand Plateaus*, 188.

[13] See the image of this painting online at www.vangoghgallery.com/catalog/Painting/374/Painter-on-His-Way-to-Work,-The.html

[14] Peter Sloterdijk, *Spheres I: Bubbles, Microspherology* (Los Angeles, Semiotexte: 2011), 343.

[15] Chiappini, *Bacon*, fig. 34, 126-27.

[16] Michael Peppiatt, *Francis Bacon: Anatomy of an Enigma* (New York: Skyhorse Publishing, 2009), 252-54.

[17] Schmied, *Bacon*, ibid., fig. 25.

[18] John David Ebert, *Dead Celebrities, Living Icons: Tragedy and Fame in the Age of the Multimedia Superstar* (New York: Praeger, 2010), 83.

[19] Although Vilem Flusser points out that the "telematic society," as he calls it, is composed of a realm, not of two-dimensional, but rather of zero-dimensional images, since its basic unit of composition is the dimensionless point. In any case, we both agree that it is a realm of *fewer* dimensions than the physical world. See Vilem Flusser, *Into the Universe of Technical Images* (University of Minnesota Press, 2011), 8-10.

[20] Chiappini, *Francis Bacon*, ibid., fig. 30.

[21] Ibid., fig. 46.

[22] Ibid., fig 44.

[23] Ibid., fig. 29.

[24] Ibid., fig. 40.

[25] Ibid., fig. 48.

[26] Ibid., fig. 49.

[27] Schmied, *Bacon*, fig. 8, 53.

[28] Ibid., fig. 56.

[29] Peppiatt, *Francis Bacon*, 391.

Damien Hirst

[1] See the collages in Damien Hirst, *I Want to Spend the Rest of My Life Everywhere, With Everyone, One to One, Always, Forever, Now* (United Kingdom: Booth-Clibborn, 1997), 69-73.

[2] Ann Gallagher, *Damien Hirst* (London, UK: Tate Publishing, 2012), 30-31; 40-41.

[3] Hirst, *I Want to Spend the Rest of My Life Everywhere*, 248-49.

[4] Damien Hirst, *The Complete Medicine Cabinets* (New York: Other Criteria, L&M Arts, 2010), 61-67.

[5] Gallagher, *Damien Hirst*, 44-45.

[6] Hirst, *I Want to Spend the Rest of My Life Everywhere*, 28.

[7] Gallagher, *Damien Hirst*, 95.

[8] Ibid., 72-75.

[9] Ibid., 46-47.

[10] Ibid., 128.

[11] Hirst, *I Want to Spend the Rest of My Life Everywhere*, 97.

[12] Gallagher, *Damien Hirst*, 130.

[13] Hirst, *I Want to Spend the Rest of My Life Everywhere*, 310-13.

[14] Ibid., 318-25.

[15] Damien Hirst and Gordon Burn, *On the Way to Work* (NY: Universe Publishing, 2002).

[16] Gallagher, *Damien Hirst*, fig. 16, 28.

[17] Ibid., 152-53.

[18] Ibid., 138-39.

[19] Ibid., 150-51.

[20] Marina Warner, "Once a Catholic..." *London Review of Books*, July 5, 2012. Found online at: www.lrb.co.uk/v34/n13/marina-warner/once-a-catholic

Anish Kapoor

[1] Germano Celant, *Anish Kapoor* (Milan, Italy: Edizioni Charta, 1998), 8-43.

[2] Ibid., XII.

[3] Ibid., 40-41.

[4] Heinrich Zimmer, *Philosophies of India*, ed. Joseph Campbell (Princeton: Princeton University Press, 1969), 338-351.

[5] Celant, *Anish Kapoor*, ibid. 84-85.

[6] Ibid., 94-101.

[7] See Ajit Mookerjee and Madhu Khanna, *The Tantric Way: Art, Science, Ritual* (Boston: New York Graphic Society, 1977), 57 for an image of the Shri Yantra together with a discussion of the *bindu*.

[8] Celant, *Anish Kapoor*, ibid., 106-07.

[9] Ibid., 92-93.

[10] Ibid., 104-06.

[11] Rainer Crone and Alexandra Von Stosch, *Anish Kapoor: Svayambh* (New York: Prestel, 2008), 24.

[12] Celant, *Anish Kapoor*, ibid., 144-49.

[13] Ibid., 204-05.

[14] Ibid., 206-08.

[15] Homi K. Babha, *Anish Kapoor* (Paris: Flammarion, 2011), 54-59.

[16] Ibid., 50-53.

[17] Ibid., 44-47.

[18] Ibid., 24-29.

[19] Ibid., 2-15.

[20] See Peter Sloterdijk, *Spheres I: Bubbles* (Los Angeles, CA: Semiotexte, 2011), 293-95 for his description of "nobjects" and "nobjective space."

[21] Peter Sloterdijk, *Neither Sun Nor Death* (Los Angeles, CA: Semiotexte, 2011), 167.

[22] Nicholas Baume, ed. *Anish Kapoor: Past, Present, Future* (Cambridge, MA: MIT Press, 2008), 122-33.

[23] Gilles Deleuze, *The Logic of Sense* (New York: Columbia University Press, 1990), 4-6.

[24] Ibid., 9.

[25] Rainer Crone, *Anish Kapoor*, ibid., 126-27.

[26] Ibid., 6-19.

[27] Homi K. Bhaba, *Anish Kapoor*, ibid., 118.

[28] Ibid., 130-31.

[29] Gilles Deleuze and Felix Guattari, *A Thousand Plateaus* (Minneapolis, MN: University of Minnesota Press, 1987), "Introduction: Rhizome," 3-25.

[30] See Homi K. Bhaba, "Elusive Objects: Anish Kapoor's Fissionary Art" in Bhaba, *Anish Kapoor*, ibid., 61-75.

[31] Hans-Georg Gadamer, *Truth and Method* (New York: Continuum, 1989), 135-36.

Jannis Kounellis

[1] See David Lewis-Williams, *The Mind in the Cave: Consciousness and the Origins of Art* (UK: Thames & Hudson, 2004).

[2] Mary Jane Jacob, *Jannis Kounellis* (Chicago: Museum of Contemporary Art, 1986), pl. 36, 58-59.

[3] Martin Heidegger, *Poetry, Language, Thought* (NY: Harper Perennial, 1981), 161-62.

[4] Mary Jane Jacob, *Jannis Kounellis*, ibid., pl. 73, 104-05.

[5] Ibid. See the article by Thomas McEvilley in this volume, "Mute Prophecies," 101.

[6] Herodotus, *The Persian Wars* (NY: The Modern Library, 1942), 36.

[7] See Heidegger's "Letter on Humanism" in Martin Heidegger, *The Basic Writings* (NY: Harper Perennial, 1993).

[8] Jannis Kounellis, *Kounellis* (Milano, Italy: Edizio Charta, 2002), 122.

[9] Fernand Braudel, *Civilization & Capitalism, Volume I: The Structures of Everyday Life* (NY: Harper Perennial, 1985).

[10] Stephen Bann, *Jannis Kounellis* (London: Reaktion Books, 2003), 147-58.

[11] Gloria Moure, *Jannis Kounellis: Works, Writings 1958-2000* (Barcelona, Spain: Ediciones Poligrafa, 2002), 224-226.

[12] Mary Jane Jacobs, *Kounellis*, ibid., 134.

[13] Ibid., 80-81.

[14] Mary Jane Jacob, *Kounellis*, ibid., 111-13.

[15] Ibid., Pl. 71, 102.

[16] Bruno Cora, *Jannis Kounellis* (Milano, Italy: Silvana Editoriale, 2010), 60-61.

[17] Mary Jane Jacob, *Kounellis*, ibid., pl. 65, 94-95.

[18] Ibid., pl. 117, 162.

[19] Ibid., pl. 59, 86.

[20] Bruno Cora, *Jannis Kounellis*, ibid., 102-03.

[21] See "Project for Artforum" in Jannis Kounellis, Mario Codognato and Mirta D'Argenzio, *Jannis Kounellis: Echoes in the Darkness, Writings and Interviews 1966 – 2002* (Great Britain, Trolley Books, 2002), 57-59.

[22] Fernand Braudel, *Memory and the Mediterranean* (NY: Alfred A. Knopf, 2001).

Christian Boltanski

[1] Catherine Grenier, *Christian Boltanski* (Paris / New York: Flammarion, 2010), 134-37.

[2] See Michel Foucault, *The History of Sexuality, Volume 1: An Introduction* (New York: Vintage Books, 1990), 135-45.

[3] Didier Semin, *Christian Boltanski* (London, UK: Phaidon Press, 1997), 12-13.

[4] Ibid., 87-88.

[5] Erwin Rhode, in his book *Psyche*, however, points out that in the days of the Mycenaeans, the ancestral dead could not have been regarded with the same kind of weakness, since the dead in the shaft graves of the *tholoi* were always equipped with their weapons and grave gear, implying that they would actually continue to use them in the afterlife. See his book *Psyche: the Cult of Souls & Belief in Immortality Among the Greeks, Volume I* (New York: Harper Torchbooks, 1966).

[6] Franz Borkenau, *End and Beginning: On the Generations of Cultures and the Origins of the West* (New York: Columbia University Press, 1981), 64-95.

[7] Didier Semin, *Christian Boltanski*, ibid., 28-29.

[8] Ibid., 35.

[9] Catherine Grenier, *Christian Boltanski*, ibid., 145.

[10] Gloria Moure, *Christian Boltanski: Advent and Other Times* (Barcelona, Spain: Ediciones Poligrafa, 1996), 82-83.

[11] Sergio Troisi, *Boltanski: Montedipieta* (Milano, Italy: Charta, 2002), 42-45.

[12] Rick Gore, "The Dawn of Humans: Neanderthals," *National Geographic Magazine*, January, 1996, 2-35.

[13] Genesis 23:7-10.

[14] Didier Semin, *Christian Boltanski*, ibid., 122.

[15] Ibid., 89.

[16] Ibid., 40-41.

[17] Jeremy Black and Anthony Green, *Gods, Demons and Symbols of Ancient Mesopotamia: An Illustrated Dictionary* (Austin, TX: University of Austin Press, 1997), 180.

[18] Christian Boltanski and Catherine Grenier, *The Possible Life of Christian Boltanski* (Boston, MA: MFA Publications, 2009), 191-93.

Printed in Great Britain
by Amazon